# THE UNWANTED

The meeting place was carefully chosen: an abandoned church in rural Ireland just after dark. For Jonathan Quinn — a freelance operative and professional 'cleaner' — the job was only to observe. If his clean-up skills were needed, it would mean things had gone horribly wrong. But an assassin hidden in a tree assured just that. Suddenly Quinn had four dead bodies to dispose of and one astounding clue — to a mystery that was about to spin wildly out of control . . .

*Books by Brett Battles*
*Published by The House of Ulverscroft:*

THE CLEANER
THE DECEIVED

BRETT BATTLES

# THE UNWANTED

*Complete and Unabridged*

# CHARNWOOD
*Leicester*

First published in Great Britain in 2009 by
Preface Publishing
An imprint of
The Random House Group Limited
London

First Charnwood Edition
published 2010
by arrangement with
The Random House Group Limited
London

British Library CIP Data

Battles, Brett.
    The unwanted.
    1. Quinn, Jonathan (Fictitious character)- -Fiction.
    2. Assassination- -Ireland- -Fiction.
    3. Women human rights workers- -Fiction.
    4. Terrorism- -Prevention- -Fiction.
    5. Suspense fiction. 6. Large type books.
    I. Title
    813.6–dc22

    ISBN 978–1–44480–346–4

Published by
F. A. Thorpe (Publishing)
Anstey, Leicestershire

Set by Words & Graphics Ltd.
Anstey, Leicestershire
Printed and bound in Great Britain by
T. J. International Ltd., Padstow, Cornwall

This book is printed on acid-free paper

In memory of
William Relling, Jr.
Friend. Mentor.
Missed.

# Prologue

The doors to the council room had been closed for hours. That wasn't unusual. Council meetings routinely went into the early hours of the morning. It was just that this was a special meeting with a single item on the agenda. One that was very important to James Hardwick.

Hardwick had been the one to propose the item to his boss. It was a huge power play for both of them, but also the right thing to do. All the pieces were in place, and if the answer was to move forward, so much would be achieved in the service of the overall plan of their organization, a group known as the LP.

While the council met, Hardwick waited in the hallway outside the meeting room, sitting on a wooden chair against the wall. He occupied his time by going over every detail of his proposal: playing out all the scenarios, imagining the possible outcomes for each stage, and working out solutions that would keep the overall focus of the proposal on what they needed to achieve.

At 2:14 a.m. the doors to the meeting room finally swung open.

Hardwick stood up, crossed his hands behind his back, and bowed his head slightly as the members of the council walked by silently. A few didn't seem to even notice he was there, but

1

most at least gave him a nod, or looked him in the eye as they passed. The fourteenth member to walk by was Chairman Vine.

'Sorry we took so long, James,' Chairman Vine said, his voice wavering. Hardwick had no idea how old he was, but he thought there was little chance the Chairman was under eighty-five.

'No problem, Mr. Chairman. It's always better to take as much time as needed in matters like this.'

The Chairman looked like he was about to say something, then stopped himself for a moment before speaking again. 'He said to give him a few minutes.'

The *him* the Chairman was referring to would be Hardwick's boss, Mr. Kidd. He was the only council member who had yet to leave the conference room. 'Thank you, sir.'

The Chairman smiled, then turned and followed the others down the hall. His footsteps echoed in the marble hallway, growing fainter and fainter until the corridor fell silent again.

It was a full five minutes before Mr. Kidd called for James to come into the conference room. Without being asked, Hardwick closed the door behind him after he entered.

His boss was sitting in a chair near the end of the large oval table that dominated the room. It was made of mahogany and stained to a dark reddish-brown. Inset into the top of the table in front of each of the fifteen chairs was a computer screen. Only the one in front of Mr. Kidd was on, but Hardwick couldn't see what was on the screen.

The room had no pictures on the walls, no

windows. Here was a place where distraction was not tolerated. Where focus on the issues at hand was all that mattered. The business of the council had been conducted that way for decades. In fact, it was in this very room where the master directive was fleshed out more than fifty years before, the plan members of the LP had been working on since that day. All the original members were dead now, but their vision remained. And it was for the fulfillment of this vision that Hardwick had developed his proposal.

'Sit down,' Mr. Kidd said. He was a robust seventy-four. Sharp, in shape, and full of an energy Hardwick himself also possessed. His face gave nothing away, though, as he watched the younger man take the seat next to him.

'How did it go?' Hardwick asked.

There was a pause, then Mr. Kidd began to smile. 'Exactly like you predicted. Your proposal was clear and to the point. Most were able to see the merits immediately. For a few, it took a little bit longer.'

Several hours longer, Hardwick knew, but only said, 'So I can get started?'

'A question first. Do you know if Mr. Rose was able to confirm the event he's selected for his target?'

'Yes,' Hardwick said. 'I'm told it's locked, and there is little chance it will be changed.'

'And the procurement?'

'I had to be careful getting this information, of course, but it appears Mr. Rose has someone he's hired from the outside already on it. I

3

understand they have already picked up,' he paused, 'children from various locations. His target number is between twenty-four and thirty.'

Mr. Kidd frowned. 'Distasteful. But necessary, I guess.'

'So Mr. Rose seems to believe.'

'Well, James, you now have the full backing of the council,' Mr. Kidd said.

'So I can start immediately?' Hardwick asked. He could feel his excitement building, but he let none of it show.

'Yes.'

'Thank you,' he said to his boss. He started to stand. 'I should go. I have plenty to do.'

'There is just one other thing,' Mr. Kidd said.

Hardwick stopped next to the chair, worried that some condition had been added to his plan that would jeopardize its success. 'What is it?'

'From now on, you can address me as Chairman.'

Hardwick stared at his boss for a moment. 'Seriously?'

'Chairman Vine . . . Mr. Vine suggested it himself, and the others agreed.'

Hardwick thrust out his hand. 'Congratulations, sir. This is fantastic.'

'Is it?' Chairman Kidd said. He didn't take Hardwick's hand. 'If your proposal doesn't work out, I'm fairly certain I'll become the shortest-term Chairman in the history of the LP.' He locked eyes with Hardwick. 'I'd appreciate it if you could make sure that doesn't happen.'

Hardwick grinned as he reached down with both hands and grabbed his boss's, shaking it with confidence. 'I guarantee it.'

# 1

The meeting location had been chosen for its isolation, an abandoned Catholic church on the east side of a little-used road fifty kilometers northwest of Cork, Ireland, near the border between County Tipperary and County Cork. The structure that remained was all but invisible from the road. One of those places only a local would know about, then forget over time.

As a bonus, no one lived within a kilometer and a half of the ruins, making it a natural choice for an exchange. In the two days Jonathan Quinn had been scouting the location, no more than a dozen cars a day had driven past, and not a single one had even slowed, let alone stopped.

The roof of the church had long since disappeared, leaving only the gray, pitted stone walls of the chapel. Encouraged by the wet Irish climate, vegetation had grown up around the building, both surrounding it and filling the inside. It was as if a congregation of flora was waiting in the open-air sanctuary for a priest who had yet to arrive.

Nearby, an untended cemetery provided the only reminder that people had once worshipped here. Quinn didn't know how long the compound had been abandoned, but the most recent grave marker he'd located had been for someone named Maureen Owens, year of death 1889. So it wasn't hard to imagine that it had been at least a century since any parishioners had gathered between the chapel walls.

Quinn did a last walk-through just after noon, careful to step only on broken stones or patches of grass to avoid leaving any trace of his presence. He double-checked to make sure all the cameras and microphones were well hidden and working. When he was satisfied, he returned on foot to the van parked a half kilometer away.

The meeting was scheduled for nine that evening. According to the agreed-upon terms, the informant was to arrive from the south, while the man from Quinn's client — an organization known as the Office — was to come in from the north.

They were each instructed to park a quarter kilometer from the location and walk the rest of the way in. They were to meet inside the church, with each participant allowed to bring one associate. Once they had all arrived, the informant would give the Office's agent certain information in exchange for what Quinn assumed was a generous cash payment.

The details of the exchange, what the information was and what the informant was earning for his efforts, were none of Quinn's business. He was a cleaner. His job was to watch and observe, and — only if necessary — clean up any mess that might occur.

As Quinn reached the back of the van, the right side door swung open. Quinn's apprentice

6

Nate was hunched inside, a Glock 19 pistol in his right hand.

'Ground check?' Nate asked.

'We're all set,' Quinn replied.

Nate relaxed. While he had no doubt been watching Quinn's approach — first on the cameras stationed around the church, then on those surrounding the van — and had seen his boss return alone, there was always the possibility someone had gotten to Quinn in one of the dead areas, and was waiting just beyond the camera's view. But Quinn had answered Nate's question with the prearranged all-clear signal.

The apprentice moved aside and let Quinn enter, then leaned out and pulled the door shut.

The van had been transformed into a mobile observation post. But unlike those fancy ones in the movies, here little attention had been paid to the human component. A half-dozen small flat-screen monitors were mounted on the right wall. Five were receiving signals from the ten cameras back at the church, each monitor assigned to two cameras, and automatically toggling back and forth every five seconds. The sixth monitor was digitally divided into four smaller screens displaying different views of the surveillance van and the surrounding area. Below the monitors, twenty-eight digital record-ers — each no larger than a paperback book — were hung in portable racks. Two recorders per feed, in case one crapped out.

And as if that wasn't enough, there was a satellite link sending a real-time signal back to the Office's headquarters in Washington, D.C.

State-of-the-art equipment all. It was the two plastic chairs and the banged-up portable ice chest that seemed out of place.

'You check in with Peter?' Quinn asked. Peter was the head of the Office, and the man who had hired them.

'Fifteen minutes ago,' Nate said as he settled into the chair nearest the back of the van. 'We did another connection test. Signal strength is steady. I flipped it to black, so they're not getting anything at the moment.'

'Any more interference from the cameras?' Quinn said.

Nate shook his head. 'Everything seems fine now. I think we're ready.'

'Keep an eye on them,' Quinn said, nodding toward the monitors. 'If anything acts up again, let me know.'

'You going somewhere?'

Quinn pushed the empty plastic chair toward the equipment rack, then stretched out on the floor. 'As far away from here as I can,' he said as he closed his eyes. 'Wake me in two hours if there aren't any more problems.'

'Yeah, sure,' Nate said. 'I'll just . . . stay here.'

'Stay alert.' Quinn tapped the cooler with his foot. 'Have a Red Bull, if you need one.'

Nate said something under his breath.

Quinn opened one eye. 'What?'

'Nothing.'

Quinn stared for a moment longer, then closed the eye. 'I could have left you in Los Angeles, you know.'

He could sense Nate wanting to say something more, but his apprentice remained silent.

* * *

At five minutes to nine, the Office's agent, a veteran operative named David Otero, arrived. With him was William Ownby, the allotted second man. Quinn and Nate watched as the two agents cautiously approached the church, then entered the abandoned sanctuary.

Peter had told Quinn that Otero and Ownby would have no knowledge of Quinn's presence. That wasn't unusual. Quinn and Nate weren't there as backup. They were there for an entirely different reason. One Otero and Ownby wouldn't have wanted to consider.

Nate glanced at his watch. 'It's three minutes after nine. Our other guest is running behind.'

Quinn nodded, but said nothing. The second party had been told the meet would take place somewhere in the south of Ireland, but had only been given the exact location three hours earlier. And the church wasn't the easiest place in the world to find.

'Hold on,' Nate said. 'Lights.'

Quinn used a handheld joystick to pan a camera that was covering the road to the south a little to the right, centering a pair of distant headlights moving toward the church. For a moment, they disappeared as the road dipped between two hills. Quinn and Nate had measured the distance that morning. The vehicle was just under a kilometer away.

A moment later, the car reappeared, and less than thirty seconds later it began to slow.

'Approaching the turnout,' Nate said.

On the screen, the car slowed to almost a crawl, then pulled off into the wide spot in the road, and its lights were turned off.

Quinn leaned forward and pushed a button on a rectangular metal box mounted in the rack. Next to the button was a speaker, and just above that a microphone was mounted on a five-inch gooseneck extender.

'Peter, you getting this?' Quinn asked, then let go of the button.

'Yes. That's got to be them.' Though Peter's voice came through the speaker, the quality was so good it sounded like he was in the van with them.

Quinn glanced back at one of the monitors covering the inside of the church. Otero had found a large block of stone to sit on, while Ownby had taken up a less visible position in a nook near the north entrance. If either man was getting impatient, they didn't show it.

Four minutes later, one of the microphones picked up the sound of footsteps approaching the church.

'Everything recording?' Quinn asked.

Nate glanced at a small LCD monitor mounted on a swivel arm next to the hard drives. He pressed one of the buttons on the touchscreen menu. The display changed to a set of green lights.

'All drives recording,' he said, then glanced over his shoulder toward the communication equipment. 'Satellite link steady and strong.'

Quinn pushed the button that connected him with the Office. 'Approaching the church now.'

'Good,' Peter said. 'Let's get this over with.'

Otero must have also heard the footsteps. He stood up, and put a cautious hand on the bulge in his jacket pocket before looking back at Ownby and pointing in the direction of the approaching sound. Ownby reached under his jacket and pulled out a gun, a Beretta 9mm. From his pocket he pulled out a long cylinder, a suppressor, and attached it to the end of the barrel.

The footsteps stopped just beyond the walls of the church. Then silence for almost a minute.

'I don't see them,' Nate said.

'They're there,' Quinn said.

'I know. But I don't see them.'

There were a series of numbered buttons on the base of the joystick Quinn was holding. He punched number 8 and began panning a camera covering the outside of the church's south end.

'There,' Nate said, pointing at the monitor for camera eight.

Quinn could see them now. There were two of them, crouched low and half-hidden by the thick brush. As Quinn and Nate watched, one of the men sprinted forward, stopping only when he reached the outside of the church wall. He then moved down the wall until he came to what had once been a doorway, and peered inside.

'Are we going to play games, or are we going to meet?' It was Otero. He was still standing in the middle of the church, not concealing his

11

presence. When there was no response, he said, 'Two minutes and we're leaving.'

The man who had been looking into the church from the doorway glanced back at his partner and waved for him to come over.

'Quinn,' Nate said.

'What?'

'I thought they were only allowed one companion.'

Quinn shot Nate a glance, then looked at a monitor Nate was pointing at. It was the one covering the north approach to the church, the way Otero and Ownby had come.

'I don't see anything,' Quinn said.

'In the tree,' Nate said. He leaned forward and touched the screen.

For half a second, Quinn still didn't see anything, then a slight movement revealed the form of a man lying prone on one of the branches, facing toward the church.

A quick glance at a monitor that gave a broader view of that side of the church confirmed Quinn's suspicion that the man was high enough to see through the missing roof into the abandoned structure.

Quinn pushed the mic button again. 'Peter, we have a problem.'

'What?'

'Check the feed to camera six. In the tree, near the top of the image.'

There was a pause.

'Do you see him?' Quinn asked.

'Yes.'

'Is he one of yours?'

'I played by the rules. Only two,' Peter said. 'He must be one of theirs.'

Quinn wasn't convinced of that, but there was no time to argue the point. On another monitor the two newcomers stepped through the doorway, entered the church, and walked a couple paces before stopping. They looked nervous, like this was the first time they had ever done anything like this.

'You need to abort right now,' Quinn said.

'We need that information,' Peter said.

'Peter,' Quinn said, 'if you don't abort, you might not get anything.'

At the church Otero said, 'You guys are going to have to come a little closer.'

The taller of the two men shook his head. 'We are fine here. I think you have something to show us.'

Otero smiled, then tossed a coin in the air so that it landed a foot in front of his counterparts.

'Your turn,' Otero said.

The tall man tossed his own coin toward Otero. This was the prearranged recognition signal. Otero had been carrying a fifty-yen Japanese coin, and the informant a 1998 Canadian half-dollar.

'Peter!' Quinn said.

'The meet's already started,' Peter said. 'They won't answer their phones until they're back in their car.'

'They might not even make it back to their car,' Quinn said, then let go of the button.

'We can start the van,' Nate suggested. 'That should throw everyone into a panic. We could

13

even fire off a shot.'

It was an excellent idea, Quinn thought. He relayed it to Peter.

There was a pause, then Peter said, 'Do it.'

Quinn pulled his SIG Sauer P226 out of the holster under his left arm as Nate moved toward the back door to open it.

Several rapid flashes from one of the monitors caught Quinn's eye. It was the one showing the close-up of the man in the tree. He glanced at the view of the church. Otero, Ownby, and the man who had been talking for the other party were all on the ground and not moving.

The final man had just exited the church and was making a run for it. Then there was another flash. The man jerked to the left, his momentum dropping him into a bush at the side of the trail. Like the others, he didn't get up.

'Stop,' Quinn said to Nate.

The door was already half opened.

'Close it. Quietly.'

Nate shut the door as Quinn sat back down.

Quinn pushed the button. 'Your op is blown.'

'I can fucking see that,' Peter said. 'Goddammit! You need to keep whoever that is from getting to the bodies. One of those guys is carrying something we need.'

'Don't know if you noticed,' Quinn said, 'but your men are probably dead. That guy in the tree's got a silenced rifle, and I'm not really interested in walking into his range.'

'Do what you were going to do before! Scare him off. He's not going to want to get caught.'

Quinn took a deep breath, then nodded at

Nate to open the door again. He checked monitor six. The assassin was holding his position, waiting to see if anyone else was going to show up.

Quinn pulled one of the remote communication sets from a bag near the recorders. He slipped the receiver over his ear, then climbed out of the van.

'Talk me in,' he said to Nate.

'You're going to try to take him out?' Nate asked, surprised.

Quinn shook his head. 'I'm just going to convince him to go someplace else.'

'You want your suppressor?' Nate asked.

Quinn paused for a second. If things went as planned, he'd need the noise of the shot to scare the guy off. But if things got off track?

'Toss it to me,' he said.

Nate disappeared for a second, then stepped back into the doorway and threw a dark cylinder to Quinn.

Quinn stuffed it in the front pocket of his jacket as best he could. Once it was secure, he nodded back at the van. 'Talk me in. You're my eyes, so try not to get me killed.'

# 2

AFRICA

The sound of the distant gunfire hardly registered on Marion Dupuis. It was at least two kilometers away, and intermittent at best.

*Just another night.*

No doubt morning would bring a report on the government-run radio station about another successful raid against a rebel cell. The same report, if it stayed true to form, would also note that the government troops would have suffered no fatalities. Just like all the other times, President Pokou's forces would appear victorious.

Only, if Pokou's army was winning, why did the violence seem to be increasing?

Marion knew the answer. She had seen the reports, the *real* reports, and she'd heard other members of the UN observer force discuss the unrest. The way she understood it, there was at least a fifty-fifty chance that within the next couple of months Côte d'Ivoire would be plunged into another full-out civil war.

And once again, no one outside the tiny West African nation would care.

More gunfire. A short burst.

Marion didn't even flinch.

The action seemed to be containing itself to the east, away from where she was, and where she needed to be. She would be willing to bet most of Pokou's troops would be moving in that direction, too. In a way, she thought, it was sort of a blessing.

As long as she didn't think about the lives that were being lost.

She checked the street ahead of her. Dark, quiet, no movement. She took a deep breath, then pushed herself off the building she'd been leaning against and crossed to the other side of the street. She paused, making sure she was still unnoticed, then headed down the street.

Driving would have been faster, but she felt safer on foot. With the 8 p.m. curfew in effect, a car's engine would have drawn unnecessary attention on the otherwise quiet roads. So she stuck to the shadows and moved silently from building to building.

Most of the homes and businesses she passed were dark. It was after midnight, so even without the curfew, much of the city would already be asleep.

Five minutes later, she reached a large avenue that went east and west through the city. She started to cross, then stopped abruptly and pulled back into the doorway of a darkened building.

She'd seen headlights coming from the east, and heard the unmistakable sounds of several army vehicles. She peeked around the edge of the wall to get another look. There were at least five vehicles: three jeeps and a couple of trucks with loud diesel engines and transmissions that ground in protest of their unskilled drivers.

She estimated they would pass by her position in less than a minute. Though she knew any delay could be crucial, crossing now would be suicide. They'd spot her the second she stepped onto the street. She had no choice but to wait until they passed.

But her current position was only slightly better than standing still in the middle of the road. If one of the soldiers decided to aim a light in her direction, she would be discovered. So she slipped out of the doorway and stayed tight to the building as she looked for someplace better. She found it half a block down, an alley no more than four meters wide between a store and what looked like an abandoned restaurant.

Signs on the outside walls of the store advertised sodas and cigarettes. Like all the other buildings, it was closed up tight, but as she turned down the alley, she noticed light seeping out of one of the back windows. Marion guessed the shop provided not only a means of income for the owner, but also a place to sleep.

About a dozen meters down the alley was a pile of rotting wooden crates. She slipped behind them, crouching down so she was hidden from anyone passing by on the road. She was able to move one of the boxes a couple centimeters to the right, creating a peephole through which she could keep an eye on the army caravan as it drove by.

The rumbling of the trucks got louder and louder until the street in front of the shop grew bright from the vehicles' headlights. She watched first as two jeeps passed, then the trucks, and

18

finally the last jeep. Each had been full of young soldiers dressed in dark fatigues and berets.

Even with Marion's limited vision, it looked to her like all the men were armed with rifles. She had yet to be able to figure out what distinguished one type of rifle from another. To her, they all produced the same result.

As the rumble of the convoy receded, Marion stood up and started back toward the street, intent on making up for lost time.

'*Qui êtes-vous? Que voulez-vous?*'

Marion froze. The voice had come from behind her. It was male, deep and urgent.

'*Répondez-moi. Que faites-vous ici?*'

She raised her hands. 'Please,' she said. 'I'm just trying to get home.' Though French was her native tongue, she answered in English. In the unlit alley, her olive-colored skin might look darker than it really was, so she wanted to emphasize the fact that she was a foreigner.

She heard the man take a step closer to her. 'Are you American?' he asked, his English slow and deliberate.

'Canadian,' she said.

'Turn. Slow.'

She did what he asked.

When she saw him, she realized he was older than she'd thought. His hair was gray, his body thin and stooped. He held a pistol, and was pointing it at her, though the tremor in his hands moved the barrel a half an inch in either direction every few seconds.

He wasn't alone, either. Behind him, peeking around his hip, was a young girl. She looked more curious than scared.

'Why do you hide behind my shop?' The man seemed to think hard before saying each word, as if he was reaching back to knowledge he hadn't used in decades.

'The soldiers,' she said. 'I didn't want them to find me out after curfew.'

'Not safe. You should not be out here.'

The little girl smiled at Marion. It was doubtful she could understand a word that was being said.

'I told you. I'm just trying to go home,' Marion said.

'No car? Alone?'

Marion looked at him for a moment, then shook her head.

'You will be killed,' the man said, but he lowered his own gun, indicating the bullet would not come from him. 'Wait until morning.' He nodded at the spot she had been hiding in when the convoy passed. 'There. You will be safe. I will not . . . give you trouble.'

'I can't,' she said. 'I have to go.'

The man's eyes grew distant, then he said, 'Wait.' Only this time she knew he didn't mean for her to hide out in the alley all night.

He turned and walked quickly away, disappearing behind the back of the shop. The little girl followed him, though more reluctantly, stealing glances back at Marion, until she, too, was gone.

Though Marion felt the need to continue her journey, she did as the old man asked. Less than a minute later he was back, this time alone. The pistol he'd held in his hand had been replaced by a rectangular box that tapered at one end and fit snug in his palm.

He hesitated a moment, then held it out to her. She took it, unsure what to do with it. Without taking it from her hand, the old man turned the device so that the tapered end lay across her palm. In this direction, her thumb fell naturally across the top of the box and rested on top of a square button.

'Touch someone with this end,' the man said, pointing at the wide edge of the box. 'Push button. Electric.'

'You mean shock?' she asked. 'Like a Taser?'

He looked at her like he hadn't understood what she was asking.

'Electric. Electric,' he said, then he shook his body, imitating the results.

'I can't take this from you,' she told him, holding it back out.

'Bring it back,' he said. 'After the sun comes up.'

She took a breath, then nodded and said, 'Thank you.'

Without another word, he walked back the way he'd come. Marion then turned and retraced her steps to the street.

★   ★   ★

For thirty minutes Marion worked her way through half-paved side streets and dirt paths, avoiding the main roads altogether. Any time there was even the slightest sound, she would

21

stop and wait until she was sure there was no threat. In her right hand she held on tight to the Taser as if it were a talisman guaranteeing her passage through the city.

It seemed to work, too. She had seen no one else on her trip. And while she had heard a few more military vehicles, they had been distant and of no concern.

That was until she turned onto the street where the orphanage was located.

There were two vehicles double-parked in front of the three-story building that housed the orphanage — a jeep and a sedan, both with headlights on, and drivers sitting at the ready. Two other soldiers stood near the open door of the building.

She was three blocks away, so they hadn't noticed her. But if she continued on, she wouldn't even make it to the next block without being spotted. There weren't enough cars to hide behind, and, in the curfew-induced stillness, any movement would draw attention.

She doubled back, then went two blocks farther away before cutting over to the dirt alley that ran behind the orphanage. Water ran down the center of the road, the last remnants of the storm that had passed through earlier that evening. Other than that, the road was quiet. There were no soldiers anywhere in sight.

Marion made her way past run-down and bullet-strewn buildings that had survived coup after coup and would undoubtedly survive at least one more. The orphanage building was as old as the others, but better cared for, someone having taken the time to slap concrete patches over the worst damage. From her previous visits, Marion knew the ground floor was taken up by a small office, a kitchen, and a combination dining room/meeting place. On the second and third floors were rooms for the staff, dorms for the children, and a few makeshift classrooms.

Roslyn's Place, that's what everyone called it. But it had no official name. Nor was it sponsored like places in other parts of the city. Those orphanages had the backing of large religious agencies or other NGOs — non-governmental organizations.

Roslyn's Place had no backing. It was just something that had been started by a Swiss woman who had visited the country twenty years earlier and had never left. Frau Roslyn had intended it as a facility where children could come, feel safe, and perhaps even learn something during the day. But when she realized that many of the kids who came to her had nowhere else to go in the evenings, she began letting them stay. It wasn't long before the occasional baby or toddler would be left at the front door. Roslyn could have turned them over to an official facility, but she never did. She felt the responsibility had been given to her, so she had no intention of passing it on.

Now, the first thing she did every morning was open the front door and look down.

With the help of a few locals whom Roslyn paid out of her modest savings, she did it all on her own. When Marion had stumbled upon Roslyn's Place two months earlier, she'd made it her personal mission to do what she could to help out. Using her position within the UN, she'd been able to arrange for a shipment of school supplies, and had even convinced a European-based aid organization to send packages of nonperishable food every few weeks. But racing through the city in the middle of the night on foot was not something she had ever foreseen as part of her commitment.

Marion ducked down and passed below the darkened first-floor windows, making her way over to the dingy door on the far side. It was the back entrance into the kitchen, where most of the supplies were brought in. She put an ear to the wooden surface and listened. The room beyond was quiet. She grabbed the knob and gently turned it. As Frau Roslyn had promised on the phone, the door was unlocked. Marion had been warned that the hinges were not the quietest, so she slowly worked the door open just enough so she could squeeze inside.

Low light seeped into the kitchen from the window near the door. But it was more than adequate for Marion's night-adjusted eyes to see. She skirted past an old wooden table covered with pans and boxes and bags, and tiptoed over to the doorway that led out into the dining hall. There was no actual door, just a flower-print drape covering the opening. At serving time, it would be moved out of the way and held in place by a hook mounted on the wall.

Marion pulled the curtain back just enough to peer into the other room. The dining hall was also unlit, but like the kitchen, there was more than enough illumination shining through the windows from outside. The tables were empty, and the ragtag group of chairs and benches were all neatly in place. Everything ready and waiting for the morning meal.

Marion pushed the curtain out a little so she could look to her right toward the front of the building, and immediately caught her breath. There was someone standing against the wall only a few feet away. Her first instinct was to let go of the drape and escape out the back door into the night. But she didn't move. Frau Roslyn's words from her rushed call earlier came back to Marion.

'They're coming back,' the old woman had said.

The call had woken Marion. 'Who?' she'd asked, trying to focus.

'It's them. The ones we talked about. They're making the rounds again,' Frau Roslyn said. 'I just got the call. They'll be here soon, I'm sure of it.'

'You've nothing to worry about. Last time they only stayed a few minutes and then they were gone.'

'We didn't have what they were looking for last time.'

It took a second for Marion to realize what Frau Roslyn was saying. When she did, she could feel the blood drain from her face. 'Iris.'

'Yes.'

That had been enough to start her on her night journey.

Marion steadied herself and took another look

25

at the person who was standing on the other side of the door. With calmer eyes, she realized the shape was too small to be one of the soldiers. It had to be one of the children from upstairs. The form shifted against the wall, turning toward the back and allowing the light from outside to play across the child's face.

Dominique. Of course.

Marion pulled the curtain open a little more, then whispered, 'Dominique. *C'est moi.* Mademoiselle Dupuis.'

Dominique didn't even jump. 'I heard you come in,' she said in French. 'Frau Roslyn sent me to wait for you.'

Marion leaned her head through the opening. 'Where is she?'

'With the soldiers.' Dominique pointed above them. 'You stay. I will get her.'

'I should come with you.'

The girl shook her head several times. 'No. She doesn't want them to see you. Wait. It will only take me a minute.'

The girl turned and ran off before Marion could say anything more. Not sure what else to do, Marion pulled her head back into the kitchen and let the drape close over the opening. She tried not to think of anything, but her mind wouldn't let that happen.

*Iris. Why would they want her?*

The girl had been left at Roslyn's Place only a week before. Not a baby, but no more than four or five. Iris couldn't tell anyone how old she was. It wasn't just that she didn't know; she had no concept of age and probably never would. She'd

26

been born with Down syndrome and would forever need the help of others to survive. What tears had been on the girl's cheeks when they found her soon disappeared in smiles and laughter as Frau Roslyn and the other children welcomed her into their family.

Marion could hear someone enter the dining room. She gripped the Taser tightly in her hand, ready in case the new arrival was not a friend. But when the curtain was pulled aside, Marion relaxed. It was Roslyn.

The old Swiss lady was short and thin with a wrinkled face and white hair that stopped just above her shoulders. And while her appearance did nothing to hide the fact that she'd seen more years than most, she exuded an inner strength, a confidence that made the toughest of men pause before deciding to take her on.

'Come with me,' Roslyn said.

Without another word, the old woman went back into the dining room. Marion followed.

'How long have they been here?' Marion whispered once she caught up to her.

'Fifteen minutes.'

'They haven't found her, then?'

'No,' Roslyn said. 'But they know she was here. Someone must have told them. They say they won't leave until they find her.'

They crossed the dining room toward the hallway that led to the office at the front of the building. Marion was about to ask another question, but Frau Roslyn held up her hand, stopping her.

'You must be quiet,' the woman said. 'They

will hear you. And if they hear you . . . '

She didn't have to finish the thought. They both knew what would happen.

As they entered the short hallway, Frau Roslyn paused. There was light at the far end where the small building lobby was located. Above them, Marion could hear the movement of several heavy sets of feet. There were also the muffled cries and voices of children unsure why they had been woken in the middle of the night.

Frau Roslyn took several quiet steps forward, passing the door on the left that led to her office, and another on the right to the makeshift first aid station. Again, Marion followed.

They stopped a couple feet shy of the end of the hallway. If anyone had walked by, the light from the lobby would have been more than enough to expose Marion's presence.

Frau Roslyn leaned to her right, looking into the lobby. The angle would give her a view of the front door. When she straightened and turned around, she whispered almost too low for Marion to hear, 'Two soldiers, but they're still outside. Come on. We don't have much time.'

She pushed past Marion and opened the door to her office. Unlike the back entrance, the hinges on this door were well oiled and made no sound. Frau Roslyn motioned Marion inside, then she closed the door, easing the latch into place.

'The soldiers,' Marion said, 'they won't hurt the children, will they?'

The woman shook her head. 'Jan is up there.'

Jan was Roslyn's cousin. A large Swiss-German man who had the benefit of being a former member of the Swiss government, something Roslyn would have made sure the soldiers knew.

'Where's Iris?' Marion asked.

Roslyn put a finger to her mouth, then turned and edged her way around the large metal desk that seemed to take up half the room. She reached up and made sure the curtains across the window on the back wall were fully closed. Then, instead of sitting down in the old wooden chair, she continued past the desk to the side wall. Like the rest of the room, the wall was painted off-white. On it were hung several framed pictures of Frau Roslyn with children who had at one time or another lived in the orphanage. They all seemed to be smiling and happy and content.

The old woman moved one of the pictures to the side and touched a spot on the wall. There was a faint click, then the wall eased open an inch. Roslyn reached around the edge of the opening and pulled the wall out like a door.

Marion's eyes widened in surprise.

'Come, come,' the old woman said.

Marion hesitated a moment longer, then moved around the desk and joined Frau Roslyn.

Since the hidden door swung out into the office, Marion had not been able to see what was inside until the door was all the way open. The space it revealed wasn't large, maybe a meter deep at best, and only as wide as the opening. It was made even more cramped by the fact that it wasn't empty.

One of the older boys was inside. He was maybe thirteen or fourteen. Marion had seen him many times before but couldn't remember his name. In his arms he held another child. A girl, much younger than he was. Her head rested against his chest and her eyes were closed in sleep.

It was Iris. There was no mistaking her.

The old woman held her hands out, and the boy gave her the child.

'Everything okay?' she asked.

'She slept the whole time, Frau Roslyn.' The boy smiled. 'She was very good. Are they gone?'

Before Roslyn could answer, the loud pounding of feet came from the stairs near the front of the building.

'Madame Krueger? Madame Krueger?' a voice called from the direction of the footsteps. Male, deep. One of the soldiers, using Roslyn's surname.

Roslyn looked back at the boy. He was still in the tiny space behind the secret door. 'Out,' she said. 'Quickly!'

The boy stepped out into the office.

'Madame Krueger?' the voice was closer.

'Take her,' Roslyn said as she held Iris out to Marion. 'Get inside. You have to hide.'

'What?' Marion said.

'There's no time,' the old woman said. 'Please. Take her.'

Marion instinctively pulled the child into her arms, careful to point the end of the stunner

30

away from the girl's back.

'Now get in,' Roslyn said.

'I don't think I'll fit.'

'They'll take her if you don't.'

Marion nodded as she realized there was no choice. She stepped past the woman and the boy into the small space in the wall.

'I'll let you out when they're gone,' Roslyn said.

'What if she wakes?' Marion asked.

'I gave her something to help her sleep. You'll be fine.'

Before Marion could say anything else, the secret door closed, entombing her and Iris in the wall. The seal was a good one. There was absolutely no light. Marion could never remember being anyplace so completely dark. For a moment she allowed the fear to shake through her like a deep chill. But then she heard the office door fly open, and she froze.

'What are you doing?' It was the same voice that yelled from the stairs, muffled by the closed secret door, but still distinct.

'One of the boys was missing,' Roslyn said, her voice calm and unhurried. 'I came to look for him.'

'What were you doing down here?' the soldier asked.

'I . . . I got scared,' the boy who had been taking care of Iris said. 'I was hiding.'

There was the sound of movement, then the scrape of metal along the floor. The desk, perhaps, being pushed back or out of the way.

'Please, no,' the boy yelled out.

31

'You want to be scared?' the soldier said.

'No. I'm sorry. I shouldn't have hid. I wasn't thinking.'

Silence for a moment.

'And you were alone here?'

'What?' the boy said. 'Yes. Alone.'

'Please,' Roslyn said. 'The boy is young. He saw his parents killed in the middle of the night, so naturally he gets scared sometimes.'

'We've all seen people killed in the night,' the soldier said. But Roslyn's words must have gotten to him. The harsh tone in his voice was gone. 'Next time, you don't hide, you understand?'

'Yes, sir,' the boy said.

'Go upstairs with the others.'

Again movement. Feet, not as loud as the soldier's, moving out of the room.

'Come with me,' the soldier said.

'Where?' Roslyn asked.

'I'm the one who asks the questions.'

'Of course.'

There was the sound of several feet walking out of the office, and then there was silence.

Marion waited, hoping that the sleeping child in her arms would remain that way.

What could the soldiers want with her? Her difference from the other children should have made her less desirable for the soldiers rather than more. Her kind was seldom wanted. Not just here in Côte d'Ivoire, but in most countries throughout the world. Yet this wasn't the first time the soldiers had come looking for a child like her.

32

The darkness made it impossible for Marion to know what time it was. She began counting off minutes in an effort to remain calm. But after a while she lost her place and gave up. Where was Roslyn?

Finally, she heard footsteps enter the office. It sounded like more than one person, but she couldn't tell for sure. She tried to angle the stunner so it pointed toward the door just in case.

The steps seemed to stop near the desk. She thought she heard someone whisper, but she wasn't sure. Then the steps came forward again, stopping less than a foot away from her on the other side of the wall.

She brushed the button on the stunner with her thumb, checking its position so she'd be ready.

Something scraped along the wall. A picture being moved.

Then there was the click again. Only it was louder inside the hidden room.

The door popped open an inch and light seeped in.

The sudden change caused Iris to move, her head rocking against Marion's chest.

'It's okay, it's okay,' Marion whispered, trying to coax the child back to sleep.

Marion could see the tips of several fingers grabbing the edge of the door. Iris twisted again, this time lifting her head up, her eyes opening at the same moment the door did.

Marion held the child tightly with one arm while the other was occupied with the Taser,

33

ready to ram it into the first piece of skin she saw.

Outside, blocking the light, was a dark form. Large, like one of the soldiers. Without even realizing it, she pushed down with her thumb, activating the weapon in her hand. Only nothing happened. There was no arc of electricity, or even a vibration that would tell her the device was on.

'I would appreciate you moving that away,' a voice said. It came from the shadow. The voice was male, speaking French like the soldiers. Only it was different. The accent was Germanic.

As he stepped backward, the weak light of the office revealed that he wasn't one of the soldiers from before.

It was Jan, Frau Roslyn's cousin.

'I don't think that works anymore, anyway,' he said.

He held out his hand. After a moment, she gave him the stunner.

As he set it on the desk, he said, 'It's safe now. You can come out.'

'They're gone?' she asked.

He nodded. 'Fifteen minutes ago.'

He helped her to step out of the space in the wall, then he closed the door behind her.

'Where is Frau Roslyn?' Marion asked.

The look on Jan's face darkened. 'They kept her out front for over an hour talking. Then they took her away.'

'What? What do you mean 'away'?'

Jan hesitated. 'I'm going to go look for her as

soon as I can find someone to watch the children.'

'I'll stay.'

'No,' he said. 'You have to get out of here. You have to take Iris with you.'

They both looked at the child. She was awake now, but she hadn't made a sound. She was looking at Marion, smiling.

'Where do I take her?'

'Someplace safe,' Jan said. 'The UN compound. They won't bother you there. But — '

'I can't just take her to the compound.'

Jan stared at her for several seconds. 'Then leave her here. I'll give her to the soldiers when they come back.'

She closed her eyes and took a deep breath. 'Of course,' she said. 'Of course, I'll take her. I'm sorry.' She paused for a moment, the beginnings of a sob caught in her chest. 'I'm just . . . scared.'

The look on Jan's face was tense. There was no smile, no friendly sparkle in his eyes like Marion had seen on previous visits. 'You should be.' He leaned down until only a foot separated his face from her. 'Listen to me. They'll keep looking for her. You need to get her away. Far away. Once you do, you need to disappear. Don't let anyone know where you are. These people will find you. And once they have the girl, they'll kill you.'

'If I can get her out of the city, they'll have to give up. They're just local soldiers.'

'Forget about the soldiers,' Jan said. 'It's not the soldiers you need to worry about. It's the people the soldiers are working for. Those are the people you need to be concerned with. They're not local. They're not even from Africa.'

She didn't understand what he meant, but it was obvious he had no intention of explaining more. Without saying another word, he guided her through the orphanage to the back door she had snuck through less than two hours before.

'Go,' he said, all but pushing her through the door. 'Iris's life depends on you.'

The door closed before she could respond.

She looked down at the child. Iris's eyelids were heavy.

'That's right,' Marion said. 'Sleep. Just sleep. I'll take care of you.'

Once the girl's eyes closed, Marion began retracing the steps that had brought her to the orphanage, not knowing how she was going to keep the promise she had just made.

# 3

Quinn used the same path he had earlier in the day when he'd returned from his last check of the church. Only this time it was dark, and if that wasn't hindrance enough, it seemed as if all the bushes that lined the trail had grown significantly larger in the several hours that had passed. He had to take extra care not to sound like a herd of roaming sheep.

In his right hand was his SIG, and in his left, the small wireless microphone that paired with the receiver hanging on his ear. Keeping his eyes on the path, he reached up and attached the mic to his collar.

'Give me a constant update,' he whispered. 'I'm not going to be able to say much, so just keep talking.'

'Got it,' Nate said, his voice overamplified and crackling.

'You're killing me,' Quinn said. 'Turn down your gain.'

There was a pause, then Nate said, 'Better?' His voice sounded almost normal.

'Yes. Thanks,' he said.

Two minutes later he came to a small open field. Though he was pretty sure the assassin in the tree wouldn't be able to see him, he kept to the dark shadows at the edge of the clearing.

'He's still in the tree,' Nate said. 'But he's moved back, closer to the trunk. Harder to see.'

*He's expecting company,* Quinn thought. *Waiting to see if his victims have backup anywhere close by.*

'I still don't see signs of anyone else. I think he might be working alone.'

Quinn wasn't ready to concede that possibility yet. He'd seen too much in his years in the business, seen too many people who had been killed because they underestimated their opponent. He removed the sound suppressor from his jacket and attached it to his weapon. Any shot Quinn took at this point wouldn't be to scare the guy, it would be to hit him.

'I've got no movement from the men on the ground,' Nate said.

There wouldn't be. They were all dead the second Quinn and Nate had seen the muzzle flashes on the screen. The assassin got the first three shots off before any of the men in the church could react. The range was not much more than thirty yards. So close it was almost cheating for a trained marksman. Kill shots, all of them. No question. The only reason there'd been a delay before the fourth man was killed was that the assassin hadn't had a clean shot. So he'd waited a few seconds for the man to panic, and run for someplace new to hide, then bang. Four dead.

'Wait,' Nate said. 'I think he's climbing down.'

Quinn had reentered the trees on the far side of the pasture and was once again fighting the underbrush. He guessed he was about a minute away from the old church grounds. From this direction, he would reach the graveyard first.

'He's on the ground, but staying close to the tree. I can see his weapon, though. Hold on, let me zoom in.' There was a pause. 'I think it's a Galil.'

That would make sense, Quinn thought. A Galil sniper rifle using subsonic rounds could be silenced effectively. Plus the weapon was light and easily portable. An excellent choice.

Ahead Quinn could see the trees thinning. Beyond would be the graveyard. He slowed as he reached the edge of the woods, and crouched down low. Less than ten feet away from where the trees ended was a ragged row of headstones. They were old and weathered, several to the point of being unreadable. Between the stones grass had grown high, and here and there a tree or a bush had taken root. But none had grown too large. Quinn guessed that every few years someone came out and cleared away the vegetation, a last act of respect for the dead parishioners who were otherwise forgotten.

'I'm here,' Quinn said, keeping his voice as low as possible. 'Behind the graveyard.'

'He's around the right side of the church from your position,' Nate told him. 'Probably about your two o'clock.'

'Okay.'

'Quinn.'

'What?'

'Peter wanted me to remind you not to let him get to the bodies.'

'That's kind of what I'm trying to do, isn't it?'

'And . . . em . . . if there's any way you can subdue him, that would be best,' Nate said.

39

'Peter said he's got a couple guys heading our way right now. Should be here in thirty minutes.'

'That's a joke, right?'

'Would you like me to patch you through to him directly?'

'No,' Quinn said, trying hard to keep his voice from getting too loud. 'I'm really not in a place where I can have a chat with —'

'Movement,' Nate said, cutting him off.

Quinn froze in place.

'What's happening?' he asked.

'He's heading toward the church. He left the rifle behind the tree, and is carrying a pistol now. Looks like a SIG.'

Quinn stood up and weaved through the graveyard toward the church, the building's bulk between him and the assassin, shielding him from view.

'I see you,' Nate said. 'You're both closing on the building at the same rate.'

Quinn sped up, moving to his left as he did, toward an opening that had probably once held a beautiful stained glass window. He knew from his earlier reconnaissance that the window would provide a clear view of the interior of the church. He crouched beneath the sill.

'Okay,' Nate said. 'You're there first. He's stopped at the body outside the church. He's checking the pockets . . . hold on . . . okay, he's rolling him over and checking the back pockets . . . the dead guy doesn't seem to have anything on him . . . okay, he's getting up again . . . now he's heading for the church.'

Quinn checked that the suppressor was

securely fastened to the barrel of his SIG.

'He's stopped just outside a doorway,' Nate continued. 'It's the one directly across from where you're at.'

Quinn pictured the interior of the church in his mind. The window he stood beside, the door the assassin would walk through, the positions of the bodies on the sanctuary floor, the possible hiding places, the escape routes, everything. Then he took in a steady, silent breath, knowing what he would do. Peter was going to owe him big-time after this.

'He's peeking around the doorway, looking inside . . . he's stepping across the threshold and . . . inside . . . heading for the closest body first. Otero. Wait a minute. He stopped, seems to be listening.'

Quinn cocked his head, then he heard it, too. A car. It was coming fast from the north. No, not just one car, but two. Distant at the moment, but approaching rapidly.

'Car,' Nate said a second later. 'Heading south.'

Quinn risked a glance through the corner of the window. The assassin was still standing rock still next to the body of David Otero. His head was turned away from Quinn toward the front corner of the church where the entrance once had been.

On the road, the cars continued to draw nearer. Quinn judged that they were less than two minutes away.

The assassin must have made the same calculation. He looked down at Otero, then glanced at the other two bodies. Quinn's plan had been to make his move when the assassin was bent down searching one of his victims. It would have put him at an advantage, and he would have had little problem guarding the shooter until Peter's backup arrived. If the assassin tried to run, Quinn would be able to take him out with a single shot.

But the cars changed everything. A second later, the assassin began rapidly retracing his steps out of the church and back to the tree that had served as his roost. Apparently he had decided to forgo searching the bodies in exchange for getting the hell out of there.

'He's on the move,' Nate said. 'Nearing the tree.'

Quinn rose and moved down the side of the church, staying tight to the wall. When he reached the corner, he turned and headed toward the far end. Beyond was an open area that ran parallel to the church and out seventy-five feet to where the brush and the trees took over in force.

The assassin's tree was there. Quinn could see it another ten feet into the wild. He just couldn't see the assassin.

'He's picking up his rifle,' Nate said. 'Now he's slinging it over his shoulder and heading . . . northwest . . . he's out of camera range now. I've lost him.'

That was it, then, Quinn thought. He wasn't about to chase the man through the wilderness without the advantage of Nate being able to watch his back. He allowed his body to relax.

'Keep an eye on the monitors in case he's just circling around,' Quinn said. 'And watch the road cams, too. See if a car shows up that seemed to come out of nowhere. That'll be him. He's got to have a ride parked around here somewhere.'

'Quinn?' Nate asked.

'What?'

'Peter wants to talk to you.'

The muscles in Quinn's face tightened. 'Fine. Put him through.'

While Nate transferred the call to the comm gear, the two cars on the road reached the point closest to the church, but neither slowed. Immediately the whine of their engines began to recede as they continued down the back road to Cork.

Static in Quinn's ear, then, ' . . . inn. Are you there? Can you hear me?'

'Yeah. I hear you, Peter,' Quinn said. 'The gunman's gone. A couple cars on the road spooked him.'

'You've got to find him.'

'Ah . . . no. I don't. I already took a chance trying to take him here at the church. He's out in the woods now. I don't have any eyes out there.'

Peter said nothing for several seconds. When he did speak, there was a tremor in his voice. He was either scared or angry as hell. 'You have to find him, Quinn. You have to stop him. Jesus, at least find a way to delay him until my men get there.'

Peter's insistence surprised Quinn. 'It's too late, Peter. He's already got a good lead on me.

Plus he's a marksman, *and* has at least two weapons on him . . . it's too much of a risk. Sorry.'

Peter took a second before he spoke. 'Our deal was no questions. That means you do what I need, right?'

Quinn could feel his own anger rising. The deal — made the previous year — was three jobs, no questions. It had been made when Quinn had been at a disadvantage and needed Peter's help. It had taken Peter six months to finally invoke the first of the promised 'no question' assignments. If the next two were similar, they would be the last Quinn ever worked for Peter and the Office. About the only good thing was that none of them were freebies. Quinn's standard rate of thirty thousand a week with a two-week minimum still applied.

'You're losing time,' Peter said.

'Fine,' Quinn said. There *was* one thing he could try that was marginally safer. 'Nate, get him off the line.'

A second later the signal cleared up.

'He's gone,' Nate said.

'I need you out on the road. You think you can do that?'

'I can do whatever you need,' Nate said, immediately defensive. 'We already went over this.'

They had. Dozens of times over the last several months. It was just that Quinn was not yet convinced. The truth was he still wasn't sure Nate was ready to be back in the field. It had only been eight months since his apprentice had

44

lost the lower portion of his right leg when it was crushed during a job in Singapore. *A personal job*, Quinn reminded himself. One he should have left Nate home on. But instead he'd brought Nate along, and in the end had been forced to give the go-ahead on the amputation while his apprentice was unconscious.

'Go south,' Quinn said. 'Listen for a car door or an engine starting. The shooter's got to have a vehicle out here somewhere. I'll go north.'

'I'm on my way.'

As soon as Quinn reached the road, he turned north and began a quick jog along the left edge of the blacktop. He knew there was no way he would have been able to find the assassin once he took off into the woods. But the guy had to have a way out. A car, probably parked along a dirt road that led into one of the fields lining the narrow highway. Similar to the one Quinn had used for the van. None of the roads were longer than a couple hundred yards, and their only outlet was to the highway.

The assassin had headed west, but the nearest road in that direction was at least two miles away. Since he had had to follow either Otero or the other party to the meet, there would have been no way for him to drive over to the distant road, then trek back two miles on foot in time to get set up in the tree and pick off his targets. So he must have come on the same road as everyone else. That meant even though he had run west, he would soon be turning either north or south to circle back to where he'd left his ride.

There was a little-used dirt road just ahead on the right. Quinn remembered it from his earlier recon of the area, but passed by it with just a glance. It was too close. Quinn and Nate would have noticed any car that would have turned down it, even if someone had come in slow with his lights off.

'Anything?' Quinn said into his mic.

'No,' Nate said. His breath sounded a little labored. 'I'm already about seventy-five yards south of the road the van's on. How far do you want me to go?'

'Until I say stop,' Quinn said. 'He's not going to be close.'

There was another break in the brush, with two parallel ruts worn into the ground heading west. Quinn slowed this time, taking an extra hard look. Around fifty feet in, there was a solid dark shape. It was out of place among the more wispy brush.

Quinn turned cautiously down the path. After only a few steps, the shape became a car, a sedan. Dark, probably blue or black. As he neared he recognized it as a Ford Mondeo.

*The kind of car Otero was supposed to arrive in*, Quinn thought. Of course, that didn't mean the man he was chasing hadn't arrived in one either.

The vehicle appeared to be empty, so he quickened his pace, stopping just short of the rear passenger door on the left side. There was still no movement from inside. He held still for a moment, listening for anyone approaching through the brush. All was quiet.

He took a step forward, then peered through the window.

No one. Only a map, half-folded and jammed between the two front seats.

*Otero's car*, Quinn decided.

The evidence wasn't perfect, but the fact that the map had been stowed between the seats instead of tossed onto the passenger seat could very well have meant there had been two people riding up front. But more than that, the half-open map itself was a better indication that this wasn't the assassin's car. The assassin would have been following Otero, not worrying about how to get to the final destination. In fact, he wouldn't even have known where the final destination was.

Quinn ran back to the highway, then headed north again.

He knew he had to be close now. If Otero had been the one the assassin followed, his vehicle couldn't be too far away. He probably had been able to place a tracking bug on the Mondeo, then had sat back and followed a mile or two behind. Any closer and Otero would have noticed. But once the Mondeo had stopped moving, the assassin would have closed the distance, parking as close as he dared without drawing attention.

'Car,' Nate said.

Quinn stopped instantly, and turned to the south as if he could see Nate on the road in the distance. 'Is it him?'

'No,' Nate said. 'It's about a mile off, heading toward us. But it'll be here in a minute or two.'

47

'Make sure whoever it is doesn't see you.'

He could hear the car now, too. It wasn't as loud as the two cars earlier had been, apparently traveling at a more civil pace.

As Quinn turned back toward the north, he heard the unmistakable sound of an engine starting. It was close, maybe another fifty feet ahead of him, and off to the right, hidden by the brush.

Quinn raced forward, his SIG in his right hand. In seconds, he saw the path the car had taken into the brush. It was another old rutted road that probably hadn't been used in years.

'It just passed me,' Nate said. 'Delivery van. One guy up front. Didn't see anyone else.'

Quinn could hear the van on the road behind him approaching. And ahead, he could also hear the assassin's car. Its engine was only marginally louder than the van's.

Almost at once there was light in front and behind him. The van was cresting a small hill and soon would be completely visible to Quinn. And on the rutted path ahead of him, reverse lights, bright in the dark night, and warning all that the assassin was about to back out.

Quinn slipped behind a tree five feet from where the dirt road met the highway. He glanced to the south. The van had come into view and was traveling down the blacktop, showing no signs of having noticed the lights from the assassin's car.

And on the dirt road just ahead of him, Quinn could hear the tires of the assassin's car begin to move along the ruts toward the highway.

48

The timing was horrible. If they didn't run into each other, then it would be damn close. And any kind of incident would bring out the local officials. Quinn couldn't have that.

He moved around the tree and pushed through a couple of bushes until he was standing at the edge of the rutted road. The highway was fifteen feet to his left, and the assassin's car was only five to his right.

Quinn raised the SIG and pulled the trigger without any further thought.

There was the all too familiar *thup* as his bullet passed through the suppressor, followed instantaneously by the crunch of the rear window safety glass as it was ripped from its frame. Red lights flashed as the assassin stomped on the brakes.

On the highway behind them, there was the double tap of a horn, a friendly 'Hey, I'm out here' from the van, then a second later the sound of the larger vehicle as it passed by and continued on in the night.

Quinn stayed focused on the assassin's car. It was a four-door hatchback that could have been picked up at any rental place on the island. Only the good people at Hertz weren't going to be too happy with the blown-out window and whatever other damage Quinn's shot had caused.

The assassin had ducked out of sight below seat level. Going for his gun, Quinn knew. But he had no idea how many people he was facing, or where they were positioned. Any defense he would put up would be a guess.

Quinn took four quick silent steps through the

brush parallel to the car. This being Ireland, the driver's seat was on the right, the side nearest him. As he drew level with the driver's side door, he could see the assassin hunched low. The man was checking his gun to make sure there was a round in the chamber.

Quinn squeezed the trigger of his SIG again, a warning shot through the driver's side window. It ripped the air only inches above the assassin, then exited through the window on the other side.

The man froze.

Quinn motioned for him to put the gun down.

Though they killed for a living, he knew of no assassin who had a death wish. When pushed into a corner, they would bide their time, and wait for an opportunity to use their skills in an attempt to extract themselves from a bad situation.

Quinn's new friend, though, seemed to be working from a different handbook.

At first he pretended to set the gun down, but as he did, the barrel turned toward Quinn.

Before the man could get a shot off, Quinn pulled his SIG's trigger for a third time. This time it was no warning. The bullet smashed through the man's palm and grazed the bottom edge of the pistol's grip, sending it spinning to the floor, out of the man's reach.

'I've gone almost a mile and haven't found anything,' Nate said in Quinn's ear. 'I don't think he's out this way. I mean, I would have seen him by now, right?'

# 4

Quinn waited until Nate got there before doing anything about the wounded man's hand. He had Nate search the trunk for something that might work as a bandage.

'He's got an overnight bag in here,' Nate said.

There was the sound of a zipper, then a few moments later Nate held up an expensive-looking black shirt.

'Hugo Boss,' he said. 'That work?'

'Perfect,' Quinn said.

Nate tossed the shirt through the window at the assassin.

'Wrap that around your palm,' Quinn said. 'Probably should make it tight. You're quite a bleeder.'

The man did as Quinn suggested. It wasn't easy, and he had to start over more than once, but no one was about to give him any help.

Quinn glanced at Nate, then looked back into the car. 'You all right?' he asked.

Nate's face was sweaty, and even in the low light Quinn thought he could see red splotches on his apprentice's neck.

'I'm fine,' Nate said.

Quinn looked over again, this time his gaze moving momentarily down toward Nate's legs.

'It's fine,' Nate said, noticing Quinn's line of sight. 'No problems. I just ran over a mile to get back here, for God's sake. You'd be sweating, too.'

*Maybe*, Quinn thought. But he said nothing. He'd only allowed Nate to accompany him this time because he was tired of saying no. That, and Orlando had argued it was time.

'If you keep putting it off,' she had said, 'you'll never know what he can do. And after a while, you're going to start hurting his confidence.'

A cleaner without confidence was either working in some other field or more likely dead. So Quinn had reluctantly agreed to let Nate come along, all the time wondering if his missing lower leg, replaced now by a man-made prosthesis — albeit state-of-the-art — would be a hindrance or just an annoyance. So far, much to Quinn's surprise, it had been neither.

'Clear his weapons,' Quinn said, nodding toward the bleeding man in the car.

Nate nodded, then walked around to the other side of the vehicle. Within a few seconds, he'd removed both the man's pistol and the sniper rifle, and had patted the man down in case he was carrying anything else.

'Clear,' Nate said. He then pulled himself out of the car and brought the weapons back around, setting them against a tree ten feet away.

'You should let me go,' the assassin said. They were the first words he had spoken. His accent was American. Midwest. Not Chicago, more like Kansas. Of course, it could have been just a put-on. 'My client won't be pleased.'

'I don't really care,' Quinn said.

'You should.'

'But I don't.'

The man grew quiet.

'You bring your phone?' Quinn asked Nate.

'Yes.'

'Call in. Get an ETA.'

'My employer's men will be here before yours,' the assassin said.

Quinn ignored him. That, he knew, was a bluff. There was no reason for anyone to come after the assassin. He either did his job or he didn't. There would be no backup or cleanup team. In this case, leaving the bodies would have been desired. They'd be a message. *Don't mess with us.*

Nate pulled out his phone and walked toward the road beyond the rear of the car.

The assassin shrugged. 'Doesn't matter. I did what I was hired to do. So whatever operation you're running is screwed.'

'The only operation I'm running is catching you. And right now I'm trying to decide if you died as you tried to get away or you shot yourself to keep from being taken.'

'My employer wouldn't like that.'

'I don't give a damn what your employer likes or doesn't like,' Quinn said.

The man's eyes narrowed. 'That would be a mistake.'

'Wouldn't be the first time,' Quinn said.

★ ★ ★

The transfer went smoothly. Peter had sent three men. Two left in the SUV they'd arrived in with the assassin restrained in the back, while the third drove the gunman's sedan away.

'Let's get to it,' Quinn said to Nate once the others were gone.

They started walking back up the road toward the church. Even though there was a lot of night left, they still had a considerable amount of work to do before the sun came up.

The bodies were first on the list. Not surprisingly, pocket checks of the dead men revealed very little. Peter's men each carried forged IDs on the off chance they got pulled over by the police. The other two men had none. The only thing the guy outside the church was carrying was a spare mag for his gun. But his partner, the one who had been inside doing the talking, was carrying a little something extra.

It was a tiny manila envelope, an inch wide by about an inch and a half long, and bulging a bit in the center. Whatever was inside, Quinn guessed it must contain the information that was supposed to have been passed on. Peter's precious haul, no doubt. The reason he'd been so adamant about keeping the assassin away from the bodies.

Quinn was tempted to leave it in the man's pocket and tell Peter he hadn't found anything. But as satisfying as that was to consider, Quinn didn't operate that way. He slipped the envelope into his own pocket, then looked at Nate. 'Ready?'

'Yeah,' his apprentice said.

One by one, they placed the bodies on top of a large piece of plastic sheeting with whatever weapons they had been carrying, then wrapped them individually, securing them with a healthy amount of duct tape. They then stacked them in the back of the van where Quinn's and Nate's chairs had been.

While Nate searched for casings beneath the tree where the assassin had been positioned, Quinn worked the blood-soaked ground, covering it with mud and loose bushes. By the time night came again, no one would notice the stains on the soil.

The body removal was the easy part. It was dealing with the vehicles that was trickier. There were three of them for only two people — the van, and the two sedans the meeting's participants had arrived in.

Quinn didn't want to take a chance driving around with a van full of dead men more than he had to, so they started with the cars first. They each took a sedan and drove south for twenty minutes before turning down a narrow back road.

After another ten minutes, Quinn spotted an opening between the trees. Not another road, nor even a cart path. Just a break in the vegetation wide enough for the sedan to navigate through. He was able to work his way almost a hundred feet into the brush before he could go no farther. It was enough. There was no way the car could be seen from the road. With any luck, it might be days or even weeks before someone stumbled upon it. By then, it wouldn't matter.

He retraced his steps to the road, where Nate waited in the other car, and soon they were heading back north.

'Kind of fitting, I guess,' Nate said after a while. 'Dying in a church.'

'Dying in church is a common thing, is it?' Quinn asked.

'Not the dying so much,' Nate said. 'But being dead in church. You know, funerals. Memorials.'

Quinn looked at Nate, all but rolling his eyes. He then pulled out his cell phone and located a number in his contact list. The line rang twice.

'Hello?'

'We're on,' Quinn said.

'When should we expect you?' the voice asked.

'Before dawn.'

'We'll be ready.'

★　★　★

Quinn and Nate separated again at the church, Nate staying in the sedan while Quinn got behind the wheel in the van. This time they headed north toward Dublin. They kept their speed steady, not too fast, not too slow, so as not to draw undue attention. But they needn't have worried. There were few other vehicles on the road. When they reached the Irish capital, they skirted around the south edge, and made their way to Dun Laoghaire Harbour.

The boat was ready and waiting. It was a private yacht, a forty-six footer that could be run by one person if necessary. A Meridian 411 Sedan. Luxurious yet practical.

The name painted near the bow read *The Princess Anne*.

The crew of two was waiting just inside the access gate to the private dock where *The Princess Anne* was moored. The men, David Baulder and Steven Howard, were people Quinn had worked with in the past and had come to trust. He had hired them and rented the yacht as a safety precaution just in case the need arose. That was part of being a cleaner, always being ready for any contingency, but not always having to activate your plans.

Dawn would arrive in less than two hours, so at best they had thirty minutes before activity at the marina picked up. The dock they were using had been chosen with care. Security in this part of the marina was lax. No cameras, no guard station, and only two motion-activated lights in the vicinity — one at the gate and a second on the dock. Both had been disabled.

Not wasting a second, they moved the plastic-wrapped bodies out of the van and onto the boat. There was no blaring of sirens in the distance, no sudden arrival of the police.

Fifteen minutes later, they motored through the marina and out into the Irish Sea.

Quinn helped Nate and Howard remove the bodies from the plastic, while Baulder piloted the boat. Once free of the wrapping, each of the dead men's torsos was bound with a steel cable attached to a set of metal weights. The pieces of plastic that had enclosed the corpses were then folded and piled in the corner. Once all the bodies had been removed, the pile of plastic was wrapped with its own cable and weights.

After they were finished, Quinn went inside

the cabin and pulled out his phone.

'Hello?' a female voice said. It was Misty, Peter's assistant.

'It's Quinn for Peter.' Though it was the middle of the night in Washington, D.C., Quinn was pretty sure Peter would still be there.

'Quinn,' Misty said, her voice mellowing. 'We were wondering when you'd call. Hold on, he's expecting you.'

There was a short pause, then Peter came on the line.

'Well?' he asked.

'The church is taken care of,' Quinn said. 'The bodies are about to disappear, too.'

'No blowback?'

'Not from my end,' Quinn said, annoyed. He was good at his job, and blowback from anything he was responsible for never happened.

'Good.'

'The shooter?' Quinn asked.

Peter hesitated. He was notorious for not wanting to share more information than he had to. But then he said, 'He's on a plane. Should be here in a few hours.' Another pause. 'You did great. Catching him, I mean. That's bonus worthy.'

'You're right. It is.'

The ship's engines suddenly died down to a low rumble. Quinn stepped out of the cabin and onto the rear deck. The sky was a mixture of dark blue and faded orange. In the east, over the sea and toward the U.K., the sun would soon peer above the horizon.

Baulder called down from the bridge. 'I've got

58

nothing on the radar for miles.'

'Hold on,' Quinn said into the phone. He looked west first, toward the lights of the distant Irish coast, then did a sweep of the horizon. There were no other boats within sight. 'Works for me.'

Nate and Howard took that as their cue. They lifted the first body off the deck and heaved it over the stern and into the water.

As they reached down for the next one, Quinn brought the phone back up.

'Consider the job done,' Quinn said. 'That's one.'

'One what?'

'Our deal. You've got two more jobs, then we're clean. Goodbye, Peter.'

'Wait,' Peter said.

'What?'

'Was there . . . anything on the bodies?' Peter asked.

Quinn hesitated. He could still throw the tiny package he'd found into the ocean with everything else, and claim there was nothing. 'I found an envelope,' Quinn said. 'I assume that's what you're looking for.'

'Yes,' Peter said, relief in his voice. 'Yes, definitely. That's got to be it.'

'I'll mail it to you when I get back.'

'I can't wait that long. I need it now.'

'Well, you can't have it now.'

'Where are you headed after this?' Peter asked. 'Back to Los Angeles?'

Quinn remained silent.

'Okay, don't tell me,' Peter said. 'But wherever

59

you're going, can you at least make a connection close to me?'

Though Quinn wasn't opposed to making life difficult for Peter, the envelope was obviously important enough for people to get killed over. The sooner he got rid of it, the better. 'Atlanta work for you?'

'When?'

'I'll email you,' Quinn said, then paused for a moment. 'If your contact in Atlanta doesn't show up on time, I'm not waiting around.'

He hung up.

The wind was beginning to pick up. It was brisk, bone chilling. As Quinn watched Nate and Howard toss the last of the bodies into the sea, he slipped his hands into his jacket pockets. The fingers of his right hand brushed up against the all-important manila envelope.

Whatever was inside had resulted in the deaths of four men. Quinn would be happy when it was no longer in his possession. But there was something that tickled at the back of his mind, that little internal warning signal he'd had since birth. This time it was telling him that getting rid of the package might not be the end of things.

He hated that feeling.

# 5

ONE WEEK LATER

Room 531 of The Geist Hotel in Washington, D.C. The only light was the blue-white glow emanating from ten wide-screen monitors. But for the three men standing together in front of the displays, that was more than enough. Peter, head of the Office, was more or less the host. It was his assistant who had arranged for the room, his techs who'd set up the equipment, and his agent standing guard near the suite's exit. But it was really the other two men who were running the show. They were his clients, after all.

His two guests stood together, separating themselves from Peter as much as possible in the small space available. Except for their age difference, and the fact that the younger one appeared to be of Asian descent, they were almost like twins. Dark tailored suits, white shirts, and expensive Italian shoes. Even their hair was cut the same, close cropped with hardly enough left on top to run a comb through. The man closest to Peter was named Robert Chercover. Older than his associate by at least three decades, he was the one ultimately in charge. His title was purposely vague: Special Assistant to the Director of National Intelligence. But Peter knew very well what it meant. Chercover was in charge of handling problems no one else could be trusted with.

The man with him had been introduced as Kevin Furuta. Peter had never dealt with the man before, but he immediately knew he didn't like him. At most, he was in his mid-thirties, yet he carried himself like he was Peter's superior. The son of a bitch probably didn't even have a quarter of the experience Peter had amassed. But Peter had to admit Furuta was in better shape, something the asshole didn't seem to have a problem emphasizing. Any time he would talk, he would turn with his whole body toward Peter with his chest puffed out, and his arms held out to the side like his muscles were too big for his limbs to lie flat against his body. He appeared to enjoy the fact that at about six feet tall, he towered a good half foot over Peter. Peter took comfort in the knowledge that despite Furuta's larger size, he would have no problem taking the bigger man in a fight. No problem at all.

In essence, the hotel room had been set up as a mobile strategic operations center. The furniture had been pushed to the side, making way for several long, portable tables. These had been arranged in a loose U shape. The ten monitors were set up on two sides of the U. On the third side were several pieces of equipment: receivers and computer-controlled hard drives both feeding and recording the images being shown.

All the screens were active. Those along the left displayed images from inside the hotel itself: the front and rear entrances, the main lobby, and the hallway on the fifth floor outside room 531.

The images on the four monitors along the bottom of the U were murkier, and from a location nowhere near the Geist Hotel. These monitors had been numbered one through four right-to-left, the numbers superimposed in the lower right corner like a television network ID.

Monitor one was an outside shot. It was focused on a neglected apartment building two hundred miles away in New York City. A light rain was falling over the neighborhood, clearing the streets of anyone interested in an evening stroll. Lights were on in a few of the windows in the neighboring buildings, but none shone from the one centered in the shot.

According to the information Peter had received, this particular building was abandoned, a fact reinforced by windows that were either boarded over or broken. A set of concrete steps led up to the front door, where a faded paper notice had been stuck on the surface. It was too far away to read, but he had already been informed that it was an advertisement for a local concert that had long since occurred.

Monitors two through four were shots from inside the abandoned building. Number two showed the small empty lobby and the inside angle of the main entrance. Number three was focused on an equally empty hallway that fell off into darkness after only a dozen feet.

The image on monitor four, though, was different from the rest. While the cameras feeding the other monitors had been stationary, each securely mounted so as to give a fixed, steady image, camera four was anything but motionless. The image was in constant movement, up and down, side to side, and never staying in one position for more than half a second. This camera was mounted in an apparatus worn by their agent on site. It rode just above the agent's right ear. As if to emphasize that fact, the sound of low, steady breathing came out of the monitor's speaker.

Peter seemed to be the only one interested in the first three monitors. Since this was a solo incursion, and the only potential backup was several miles away, Peter knew he was all the protection the agent had. It was up to him to raise a warning if he saw anyone else on one of the screens. He had argued that this operation should have waited until an adequate team could have been put in place, but he had been outvoted.

'Agent Douglas knows what she's doing,' Chercover had said.

'And we want to keep this low profile,' Furuta added.

It wasn't the way Peter liked to run things, but he didn't have much of a choice. Perhaps if he had been the one to hire the agent, he could have pulled rank. But she was CIA, and part of the National Intelligence apparatus. That made her Chercover's responsibility. Peter's search team had been following another lead that had taken them north into Canada, and Chercover hadn't wanted to wait until they could return.

The only concessions Peter was able to get were to equip Douglas with the surveillance equipment they were now using to watch her movements, and to delay the incursion long enough so that Peter could send a small strike team up from D.C. to act as backup if necessary.

The image on monitor four stopped in front of a doorway.

'I think this is it,' Agent Douglas said, her voice coming over the speaker. 'Someone's tried to distress it, but it still looks out of place. Don't know if you noticed, but most of the other doors were wood. This one's metal.'

Chercover glanced at Peter. 'Locked?' he asked.

Peter raised the small microphone he was holding to his lips. 'Is it locked?'

A hand shot into the frame and grabbed the knob. Agent Douglas tried to twist it, but it moved less than a quarter inch before stopping.

'Yes, locked,' she said. 'I think I should take a look at what's inside. Am I cleared?'

Peter looked at the two men. Without moving his gaze from the monitor, Chercover nodded once.

'You're cleared,' Peter said into the mic. Then added unnecessarily, 'Be careful.'

Agent Douglas pulled out a lock pick set, then set to work on the keyhole. Peter glanced again to the other monitors, making sure she was still alone. His gaze lingered on the lobby shot displayed on monitor number two. It seemed as though something was different. A shadow perhaps, but everything was dark on darker, so there was no telling for sure.

'If it doesn't feel right, get the hell out of

there,' he said as he returned his attention to monitor four.

'I'm fine,' she said, her tone displaying her displeasure at being interrupted.

After several seconds, she stopped what she was doing, then turned the knob again. This time it moved.

'Got it,' she said. She stood up. 'Okay. I'm going in.'

'I'm not liking this,' Peter said, both into the mic and to his two guests. If the door was hiding something important, it shouldn't have been this easy to open. 'Something feels wrong. I'm sending the strike team over.'

'It's fine,' Agent Douglas said. 'A strike team isn't trained to look for things the same way I am. They might unintentionally mess up something we need.'

'My men are trained for all sorts of situations. They'll be okay.'

'If she says she can handle it on her own, then we should let her,' Chercover said. He leaned toward the microphone in Peter's hand. 'Agent Douglas, do you feel you need assistance?'

'No, sir,' Agent Douglas replied. 'The first sign of a problem, I'll pull myself out.'

'You may proceed then,' Chercover said. He straightened back up and looked at Peter. 'Your concern is noted, but this is a special circumstance.'

'It's always a special circumstance,' Peter said, knowing very well he'd used the same excuse himself several times in the past.

'Of course it is,' Furuta said.

All three men watched as Agent Douglas pushed the door open. The room beyond showed up as pitch-black on the monitor. Whatever light there was filtering in from the hallway didn't make a dent in the abyss.

'Can you see anything?' Peter asked.

'Hold on,' she said.

A few seconds later a bright light swept across the wall next to the doorway, then a flashlight came into view in Agent Douglas's hand. She aimed it through the new opening. At first it seemed to have no effect, then the camera moved closer to the threshold and tilted downward.

'Can you see it?' she asked.

There was a short landing, then five or six steps descending into the darkness.

'A stairway?' Peter said.

'Yes,' she confirmed. 'Appears to be pretty solid. Made of wood, I think.'

'Can you see how far down it goes?'

The image from the camera moved through the doorway, then tilted downward with the slope of the staircase. Even then, the optics and the compression caused by the satellite transmission kept most of the room's details in darkness.

'It goes pretty far. Definitely more than one story.'

'What do you mean?' Peter asked, trying to imagine what she was describing in his mind.

'The floor of the room is a good one and a half to two stories down. The stairs double back halfway down so they can fit.'

'Can you make out anything on the floor below?'

'Not really,' Agent Douglas said, then paused. The view on the camera swung methodically from side to side and up and down as she examined her surroundings. 'Okay. I'm heading down.'

The camera bobbed upward once, then angled down as Agent Douglas moved her right foot onto the top step.

'So far so good,' she said.

Her left foot came into view, then settled on the next step down. Peter could hear her breathing, deep but steady.

Another step down.

Then another.

Then, 'Shit!'

Before Peter had even registered what she had said, a bright flash and loud explosion overpowered the monitors, turning the image on the screen into a blur of whipping shapes and colors. There was nothing recognizable or coherent.

'Agent Douglas!'

The roar from the speakers became a series of booms and crashes.

Then, just as suddenly as the incident began, it stopped, the image from the camera now as still as those on monitors one, two, and three. And the only noise was an occasional creaking or muffled thud.

'Agent Douglas?' Peter repeated into the mic.

There was no response.

'Tasha,' he said, using her first name. 'Can you hear me?'

She remained silent.

# 6

'I'm sending in the strike team,' Peter said.

'Hold on,' Chercover said. 'We need to think about this for a moment.'

'For God's sake, she might still be alive. I don't give a damn what you want to do. I will not leave an agent down.'

Peter snatched up his cell phone from where he'd left it earlier, next to monitor three. He had prepped it for just such an emergency, and only had to touch the screen once to connect the call.

The strike leader answered after a single ring.

'Situation's gone critical,' Peter said. 'Move in fast. Agent down, condition unknown. Booby-trapped, but no hostiles have been spotted. Go. Now.' Once he was off the phone, he looked back at his clients. 'Next time maybe you'll listen to me when I have concerns about an operation.'

Furuta turned toward Peter, slow and deliberate. There was no concern at all in the man's eyes for the situation. 'Risks are part of the job. Agent Douglas has always been aware of that. We would assume you would be, too. But if you are unwilling to take those risks, maybe we need to rethink our working relationship.'

As Peter was about to respond, a movement on one of the monitors caught his attention. He turned to get a better look.

'What is it?' Chercover asked, looking at Peter.

'I thought I saw something.'

He was pretty sure it had been monitor three, the hallway view. But it was empty now, like it had been before. Perhaps it had just been a glitch in the transmission, some digital artifact that had appeared on the screen for a split second, drawing his attention.

He had almost convinced himself that was it, when a man appeared on monitor two. He was thin, and was dressed neat enough that Peter guessed he wasn't homeless. But with the low light, making out facial features was out of the question, as was detecting skin tone or hair color. He was a shadow in clothes.

'Who the hell is that?' Chercover asked.

Peter didn't answer.

The man ran into the lobby, then pulled the door open just enough to peek through and make sure there was no one on the stoop waiting for him. Once he saw that it was clear, he jerked it open the rest of the way and stepped outside.

Peter switched his attention to the exterior shot of the building. The man closed the door behind him, then ran down the steps and took off west on the sidewalk. Within seconds, he was no longer visible.

'Who *the hell* was that?' Chercover repeated.

Again, Peter said nothing. They'd all been watching the same feeds, so they all had the same amount of information.

Peter gritted his teeth. If Chercover had only waited for him to get a team in place, like he wanted, then maybe the explosion could have been prevented.

Peter glanced at his two guests. They were both staring at the monitors, no emotion on either of their faces. Real pros. Undoubtedly each had witnessed agent-down situations before. Peter had, too, countless times it seemed. And while he also tried to keep his emotions suppressed, he was only partially successful. He could feel a tick under his right eyebrow, a twitch that only flared up when things got out of control.

He raised the microphone back to his mouth. 'Agent Douglas?' he said.

If she could hear him, she wasn't responding. Chances were, during the fall, her earpiece had been dislodged, and she wouldn't have been able to hear him no matter what.

'Agent Douglas,' he said again.

'Leave it alone,' Chercover said. 'She's probably dead.'

Peter looked over at the old man, then raised the mic to his mouth again, his eyes locked on Chercover's. 'Agent Douglas?'

'Is that your strike team?' Furuta asked.

He was pointing toward monitor one. On it, a dark van had pulled up in front of the abandoned building.

The phone Peter had used to call the team began to vibrate. He picked it up and pressed Accept.

'We're here,' Perkins, the team leader, said.

'You're looking for a room in the basement. There was an explosion, so there'll probably be some damage in the hallway. But it should also lead you to the right room. Be careful. The

71

staircase that was just inside the door is damaged, and the floor is nearly two stories below.'

'Copy that,' Perkins said.

'Agent Douglas is down there somewhere. Find her, and get her out.'

'Anything else?'

'A man left the scene about two minutes ago. I don't expect him to come back, but there might be others. If you find someone, take them alive. I want to talk to them.'

'Got it.'

Peter gave him the signal settings he'd been using with Agent Douglas so they could communicate by radio, then hung up.

'They should search the building,' Furuta said. 'This is obviously the place we've been looking for. There's got to be something there. Something that will help us identify Primus.'

'Seems to me, Agent Douglas might have already found it.'

'Found where it is, perhaps,' Chercover said. 'But what exactly did she find?'

'That's not this team's job,' Peter said. 'They'll get Agent Douglas out, then we'll figure out our next move.'

'We need to figure that out now,' Furuta said. 'We don't have a lot of time on this. The man who got away could be informing his contacts about what happened right now.'

'We'll get Agent Douglas out first,' Peter said, his tone telling the others that this was non-negotiable.

On the monitors, the team had already begun

72

to move into place. On number one, two men dressed in dark clothing stood near the front door watching the street. Though there were no weapons in sight, Peter knew they were each armed and ready to jump into action if needed. The interior shot on two showed one man standing in the small lobby. But unlike his friends outside, he had his weapon out and ready. Number three still showed an empty hallway, and on number four, several dark, unidentifiable objects, but no movement at all.

Peter brought the mic up near his mouth. 'Perkins, you're out of our camera range. What do you see?'

'Just a dark hallway.' Perkins's voice came over monitor three's speaker. 'The door Agent Douglas entered should be down the next corridor.'

'Do you hear anything?'

'Nothing. Dead quiet.' There was a moment of silence. Then in a whisper, 'We're at the intersection now. Hold while we check.' More silence. 'All clear. We're approaching the doorway now. There's a lot of dust and smoke in the air. Visibility down thirty percent. Okay, just like you thought. Damage to the floor outside the doorway. The door itself is gone.' Pause. 'I'm looking in now. Damn. You said there was a staircase, right?'

'Yes,' Peter said.

'Not now. Morgan, fire up the spot.'

Five seconds later there was a flare of light on monitor four, the one that displayed the feed from the camera Agent Douglas had been carrying. The dark shapes that had been filling the screen suddenly became bits of concrete and pieces of wood. But there was no sign of the agent.

'Sir, it's a mess down there,' Perkins said. 'Looks like the whole stairway has collapsed.'

'Do you see Agent Douglas?'

'If she's there, she's buried. I'll take one of my guys down with me.'

There was a few minutes' delay while the gear was prepared.

'Rappelling down now,' Perkins said. For several seconds there was only the muffled sound of someone sliding down a rope. Then, 'Okay, we're on the ground.'

'Watch your step,' Peter said. 'There could be other traps.'

'Copy that.'

Light ebbed and flowed on monitor four as the team searched the debris.

'Stop!' Peter yelled.

A foot had just passed within view of the image on the monitor.

'One of you is near her camera. Both of you take one step back.'

The foot reentered the frame.

'Okay, hold there for a second,' Peter said. 'Perkins, you move your foot first.'

'Copy.'

The foot in the screen remained stationary.

'Anything?' Perkins asked.

'Have your man move now.'

There was a second delay, then the foot began to rise.

'That's it,' Peter said. 'About three feet to your man's right.'

The image remained stable for half a minute, then it rose into the air and whipped around the room until it stopped on the face of a man with short brown hair.

'Must have gotten dislodged as she fell.' Perkins's lips moved on monitor four, but his voice still came out of the speaker on monitor three.

'Chances are she's in that same general area,' Peter said.

Perkins set the camera down on something elevated, giving the three men back in the hotel suite a broad view of the room. It seemed to be some sort of old machine room. Unfinished cement walls and floors, and to the left the edge of a rusty furnace. But the dominant feature was the pile of rubble in the center of the room. The majority of debris appeared to be the wood that had made up the staircase, but there was a good bit of concrete mixed in. It must have been dislodged from the ceiling and walls by the blast.

Perkins and his man worked their way through the pile, pulling away planks and chunks of concrete. After several minutes, Perkins's partner stopped and bent down.

'I've got a hand,' he called out, his voice distant over Perkins's microphone.

The two men began working together to move everything surrounding the spot. Soon Peter thought he could see an arm, then a shoulder.

Perkins leaned down and placed his fingers on the exposed wrist.

'Pulse?' Peter asked.

'Faint, but she's alive,' Perkins said.

Obviously listening in on the conversation, Perkins's men on monitor one jumped into action. They moved over to the van and pulled a stretcher out of the back. One of them then stayed on the stoop while the other took the stretcher inside the building.

'Stretcher on its way to you,' Peter said. 'I'll call ahead to get medical set up.'

'Copy that,' Perkins said.

For the next several minutes the team worked quickly and efficiently. Soon Agent Douglas was in the van, heading for medical attention. Thankfully, for the moment at least, she was still breathing.

The images on the monitors were now still and quiet.

'We can't let this opportunity slip out of our hands,' Furuta said, his voice rising. It was the first emotion Peter had seen from the man.

'I agree,' Chercover said. He looked at Peter. 'You need to get someone in there tonight. You can do that, can't you?'

Peter was silent for a moment, then nodded. 'Yes.'

'So you have someone in mind? Someone close?' Furuta asked.

'Yes.'

'Who?' Furuta said.

'That is something you don't need to know,' Peter said.

Furuta was about to respond when his boss put a hand on his shoulder. 'I think we're done here,' Chercover said.

Reluctantly, Furuta nodded. 'Keep us posted on what you find,' he said.

'What about Agent Douglas?' Peter asked as the other two began walking toward the door. It was an unnecessary question, but Peter couldn't help pushing.

Chercover stopped and looked back at Peter. 'Of course,' he said. 'Keep us informed on her condition also. We're not exactly heartless, but this is much bigger than her life, or even any one of ours.'

Peter stared at them as they turned and left, his lips now closed.

The truth was Chercover was right.

# 7

Quinn and Nate had not returned to Los Angeles after Ireland. They were in the States, but still thousands of miles from home. After handing off the envelope to Peter's contact at the Hartsfield-Jackson Airport in Atlanta, they boarded a flight north instead of west, landing several hours later in Boston.

It was another job. The new client required only some electronic and visual surveillance, no body removals. It was a gig that suited Quinn just fine for the moment. The fiasco in Ireland was still fresh in his mind, and his annoyance with Peter for forcing him to risk his life to catch the assassin had yet to abate.

*Whoever that assassin was, he'd better be talking*, Quinn thought.

Boston turned out to be the easiest job he'd taken all year. A big part of that was due to the fact that he was working with Orlando again. She'd flown in early while he and Nate were still across the Atlantic, and set everything up. It made the assignment go smooth and simple.

The fact that he didn't have to sleep alone anymore was a bonus.

'This is really what you wanted me here for, isn't it?' Orlando had asked him as they lay sweaty and panting beside each other on their hotel bed, the sheets and the blankets pushed to the floor. 'You just wanted sex.'

'That took you long enough to figure out,' he said, trying not to break a smile.

Her shoulder-length black hair was draped partially over her face. With her right hand she tucked the loose strands behind her ear.

'Oh, I knew it. I just wanted to hear it from your lips.'

'Don't play innocent. You want it just as much as I do.'

'Oh, you think so?'

'I know you do.'

'You're wrong,' she said, a glimmer in her eye. 'I want it more than you.'

'That I'll never believe.'

She pulled him to her, their lips meeting soft but urgent, their bodies crushed together as if they wanted to meld into one.

For several years, Orlando had been living in Ho Chi Minh City, Vietnam, with her son, Garrett. Her mixed ancestry helped her to blend in — her mother Korean, her father Thai-Irish. The result was a look that allowed her the ability to claim she was from almost anywhere in Asia. But now that her relationship with Quinn had developed into more than just friendship and business, she had been spending an increasing amount of time in the U.S. at the house her aunt Jeong had left her in San Francisco the previous year. Conveniently, it was only an hour plane ride up the coast from Quinn's home in Los Angeles.

But even with this new accessibility, it had been several weeks since they'd spent any time together. Jobs and life seemed to have gotten in their way. So even though the Boston job was finished, they decided to stay on a few extra days.

Nate, on the other hand, had been able to get ahold of tickets for the Yankee-Detroit series at the new Yankee Stadium in the Bronx. So Quinn had let him go to New York, while he and Orlando remained. His only instructions were for Nate to keep his phone close, and answer if Quinn called. In this business, you had to be ready all the time.

Being with Orlando now, Quinn could feel the stress he'd been carrying drain away, if only for a night. The stress had been building since Singapore and Nate's accident, all due to guilt over what had happened to his apprentice. Guilt that he was having a hard time shedding. Guilt that, because of the amputation, Nate would never be whole. Quinn had put him in a position to be hurt, and had made the call to cut off the damaged part of his limb. He knew at the time it probably meant the end of Nate's career as a cleaner. And though he had kept Nate on, he couldn't help but feel like he was waiting for the moment he would have to let his apprentice go.

But he also couldn't hide the fact that Nate's situation wasn't the only thing that had added to his stress. It had been two weeks since he'd received the call from Liz, but he could still remember every word. It was the first time he had talked to his sister in nearly five years. She was younger than he was by eight years, so they had always traveled in different circles, and weren't close.

'First, everything is fine, okay?' she'd told him.
Instantly he was on alert. 'What is it?'

'Dad went in for some tests.'

'Tests? For what?'

He could hear her take a deep breath. 'The doctor thought he might have had a small stroke.'

'A stroke?'

'Take it easy, Jake. I said a small stroke.' Jake. The nickname his father had given him. And like the name Jonathan Quinn, Jake had no relation to Quinn's real name. 'Turns out it wasn't a stroke at all.'

'What was it, then?'

'They're not sure. Maybe a virus. He's fine now. Well, his blood pressure is high, so he's taking some medication for that. But otherwise he's fine.'

Quinn wasn't sure how to feel. His relationship with his father was an odd one. They had never been close, even when Quinn was a child. It wasn't from lack of trying on either of their parts. They just didn't have anything in common. Quinn knew the real answer why, but he never spoke it out loud. His dad was the only father he had ever known, but genetically they weren't related. So their core points of references for life were different, and neither could really understand the other. Still, he cared about his father, because he knew his father loved his mother deeply.

'How's Mom?'

His sister — technically his half-sister — sighed. 'How do you think she is? She's glad

81

he's better, but she's still concerned. She keeps checking on him to make sure he's all right.'

'I was just asking, Liz.'

There was silence for a moment. 'She tells me you haven't visited them for a long time. You need to come out here.'

At the time, he was just getting ready to leave for Ireland. 'I can't come right now.'

'Of course not.'

'But I will come soon. In a few weeks.'

'Whatever. Do what you need to do, Jake. I just thought you'd want to know.'

Before he could say anything else, she'd hung up. He'd called his mother next, but she was evasive, doing her best, as always, not to burden Quinn with anything she felt he didn't need to worry about.

Now that the jobs in both Ireland and Boston were complete, he knew he had to go see his parents. They'd be in Minnesota now, summering in the home Quinn had grown up in. He'd stop by on the way back to L.A.

★ ★ ★

'What are you thinking about?' Orlando asked.

'Nothing,' he said as they stepped out of Strega, an Italian restaurant in Boston's North End. He hadn't told her about the call from his sister.

There was a slight chill in the air. Quinn could feel Orlando shiver under his arm, so he pulled her small frame closer to help warm her up.

'Thanks,' she said.

She tilted her head up, and he leaned down and kissed her.

'Well, I *was* thinking about something,' he said as they walked down the street with no specific destination in mind.

'Thought so,' she said, an eyebrow raised. 'I assume it hurt. Maybe you should leave the thinking to me.'

It was a playful argument they'd had often, each claiming to be the more intelligent one.

'I've been thinking,' he said again, 'about our location problem.'

'What location problem?'

'The fact that you're not geographically available to me when I need you.'

'Wait,' Orlando said, the hint of a wicked smile on her face. 'You need me?'

'Shut up,' he said. 'You know what I mean.'

'We're a hell of a lot closer than we used to be,' she said.

'True enough,' he said. 'But I was just — '

'Hold on.' She pulled away a little. 'We're not moving in together. Not yet. We've already talked about that.'

'I know that.'

He eased her back against him. But as he was about to explain what he meant, his phone began to vibrate in his pocket. Annoyed, he pulled it out and looked at the display, then glanced at Orlando.

'It's Peter,' he said.

Her eyes narrowed. 'Maybe you should just let him go to voice-mail.'

It was a good idea. Quinn tapped the Reject

prompt on the phone's touch screen, then put the device back in his pocket.

'I didn't mean move in together,' Quinn said. 'But I thought maybe I could get a place up there. I don't have to be there all the time. I mean I'd definitely not be there when you're in Vietnam, but when you're in town . . . you know, I could, I could be up there, too. Close by. It'll make things easier for us.'

He looked down at her, expecting some resistance. What he'd learned since they'd become involved was that she had a fierce independent streak, and was very protective of her own space. A product, perhaps, of her previous relationship experience with Quinn's late mentor, Durrie.

But both her lips and her eyes were smiling. 'I like that idea.'

'You do?'

'Yeah. What? You thought I wouldn't?'

'I . . . eh . . . I don't know what I thought.'

Quinn's phone began vibrating again.

'Dammit,' he said. He pulled it back out. 'Peter again.'

'Let him leave a message.'

'That won't work,' Quinn said. 'He'll just keep calling until I finally answer. He's done that before.'

'Then whatever he wants, just tell him no.'

'Like that's an option.'

Quinn touched Accept on the screen.

'What?' Quinn said.

'I need you in New York,' Peter said. 'I have something for you tonight.'

84

'I can't make it there tonight. I'm not even close.'

There was a second of silence. 'You're in Boston, Quinn. I have a plane waiting. You can be here within an hour and a half.'

Quinn could feel his tension returning. 'How do you know where I am?'

'Does it really matter? Remember our deal. No questions.'

'You're a son of a bitch sometimes, you know that?'

'I'll text you with the plane info as soon as I get off.'

'What if I'm busy?'

'You're not.'

Quinn started to tighten his hand around the phone, but made himself stop. 'This is number two,' he said, knowing this would mean delaying the trip to see his parents for a few more days. But getting Peter that much closer to being off his back would be worth it. 'That leaves one and we're through.'

'I can count,' Peter said. The line went dead.

'So,' Orlando said as Quinn slipped the phone back into his pocket. 'We're going somewhere?'

★  ★  ★

Quinn and Nate stood in the hallway of an abandoned apartment building in New York, a few feet away from a doorway that had been blown out by some kind of explosion. There was debris everywhere: splintered chunks of wood, a twisted metal door frame, and bits and pieces of

85

plaster. The room beyond the gaping doorway was a pit. A nub that had once been the concrete landing stuck out no more than a foot and a half into the room, but beyond that there was nothing.

Shining his flashlight inside, Quinn was just able to make out a pile of wood and concrete approximately twenty feet down. It wasn't an entire floor's worth of wreckage, but it was enough for a staircase.

'It looks like the best places to attach the ropes are there and there,' Nate said, pointing up at the ceiling.

Quinn looked up at the spots his apprentice had indicated, happy that Nate was talking about something other than the Yankee game Quinn's phone call had pulled him away from.

Nate had found a couple of large gaps in the ceiling that exposed some of the building's support structure. The damage looked old, perhaps caused by water, or vandals, or neglect.

'Do it,' Quinn said.

Nate picked up the end of one of the ropes. 'I need a boost.'

Quinn laced his fingers together and moved up next to the hallway wall. Nate put his free hand on Quinn's shoulder, then raised his left foot and put it into Quinn's palms.

'One, two, three,' Nate said, then pushed himself up, straightening his left leg — his good leg — so that his head almost reached the ceiling. 'Good. Hold me steady.'

Quinn tilted his head up and watched as his apprentice looped the rope through the gap and around one of the beams before tying it off. As Nate stepped down, he tried to hide a wince, but Quinn noticed.

'I'm fine,' Nate said.

'That's not what it looked like to me,' Quinn said but immediately regretted it.

'I'm fine. A cramp.' Nate's face was tense, serious. 'We all get them.'

As if to emphasize his point, he reached down and picked up the end of the second rope.

'I'm ready, let's go,' Nate said.

Quinn moved three feet to his left and made another cradle with his hands. Nate repeated the task with the new rope. When he stepped down this time, he stared Quinn in the face and didn't wince. But it didn't matter. Quinn couldn't help remembering Nate lying unconscious on a Singapore street, his foot mangled by a car that had purposely rammed into him. It had been Quinn's call to remove the foot. It had been the right decision, but that didn't make Quinn feel any less responsible.

'Shall I unroll it?' Nate asked.

'Please,' Quinn said.

The end of each security line was attached to a rope ladder sitting next to the empty doorway, waiting. Nate walked over and maneuvered the ladder so that it was centered in the opening, ready to roll over the edge into the darkness.

Another hour, two tops, and they'd be done, Quinn thought. And even more important, one more job would be ticked off the Peter payback list.

So far this one had been easy, if not a little

unusual. Peter had arranged for a sedan to be waiting for them at the airport, complete with a trunk full of the equipment he thought they might need: flashlights, gloves, crowbars, the rope ladder, and handguns for each of them.

Peter hadn't been the one to greet them, though. Quinn wasn't even sure if he was in the city. It had been one of his agents, a woman named Ida. Quinn had met her briefly once before. She gave Quinn and Orlando the brief as they drove into Manhattan. It basically boiled down to a mop-up job in an apartment building, with a little recon work thrown in. Apparently an agent had run into a little trouble. While the agent had been extracted, there was the possibility that evidence had been left that could link the agent to the building. Peter wanted Quinn to make sure any link was severed. While they were at it, they were also to keep their eyes open for anything unusual.

'The agent was interrupted before the recon was complete,' Ida had said, just before they'd dropped her off near Columbus Circle.

'Recon is not one of our normal services,' Quinn told her.

'We both know that's not true.'

Quinn had almost argued the point, but let it go. Doing this job meant he was almost done with Peter and the Office. Once he finished the third of his promised jobs, he was going to stop taking Peter's calls. Enough was enough. The last few years had proved that.

Nate pushed the ladder over the edge of the opening. There was a *thud-thud-thud* as it

88

unrolled itself on the way down, then the support ropes they had just tied off snapped taut.

'We're almost set here,' Quinn said, subconsciously turning his mouth toward the mic attached to the collar of his shirt.

There was no response.

'Orlando? Did you hear me?'

There was a second of nothing, then Orlando's voice in his ear. 'Yeah, just a minute.'

'What's up?'

Earlier, while Nate and Quinn had lugged the ladder inside and set it up, Orlando had volunteered to begin the recon of the first couple floors.

'I think I found something,' she said.

'What? Where?'

Instead of a reply, Quinn heard footsteps coming from his left down an intersecting corridor. Turning toward the sound, he could see the beam of Orlando's flashlight cut through the darkness, then angle in his direction.

'It might be nothing,' she said, her voice still coming through the receiver in his ear. 'We can check it out later if we need to. I'll be right there.'

While they waited for her to arrive, Nate checked the ladder and the ropes to make sure everything was secure.

'Who wants to go first?' Nate asked, the moment Orlando rejoined them.

'You do,' Quinn told him.

★ ★ ★

89

'Check this out,' Nate said.

Quinn and Orlando walked over as Nate worked a wooden riser loose from one of the piles of junk. Nails stuck out in a line along both short ends, and one corner had splintered off, but otherwise it was intact.

'See?' he said after he flipped the piece of wood over.

Quinn had to look closely to see what his apprentice meant. There was a circular patch in the center of the tread that was just a shade or two darker than the surrounding wood. Nate pressed against it, and it pushed in half an inch, then sprang back when he let go.

'Pressure trigger,' Orlando said. 'Good catch.'

'Peter's agent must have stepped on this,' Nate said. 'That probably sent a signal to the explosives.'

Orlando smiled. 'You've been studying.'

Nate shrugged. 'Had a lot of time on my hands.' He glanced up at the doorway high on the wall above them. 'Jesus . . . do you think he fell all this way?'

Quinn's eyes were drawn to something several feet away. It flashed white as his light passed over it. He walked over, picked it up off the ground.

'I'd say there is a very good chance the agent fell the whole way,' Quinn said. He held up the item he'd found. 'I also think there is a pretty good chance that he is a she.'

In his hand was a pair of decidedly feminine glasses, complete with camera attached to the side.

'She was apparently here for a reason,'

Orlando said. 'But has anyone found out what that might have been?'

Neither Quinn nor Nate had an answer for that. So they began looking in the only place they had yet to check, under the wrecked stairs. They moved things around so they could be sure there was nothing hidden underneath — trap-doors, hidden storage spaces. But there was nothing.

'Red herring,' Nate said.

'Looks that way,' Quinn said.

'Then we're out of here?' Nate asked.

Quinn shook his head. 'Not yet. I want you to photograph everything in here. Normal and infrared. Just in case.' Quinn looked over at Orlando. 'While he's doing that, why don't you show me what you found earlier?'

★ ★ ★

Orlando led Quinn to a hallway that ran along the back of the building. About a third of the way down, she stopped in front of a door on the right-hand side. The other doors along the hallway were all wooden and rotting. And, for the most part, all were also open. This door was different. It was metal, though it had been painted to look older than it really was.

'Look familiar?' Orlando asked.

Quinn nodded. It looked nearly identical in both texture and color to the metal remains of the door that had been torn and twisted by the explosion.

'I haven't seen any others like it,' Orlando

said. 'Peter's instructions *were* to look for anything unusual. Thought this might qualify.'

'Definitely.'

Quinn touched the knob, then attempted to turn it. It moved a fraction of an inch before stopping.

'So?' she said. 'Do we try to get in?'

Though Quinn thought it might be better to just walk away, that would be neglecting the assignment. And as much as he was annoyed to be here in the first place, that was just not something he would do.

'Not through here,' he said.

He took a few steps down the hall away from the door. As he did, he let his fingers brush against the wall, tapping the surface every few inches. After ten feet he stopped, returned to the door, then did the same thing along the other side.

'Think this is rigged like the staircase?' Orlando asked when he finished.

Quinn looked back at the door, then frowned. 'What's your gut?'

'I think we'd be stupid to think it wasn't.'

Quinn smiled in agreement.

He took a few paces forward, then stopped at a spot four feet to the right of the door. He touched the wall again. Like elsewhere, it was plaster, probably supported by ancient wooden slats underneath. Only the wall had given in a little at this spot as he pressed against it.

He moved his light through the hallway. Like elsewhere in the building, random junk was scattered along the floor: an old shoe, dozens of empty food containers, newspapers, cardboard boxes, and several pieces of wood in varying shapes and conditions. He wished he'd brought along one of the crowbars Peter had gotten for them, but that would mean a trip back to the car. He almost decided he didn't have much of a choice, when the beam of his light caught something that looked promising.

It was a two-by-four, about three feet long. Quinn picked it up with one hand, then tapped it against the ground, testing its strength. It was solid, no sign of rot.

*Should work*, he thought.

'Let me hold your flashlight,' Orlando said.

He handed it over, not even registering the fact that she'd figured out what he was going to do. That was just the way they operated, more often than not having the same ideas at the same time.

He found the soft spot on the wall again, then grabbed hold of the two-by-four with both hands and arced it back until it almost touched the other side of the corridor.

'What's that?' Orlando asked, her voice hushed.

Quinn paused, his battering ram suspended in the air, ready to smash into the wall. It took him a second before he heard it. Something shuffling along the floor.

Footsteps. And heading in their direction. But not in their hallway, in one intersecting it.

'Nate,' Quinn whispered. 'What's your position?'

'I'm nearing the top of the ladder,' Nate said.

There was a pause. 'Please don't tell me you want me to go back down.'

'No. Just hold your position when you reach the top.'

'Copy that.'

Orlando doused both of the lights, plunging the hallway into complete darkness. Careful not to make any unnecessary noise, Quinn lowered the two-by-four to the floor, then pulled out his SIG. Beside him, he could hear Orlando freeing her own weapon.

Once armed, they stood rock still as the steps grew closer. There was a muffled thud like someone bumping into a distant wall, then the steps were suddenly in the same hallway as they were.

Quinn raised his gun in the direction of the noise, then whispered, 'Now.'

Orlando flipped on one of the flashlights.

'Shit! What the hell?'

Caught at the very far end of the flashlight beam's reach was a man. He appeared to be about the same height as Quinn, but that was about all the detail they could make out. A moment after being lit up, he was gone, running down the corridor away from Quinn and Orlando.

'Hey!' Quinn yelled. 'Stop!'

But the man's pace only increased.

'Dammit,' Quinn said. Both he and Orlando started running at once. 'Nate. There's a hostile in the building. He's heading your way.'

'Copy that.'

'Not sure if he's armed, so be careful.'

'You want me to take him out?'

'No,' Quinn said. 'Just . . . try to stop him, or at least scare him back in our direction.'

'Copy,' Nate said. 'I hear him. Hold on.' Quinn could hear Nate breathing. 'He's just around the corner.'

'Be careful,' Quinn said.

'Stop right the — '

Nate's command was interrupted by a loud smack, and the sound of something rubbing against the microphone.

'Dammit!' Nate yelled.

Quinn increased his speed, sprinting toward the intersection with the hallway Nate was in.

'What's happening?' Quinn asked. 'Are you all right?'

'The asshole just head-butted me in the cheek.'

'Where is he now?'

There was silence for a second.

'He's . . . ah . . . on the ground.' Nate paused again. 'I think I knocked him out.'

# 8

The unconscious man could have been anywhere from twenty-five to his early forties. His face, weathered and wrinkled prematurely, had been beaten into a shape he hadn't been born with. But though his clothes were old and thin in some spots, they were clean. And he obviously cared about his appearance enough to tuck his shirt in, comb his hair, and take a shower once in a while.

Not quite a street bum, not quite part of society, either. The guy probably existed somewhere in between.

His face also sported a new addition, a large red spot in the middle of his forehead, the remnant of his collision with Nate. Quinn knew it would turn into a bruise before long.

'Smells like he's been drinking,' Nate said.

Quinn had noticed it, too, a faint hint of alcohol, not like the guy had been sucking anything down in the past hour, but within the last several. Sour, like beer.

'Here.' Quinn held his gun out to Nate.

He grabbed it and aimed it at the man on the ground.

'What the hell is he doing here?' Nate asked.

'Kind of hard to tell at the moment.' Quinn said. 'But at least we know one thing.'

'What?' Nate asked.

'We know that hard head of yours is good for

something,' Quinn said, a small smile on his face.

'Ha, Ha. Hilarious.' There was a red spot on his cheek that was a near match to the spot on the unconscious man's forehead. Nate raised his hand and began rubbing it. 'Hurts like hell.' His hand stopped in mid-motion. 'Damn. I think one of my teeth is loose.'

Quinn knelt down and searched the man. The only things the guy had been armed with were an old black plastic comb and a set of ten keys. Definitely not a street person. They'd have no need for keys.

Quinn put his hand on the man's cheek, then rocked the man's head back and forth.

'Hey,' he said. 'Wake up.'

Not even a twitch. Quinn raised his hand a few inches, then slapped it down on the man's cheek, not too hard, just enough so that it would sting.

'Wake up,' he repeated. 'Come on.'

A low groan started in the man's chest, then escaped through his mouth. A moment of nothing, then another groan, and another. Finally, he started to move his head in a slow circle on his own.

Quinn kept his hand on the man's cheek, his thumb wrapped around the bottom of the guy's chin. All of a sudden, the man's eyelids squeezed together as a grimace of pain shot across his face. One of his hands reached up and touched his injured forehead.

He grunted, then all of a sudden he froze. Reluctantly, as if it was the last thing he wanted to do, his eyelids parted.

'Oh, God. Please. I'm sorry,' he said, his voice clipped and nervous. 'Just leave me alone. I ain't got nothing.'

'What's your name?' Quinn asked.

'No,' the man said. 'You don't need that. Just let me go, okay? Do whatever you want. I don't give a shit.'

'What's your name?' Quinn repeated.

The man looked at Quinn for a second, licked his lips, then said, 'Al.'

'Al what?'

More hesitation. 'Al Barker.'

'Okay, Al Barker. What are you doing here?'

'I live here,' Al said as if it should have been obvious.

'No one lives here,' Quinn said.

Al's gaze flicked beyond Quinn at Nate and Orlando. 'Do you have to shine that thing in my eyes?'

The beam of Orlando's flashlight moved off the man's face and onto his chest.

'Better?' she said.

'Shit, man, you guys got guns!' Al had apparently just noticed the pistols in Orlando's and Nate's hands. 'What the hell are you pointing guns at me for?'

Quinn squeezed Al's chin and turned it to the right. 'Over here, Al,' Quinn said. 'What are you doing here?'

Al glanced back at Orlando and Nate, then refocused on Quinn. 'I told you. I live here.'

'The building's empty, Al.'

'You don't have to keep saying my name.'

98

'I just want to make sure you know I'm talking to you.'

'I know you're talking to me,' Al said. 'And I do live here. The owner pays me to stay in one of the rooms upstairs. A couple hundred bucks a month, and I get the place for free.'

'So you're the caretaker,' Quinn said.

'I guess. Yeah, sure. The caretaker.'

'So if you're the caretaker, where have you been all day?'

'I was upstairs . . . listening to the radio . . . building's got no electricity, so no TV.'

'You were upstairs all day?'

'Sure.'

Quinn stared at him for a moment. 'Al, where were you today?'

'I was he — '

'Don't lie to me,' Quinn cut him off.

Al licked his lips again. 'I left, okay? Went for a walk.'

'All evening?'

'Yeah. Okay? All evening,' Al said.

'Why did you leave?'

'I can go out when I want,' he said defensively. 'I don't have to be here all the time. Mr. Monroe told me that when he let me live here.'

'Who's Mr. Monroe?'

'He owns the building.'

'Why did you leave today, Al? Did you hear something you didn't want to? Then decided it was better to find something else to do?'

The caretaker's pause was all the confirmation Quinn needed.

'Tell me the truth, or I'll have my friend here,

the one you hit with your head, shoot you someplace that won't kill you, not right away, but it'll hurt like hell.'

Al took another look at Nate. The sight must have been enough to convince him.

'I heard her come in, okay?' he said.

'Her?' Quinn asked.

'A woman. It was around sunset.'

'How do you know it was a woman if you only heard her?'

'I, eh, snuck downstairs. Sometimes we get kids in here. You know, try to trash the place. If I surprise them, it scares the hell out of them, and they leave. So I come down to do the same thing, okay? Only when I come down to the basement and peek around the corner, it's not kids. It's a woman. And she looks like she ain't here to trash the place. But she got that door open, you know? That door you're not supposed to go through. I was going to warn her, but she was already stepping inside. Then . . . boom.'

'How did you know you weren't supposed to go through that door?'

'Shit. I don't know . . . I just know it, okay?'

'Not okay, Al. How did you know?'

Al closed his eyes. 'Goddammit,' he said under his breath.

'Al.' The sharp tone of Quinn's voice brought the man back into the here and now.

'He told me, all right? He told me about the room.'

'Who?'

'Mr. Monroe,' Al said. 'Who else?'

'What exactly did Mr. Monroe tell you about

the room?' Quinn asked.

'That it was dangerous. You'd die if you went in there.'

'So you never tried to see for yourself?'

'Hell no,' the man said. 'He made it very clear if you went in there, you wouldn't come out. He was right, too. Jesus, what a mess.'

'And you didn't stay around to see if she might need any help?' Quinn asked.

'A fall like that, I figured she was dead. Didn't want to be here when the cops came and found her.'

'So you left.'

'Yeah.'

'Where'd you go?' Quinn asked.

Al hesitated.

'You went to a bar, didn't you?'

Al moved his gaze away from Quinn, then nodded. 'I needed a drink, you know?'

'Why'd you do that?'

'Mr. Monroe is not going to be happy about this,' Al said. 'I was going to get the hell out of here, then I passed the bar, and decided getting drunk would be a first good step.'

'You don't seem drunk.'

Al licked his lips like he wished there was a bottle nearby. 'I stopped after three.'

'Why?'

'Got to thinking about that woman.'

'You felt guilty and decided to come back and check on her?'

'Something like that.'

'Or did you decide you wanted to see if she had anything valuable on her you could hock?'

101

Al pushed himself up on his elbows, his head shaking side to side. 'No. That wasn't it. Like you said before. I wanted to make sure she was all right. I may be kind of on a downswing, you know, but I ain't a thief. Never been a thief.'

'So what happened when you came back?' Quinn asked.

'You hear me? I'm not a thief.'

'I heard you. Tell me what you found when you returned.'

Al bit his lower lip, then took a deep breath. 'I . . . I could tell someone else had been here. There were lots of footprints in the hall-way. They weren't there before. When I looked down into the room, I didn't see the woman anywhere. Figured someone had come and gotten her.'

'So you decided then it was okay to stay? Your boss is still going to find out about the mess.'

'I know that! I went back upstairs to pack my things. I was sitting around wondering if I could stay the night or should just leave. That's when I heard you all down here.'

Quinn stood. 'You can get up, but I wouldn't move around much.'

Quinn nodded toward Orlando and Nate, then made the shape of a gun with his fingers, and moved his thumb back and forth a couple of times like he was shooting. The look in Al's eyes told him the caretaker was going to be very cooperative.

Quinn moved down the hallway so that he was out of Al's earshot, then pulled out his phone and called Peter.

'Find anything?' Peter said.

'Your agent was a woman,' Quinn said.

'I never told you otherwise.'

Quinn was silent for a moment. 'She was looking in the wrong room.'

'What do you mean?'

Quinn described the door Orlando found.

'You think you can get in without tripping any explosives?'

'There might be a way. But people will know someone's been there. I won't be able to cover it up.'

Peter didn't even hesitate. 'Do it.'

'Fine,' Quinn said. 'Then what would you like me to do with the eyewitness?'

'What eyewitness?' Peter asked, surprised.

Quinn smiled to himself. *Didn't expect that, did you, Peter?* 'Says his name is Al Barker. Said he saw your agent go into the room just before the explosion.'

'He was there?'

'Says he left right after.'

'Describe him.'

Quinn gave him a quick snapshot of Al's vitals.

The tone of Peter's voice changed from one of surprise and concern to one of controlled anger. 'Hold him there. I'm sending someone to pick him up.'

'All right,' Quinn said. 'You can probably get a description of this Monroe guy out of him, but I doubt much more.'

'Find anything else I should know about?'

'No. That's it.'

Peter hung up.

'Please,' Al said. 'Don't open it. We'll die like that lady did.'

They'd brought Al and Nate with them when they returned to the other doorway. Once Al saw where they were going, he'd tried to stop walking. But Nate's gun in his back was enough of a prod to keep him moving forward.

'Do you know what's behind this?' Quinn asked the caretaker.

'No,' Al said. 'Always been locked. You should leave it that way.'

'I'm planning on it.'

Quinn picked up the two-by-four he'd left on the floor earlier.

'Move him back a few feet,' Quinn said.

His apprentice nodded, then pulled Al out of Quinn's swing zone.

'What are you going to do with that?' Al asked.

Quinn held on to the middle of the two-by-four with one hand, and wrapped the other hand around the end pointed away from the wall. He pulled it back high behind his head, then swung it forward. Like a battering ram, the two-by-four smashed into the soft spot of the wall.

There was a loud crack as the plaster and the wooden slats beneath it shattered under the force of the blow.

'Hey! Stop it,' Al said. 'Mr. Monroe is going to be pissed.'

'According to you, Mr. Monroe is already pissed,' Quinn said. He pulled the two-by-four back, raising it high again. 'What's behind the door?'

'I don't know! I swear!'

Quinn drove the board into the wall again.

'Ah, man,' Al said. 'No one's supposed to go in there.'

'What's inside, Al?'

Al's shoulders slumped. 'You might as well finish it. I don't know.'

Instead of taking another large swing, Quinn began punching his ram into the wall, over and over, until there was a hole approximately two feet in diameter passing all the way into the room beyond. It was just big enough to stick his head through. He set the board on the ground, then held out his hand to Orlando. She gave him one of the flashlights.

Letting the light lead the way, he leaned in.

At first it didn't look much different from the room Peter's agent had nearly died in. The notable exception was the floor. Though it was lower than the level of floor in the hallway, it was only by a couple feet, not twenty.

The wall across the room from the hole appeared to be made of concrete. *The exterior wall*, he guessed.

The wall to his right was closest to his position, about five feet away. It appeared to be constructed of the same material as the wall he'd busted through: slats and plaster. Long ago, someone had painted a red stripe at waist level along the entire side, but it was faded now. Given a few more years, it might not even be noticeable.

Stacked along the far side to the left were several cardboard boxes. Judging from the water stains on the sides and the way they sagged into each other, they appeared to have been there a long time.

Nothing obvious caught his attention. Certainly nothing that would have warranted locking the door. Perhaps it was another red herring. Perhaps the whole building was nothing but something to throw Peter's people off the track of whatever it was they were working on.

Quinn moved the light all the way to the left so he could get a look at the door. He scanned up and down twice, then pulled back out of the hole and straightened up.

'Anything?' Orlando asked.

'The door's wired,' he said. 'There's a block of something on the floor with some wires leading from it and running up the jamb.'

'So what are they trying to hide?' she asked.

'Good question. There're some old boxes stacked against the wall, but that's about it. And even those don't look promising.'

Quinn thought for a moment, then picked up the two-by-four again.

'This mean we're going in?' Orlando said.

'Yeah.'

'I'm not going in there,' Al said, not hiding an ounce of his fear.

'Watch him,' Quinn said to Nate, then looked at Al. 'Don't worry. You're not going anywhere. I want you on the floor right now. Hands behind your back.'

'So I don't have to go in?' Al asked.

'Don't make me say it again.'

Al dropped to the floor, leaned against the wall, and slipped his hands behind his back.

Quinn used the two-by-four to punch at the wall again, this time widening the hole until it was large enough to crawl through. He exchanged the board for his flashlight, then he stepped backward through the hole and into the room. Given the difference in floor levels, the first step was a big one, but he managed it without falling.

Once he was down, he reached up and helped Orlando through.

'Musty,' she said, wrinkling her nose.

Quinn approached the steps leading up to the door, stopping a respectful three feet away. Stuck to the steps at floor level was a whitish glob of what looked like clay. Quinn had seen plenty of it over the years. C-4, a malleable plastic explosive that was the first choice of many a demolition expert. The wire that would set off the explosive ran from the glob along the steps, then up the wall and into a small plastic box attached to the doorjamb. Just opposite the box, on the door itself, was a small plate, its width and length equal to that of the switch. With the door closed, the plate and the box lined up perfectly.

Additional wires led out of the box to other mounds of C-4: one on each hinge, one along the base, and a last bit in the middle of the door itself, an arrangement sure to shred anyone standing on the other side into tiny pieces.

It was a pretty simple setup. Someone opens the door. The switch and the plate move out of sync. An electronic jolt is sent out.

And boom.

Dead and destroyed.

Whoever it was who actually used the door must have had a remote device that turned the switch off when necessary.

Quinn checked the setup again, making sure there were no hidden backup switches. Luck was with him. Everything looked pretty straightforward. Since there was only one perceived way into the room, no extra security measures would have been needed. The booby-trap maker would never have expected someone to come through the wall to get at his handiwork.

Quinn started with the C-4 next to the steps. He separated it from the wire, then repeated the procedure with the other mounds.

'You could have just left it,' Orlando said.

'I didn't feel like climbing back through that hole to get out,' Quinn said. 'Besides, this way some wino won't stumble into it someday.'

Orlando cocked her head and smiled. 'I knew there was a reason I loved you.'

'If that's the only reason, then we're both screwed.'

Quinn opened the door and stuck his head into the hallway. Al looked over at him, his eyes wide with fear. Nate looked over, too, but he seemed considerably less surprised.

'Everything all right out here?' Quinn asked.

'Couldn't be better,' Nate said.

'You want to bring him in here?'

'I'm not going in there!' Al said, fear in his voice.

108

'It's safe now,' Quinn said.

'I'm not. I told you I'm not. I'm not going in there.'

'We're okay,' Nate said to Quinn.

'Quinn?' It was Orlando.

Quinn pulled himself back inside. Orlando was across the room, next to the gap between the stack of boxes and the exterior wall in the far left corner. She was looking at the floor.

'What is it?' Quinn asked.

'I think this might be the room Peter's agent was looking for.'

Quinn hurried over. Instead of concrete like the rest of the floor, here was a four-foot-square piece of metal. It was dark and showing signs of rust along the edges, but otherwise was in remarkably good shape. There were hinges along the left side and a latch on the right. Through a loop on the latch was a large, very new padlock.

'Shall I?' Orlando asked.

'It might be wired also,' Quinn said.

'Should be easy enough to check,' she said. 'The metal's warped at this end.'

Without waiting to hear what Quinn thought, she got down onto the floor and pressed the side of her face against the concrete. She moved her light so that it played into the opening, moving it back and forth several times. After a minute passed, she sat back up.

'Clean,' she said.

'You're sure?' Quinn asked.

'Enough to stake your life on it.'

'My life?'

She moved over to the padlock, removed her set of lock picks from her backpack, then set to work. It took her less than thirty seconds to open it.

'This is the part where you open the door,' she said after she removed the lock from the loop on the latch.

'Maybe Nate should do it,' Quinn said.

She stared at him. 'You trust me that little?'

Quinn let out a short laugh, then reached down. 'You might want to stand back. Just in case you're wrong.'

'Oh, I'm not wrong,' she said. But she took a few steps back anyway.

Quinn smiled, then pulled the trapdoor up. There was a loud groan as the hinges protested under the weight of the metal door. Quinn swung it all the way open so that it was leaning against the back wall.

'You guys all right in there?' Nate called.

'We're fine,' Quinn and Orlando said in unison.

Orlando shone her light into the opening, revealing a steep, narrow concrete stairway.

'Nate,' Quinn said, voice raised. 'We'll be on radio.'

'Radio?' Nate said. 'Where are you going?'

'That's a good question.'

Quinn looked at Orlando, then mounted the steps and started down. He could hear her following him a few feet back.

'What's going on?' Nate said in his ear.

Quinn gave him a quick description of what they'd found.

'So I just wait here while you guys have all the fun?'

'Call Peter,' Quinn said. 'Get an ETA on his men.'

'Okay,' Nate said. 'What if he asks me what we've found?'

'Tell him I'll call him when we're done.'

The steps of the stairwell were made of stone and spiraled downward. It reminded Quinn of some he had climbed in old European churches, just tread after tread surrounded by walls and ceiling. A curving tunnel leading to God knew where.

When they reached the bottom, there was only one way to go, a brick-lined tunnel leading away from the stairs. Unlike the cramped space of the staircase, this tunnel was wide enough for them to walk side by side, and the gently curving ceiling just tall enough for them to stand upright without being concerned about head injuries. In the distance they could hear a low rumble, almost more a feeling than a noise.

'So someone was trying to hide a secret entrance into the building,' Orlando said.

'Or a secret exit,' Quinn said. 'Say you're afraid of being followed. You could duck into this building, come down to this tunnel . . . and from here you can probably get anywhere.'

'Should we stop?' Orlando asked. 'Or should we see what's ahead?'

'Let's go on a little longer. I'd like to see where this lets out.'

There was a trickle of water running along the floor heading in the same direction they were,

111

indicating a downward slope. The bricks of the walls and ceiling looked old. Quinn guessed the tunnel might be even older than the abandoned building above, perhaps from the early 1900s or the late 1800s.

'Quinn,' Nate's voice said in Quinn's ear. 'Should . . . think?'

'Nate, repeat. I missed that.'

'Can't . . . you.'

'The signal doesn't travel well down here,' Orlando said.

'Nate, hang tight.'

'What?'

'Hang tight,' Quinn repeated.

'Copy . . . '

'Nate?' Quinn said.

There was nothing but dead air. They had moved out of range.

Ahead, the tunnel seemed to go on forever. The beams of their flashlights pushed the darkness back only so far before the black took over again.

'What *is* that?' Orlando said, cocking her head.

It was the rumble. It had grown louder as they moved deeper into the tunnel.

'Subway,' Quinn said.

Though the noise was basically constant, it ebbed and flowed like trains would do as they moved through the busy New York system.

'Something up there,' Quinn said.

An opening in the wall along the right.

As they neared it, Quinn's first guess was an intersection tunnel. But soon he saw that whatever it was, it was covered by an old wooden door. Decades of dampness, with an assist from unseen termites, meant at best it had only a few more years before it fell apart on the spot.

But the door wasn't the only thing that was deteriorating.

'Smell it?' Quinn said.

'Yes.'

He shoved at the door with the end of his flashlight. It resisted at first, then began to swing open, scraping the floor as it did. The smell was stronger now, almost overpowering. What made it worse was the noise that accompanied it, a combination of smacking and chomping.

As Quinn shone his light into the room, dozens of rats scattered in every direction. Several even headed out the door and between Quinn's and Orlando's feet.

'Dammit!' Orlando said as she jumped to her left.

'You all right?' Quinn asked.

'I swear to God one of them tried to crawl up my leg.'

Quinn scanned the room with the light again. Except for the most tenacious ones, most of the rodents were gone now. Those that remained glanced up every few seconds, seeming to dare Quinn to try to make them leave.

In the center of the room was the feast they'd all been enjoying. The body of a man.

Quinn stepped across the threshold. Again the rats looked up but didn't move.

The space appeared to be an old equipment room, long retired. There were bolts extending up out of the floor where machinery had once been secured. Pipes, some as wide as six inches, stuck down from the ceiling in a group. They were all truncated, their open ends either once connected to the long-gone machines or created that way to serve as conduits for cables and wires to pass through to the world above. There were no other doors out, no storage cabinets, no tunnels in the floor. Just the rats, and the memory of the machines, and the dead guy.

'Too well dressed to have been living down here, don't you think?' Orlando said.

She had come in behind him, and was following close, flashlight in one hand and gun in the other. Quinn thought if another rat came within a few feet of her, she'd shoot it.

'Yeah,' Quinn said.

The body was wearing a suit. Dark gray, and made with expensive-looking material. And the man's shoes. Mezlans. At least three hundred dollars a pair. Not the kind of outfit you'd expect a tunnel dweller to be decked out in.

The man was lying on his back. His suit was open, and the shirt had been ripped by the rats to get at the flesh underneath. There was even more damage along the man's neck and jaw, but his face was largely still intact.

'I think we can rule out natural causes,' Quinn said.

The corpse's most prominent facial feature was not one he'd been born with, nor one caused by the rodents feasting on him. It was a bullet hole, a half inch above his right eye.

'He look familiar to you?' Quinn asked.

Orlando shook her head. 'Someone you know?'

'I'm not . . . sure.'

He took a step forward and looked hard at the man's face.

The state of the dead didn't always resemble that of the living. It was in the way the muscles let go, relaxing for the last time. But Quinn had seen plenty of dead, and had learned how to see the living in the decaying flesh.

And there was something familiar about this guy. Not the familiarity of someone Quinn knew personally, but more like someone he'd seen before. In pictures, or on TV, or something like that.

But no name came to him.

Quinn shooed a couple of the rats away with his flashlight, then leaned down and patted the man's jacket. The pockets were all empty.

He opened the jacket and moved it out of the way so he could check the pants pockets. In the left front pocket was a thin card carrier, the kind some men used instead of a wallet. Less bulk. More streamlined. Inside were two credit cards, an insurance ID, four business cards, and a driver's license.

The license gave him a name. Christopher Jackson. But it was the business cards that connected with Quinn.

Quinn stared at the top one for a moment, not sure he wanted to believe what he'd read.

'Who is he?' Orlando asked.

Quinn told her the man's name.

There was still a question in Orlando's eyes. It

was to be expected. Even if she hadn't spent so much time out of the country, there was a good chance she wouldn't have known who he was. Quinn hadn't gotten it on the name, either. Though Jackson had a high-level job, he kept a very low public profile.

'The DDNI,' Quinn said.

Her eyes grew wide. There was no need to explain to her what the initials meant.

DDNI — Deputy Director of National Intelligence.

# 9

On most jobs the disposal of the body was the easy part. It was the time spent at the incident scene that could be the most problematic. The situation had to be assessed, cleaned up, and the body moved to the transport vehicle before anyone could come snooping around. It was during that segment of the job when the chance of discovery was at its highest. And if that happened, things could get really messy.

A body safely stowed in the back of a van or the trunk of a car, and the vehicle racking up the miles from where the corpse had been found, lowered the risks considerably. From there, it was straight to a preplanned disposal site. The Irish Sea for one, or an after-hours crematorium, or a deep hole in some out-of-the-way spot. Usually Quinn would have two or three options lined up. Often, as had been the case in Ireland, there would be a team on standby to help him. Being prepared was what made him one of the best.

Unfortunately, none of that applied to the body riding in the trunk of their sedan.

'Christopher Jackson. Born March 6, 1949, in Tampa, Florida,' Orlando said.

She was in the front passenger seat, her laptop opened on her lap, as Quinn drove through the city. Nate was in the back seat, quiet but looking worried.

'He had been with the agency since the late eighties,' she continued. 'Worked his way up. Did some time in Germany, Saudi Arabia, Lebanon, and South Africa before settling in at Langley. Seemed to be a specialist-at-large, moving from one division to another. Eastern Europe, Mideast, Latin America.' She looked up from the computer for a moment. 'Building quite a résumé. Must have already been thinking about higher office.' Her gaze returned to the screen. 'He was number two in the office of Russian and European Analysis on 9/11. He quickly moved up from there. Became Deputy Director of National Intelligence two and a half years ago. Married. Two sons. One's still in college, Penn State. The other's just passed the bar exam in D.C.'

'Politics?' Quinn asked.

'Nothing concrete here, but reading between the lines, he appeared to be a little right of center, but not much.'

'And nothing about him being missing?'

'Nothing.'

*Then someone's keeping it quiet*, Quinn thought. The body was at least forty-eight hours dead. 'Try Peter again,' he said.

They had already tried calling the head of the Office twice since leaving the not-so-abandoned apartment building, but both times no one had answered. The last time Quinn had talked to him had been in the building hallway after Peter's men had arrived to pick up Al Barker. When Quinn told him about Deputy Director Jackson's body, Peter's initial reply was a shocked silence, followed by a quick 'Get him out. I'll call you back.'

Orlando switched her phone to speaker so they could all hear. After the fourth ring, Quinn was sure they'd be redirected to the generic voicemail message again. But then there was a click.

'Hello?' It was Peter.

'Where the hell have you been?' Quinn asked. 'We're driving around with the — ' He stopped himself from saying, 'the DDNI.'

The chance anyone would be able to tap into his line was minimal. But minimal wasn't impossible. 'With . . . someone we're not really interested in hanging out with much longer.'

'I've been making arrangements,' Peter said. 'This is a delicate matter.'

'You think?' Quinn said, unable to subdue his annoyance.

'It's not something that can just disappear,' Peter shot back.

'Stating the obvious, Peter. I need a location. Someplace I can drop him off.'

There was a pause. 'I've been on the phone with a friend from Washington.'

Quinn tensed. He didn't like the idea of bringing more people into this. 'And?'

'And he's going to take care of it.'

'Exactly when is that supposed to happen?'

'He's to call me back in five minutes with an address. You'll leave the car there, then walk away.'

'This is someone you trust?' Quinn asked.

'Yes.'

119

'You're not setting me up, are you?'

'No. Of course not.'

Quinn paused. 'Five minutes?'

'Yes. I'll call you back as — '

Whatever Peter was going to say was drowned out by the crunch of a car ramming into the sedan's rear bumper.

'Shit!' Nate said.

Quinn kept his foot on the gas. In the rearview mirror he could see the other car. It was a Ford Explorer SUV. One of its headlights had been damaged by the impact and had gone out. But that didn't seem to discourage whoever it was behind the wheel. He was coming at them again.

Quinn pushed the pedal all the way to the floor, but it wasn't enough. The SUV slammed into them again.

He glanced at the rearview mirror again, expecting to see the grille of the Ford preparing for a third hit, but the truck had dropped a car length back, and seemed content for the moment to just follow.

'Nate,' Quinn said. 'Get a visual.'

There was a pause, then Nate said, 'The front window's tinted. I can't see inside.'

'How long has he been behind us?' Orlando asked.

Quinn shook his head. 'Not long. I checked less than a minute ago, and he wasn't there.'

As always, Quinn had been keeping watch on the road both in front and behind. Twenty seconds before the initial hit, Quinn was positive the SUV had not been following them.

Orlando's phone began to ring. It must have

gotten disconnected sometime during one of the collisions.

'It's Peter,' Orlando said, looking at the display on the mobile.

'Tell him we'll have to call him back.'

Quinn looked back into the mirror as she talked to Peter. The SUV was approaching again. Quinn switched his gaze to the road ahead. The end of the block was coming up quick.

'Hold on,' he said.

He waited until the last second, then whipped the wheel to the right, taking the turn at near full speed. The Ford grazed the corner of his bumper as it shot by, causing Quinn's car to weave to the left.

The sedan's tires screeched as they tried to grip the surface of the road, then the car rocked in protest as Quinn straightened the wheel before it settled down.

Quinn looked in the mirror again. The truck had missed the turn and was no longer behind them. He flicked his gaze back and forth from the road to the mirror, expecting the truck to reappear. But it never did.

A half block ahead, several taxis were parked near the entrance to a small hotel. Quinn slammed on the brakes, bringing the sedan to a stop.

'Out! Both of you,' he said. 'Grab a cab and follow me. If that guy comes back, see if you can get a visual. Coordinate with Peter. He should be able to get us some backup.'

Nate was out the door before Quinn finished

speaking. Orlando hesitated only a moment longer.

'Be careful,' she said.

'Go, go,' he said.

He waited until they were climbing into the cab at the front of the line, then pressed down on the accelerator again.

If Quinn had been the follower, he would have gone up another block and circled around so that he might be able to catch up to his prey at the next intersection. As he neared the end of the street, he slowed and looked left, hoping to get an early glimpse of the truck if it was there.

It being night in New York City, he couldn't be one hundred percent sure. There had to be dozens of cars within a one-block radius. The majority were cabs, but there were still plenty of private vehicles, including a fair share of SUVs. None, though, were missing a front headlight.

He turned right onto Park Avenue, heading south toward Grand Central Terminal. A few seconds later, he saw Orlando and Nate's cab pull onto the road behind him.

Still no sign of the one-eyed SUV.

Quinn reached into his pocket and pulled out his phone. He placed his thumb on the touch screen, deactivating the security lock. Glancing back and forth between road and phone, he found Orlando's number in his quick call list and touched it. As the line began to ring, he engaged the speakerphone, then set his mobile on the passenger seat, securing the end in the crevice between the back and the bottom cushions.

'As far as I can tell, the tail's gone,' Orlando said.

'Slow down a little,' Quinn said. 'See if he's hanging farther back.'

'Okay.'

He could hear her relay the instructions to the driver. There was a few seconds' delay, then the cab slowed.

'Still nothing,' she said a minute later. 'I think he's gone.'

Quinn turned west on Forty-seventh Street, then south again on Fifth Avenue, each time relaying his actions to Orlando. As he crossed Forty-second Street and came abreast of the New York City Library, his phone beeped, indicating he had another call.

'Hold on,' he told Orlando. He switched the calls. 'Yes?'

'What kind of car are you in?' It was Peter.

'What? Why?'

'Just tell me.'

Quinn thought for a second. 'Buick. A Lucerne, I think. Silver or gray.'

'You need to find someplace to hide that car now!'

'What's going on?'

'An APB was just issued by the NYPD for a gray Buick sedan with rear bumper damage. Sound familiar?'

'Son of a bitch,' Quinn said.

'They even have the license number. The bulletin says the driver is wanted in connection with a murder. It's been given top priority.'

Quinn's eyes narrowed. He'd been set up. He

was driving through the streets of New York City with the body of one of the country's top-ranking intelligence officers in his trunk, and now every member of the New York Police Department was going to be looking for him. Despite the urge to go faster, he slowed down so as not to bring any extra attention to his vehicle.

'I'll park it and let you know where it is,' he said.

'No. You've got to put it someplace no one will find it. We can't risk someone discovering the body.'

'That's a little easy for you to say right now, Peter. You're not the one looking at a federal death sentence.'

'Find a parking garage. All the hotels have them.' When Quinn didn't respond right away, Peter said, 'Are you still there?'

'Yes,' Quinn said. 'But it might be a little too late for parking garages.'

One of NYPD's finest was parked in front of a closed-up newsstand on the left side of the road just ahead, near the corner of Fifth Avenue and West Thirty-sixth Street. There was no chance for Quinn to avoid him, no street he could turn down before passing the patrol car. And pulling over to the curb would only delay the inevitable.

'I'll call you back,' he said, then switched back to Orlando. 'We've got a problem.'

He told her Peter's news while keeping an eye on the cop car as he drove by. Inside there were two officers. They seemed to be talking to each other, not noticing the traffic around them.

There was a moment when Quinn thought

he'd made it. But as he checked his rearview mirror to be sure, he saw the cop in the passenger seat look over and point at the sedan.

There was no reason to wait around to see what happened next. Quinn floored it.

'He's on you,' Orlando said through the phone.

'Yeah . . . I noticed that.'

Quinn could see the cop car pulling away from the curb, lights flashing in his mirror. He had a half a block lead. He only hoped it was enough.

At first the traffic lights were in his favor. He made it past Thirty-fifth and Thirty-fourth in seconds. But ahead, the light was turning yellow. He slowed only enough to make a wide turn onto West Thirty-third Street. His momentum carried him up onto the first foot of the sidewalk on the left side. If the Starbucks at the corner had still been open, the people inside would have gotten quite a rush.

Quinn straightened the sedan and sped off down the center of the street. He'd just passed the back side of the Empire State Building when the police car rounded the corner from Fifth Avenue. Quinn's gaze changed from the mirror to the road, and he saw in an instant that his main problem wasn't behind him, it was ahead.

Instead of cars just being parked along the left side of the road, now there were empty vehicles lining both, cutting the usable road space down to no more than a lane and a half.

'Orlando, where are you?' Quinn asked.

'On Fifth,' she said. 'We're having a little . . . problem with our driver.'

'Switch cabs. Meet back at the safe point. I'll be there soon.'

'What are you going to do?'

Quinn hesitated. The light at the upcoming intersection was red. There were half a dozen cars waiting for it to change, blocking the way. Behind him the cop car was coming on fast. He was about to be boxed in.

'Just go. I'll be there.'

He picked up his phone, hit disconnect, then shoved the device in his pocket.

There was really only one choice. He was going to have to run for it, and hope the cops wouldn't risk hitting innocents by opening fire on him.

As he eased off the gas, he reached under his seat, pulled out his SIG, and placed it on his lap. With his left hand, he reached for the door handle, but stopped before opening the door.

Ahead to his right, an opportunity.

He jammed down on the accelerator, turned the wheel hard to the right, then left again as he negotiated the narrow gap between two parked cars onto the sidewalk. There was the screech of metal on stone as the side of Quinn's sedan slammed against the marble-tiled building before centering itself on the walkway.

The drivers in the other cars gaped at him as he raced by. Near the corner there was a couple walking down the sidewalk with their backs to him. Quinn jammed his palm down on the horn. The couple turned, their eyes growing wide. At least the woman had sense enough to pull her companion between two parked cars a second before Quinn raced by.

Ahead on the intersecting street, Broadway, cars drove from right to left, unaware of his approach. As he reached the GameStop store on the corner, he glanced in the mirror again. The cops had slowed at the back of the traffic and were trying to maneuver onto the sidewalk behind him. But their driving skills were nowhere near as good as his, and they were finding it more difficult than they'd anticipated.

The intersection was only ten feet away. Quinn pressed the car's horn with one hand and turned the wheel to the left with the other as he flew off the end of the sidewalk into traffic. His horn was soon joined by others.

Then there was the screech of tires.

Then the crunch of impact.

The sedan had been jolted to the left as a cab slammed into the passenger side. He could feel the Buick wanting to flip over, but it remained upright. Quinn looked over his shoulder. The driver of the cab was staring at him in a daze, the front end of his taxi still touching Quinn's car.

Quinn pressed down on the accelerator and tried to pull away. But as he did, he could feel the cab wanting to come with him. He threw the Buick into reverse and pushed down on the gas again. That did it. The cab groaned as it spun away, setting Quinn free of the unwanted obstruction. Quinn shoved the transmission back into drive, then took off down Broadway.

Behind him was chaos. Cars scattered all over the place. People standing in the middle of the street. And two cops rounding the corner on foot, guns in hand, but with nothing to shoot at.

For the moment he was alone, but he knew that wouldn't last long.

He needed to dump the car. Fast.

He turned down West Twenty-seventh and found a spot in front of a jewelry store on the right. It was just large enough for him to fit, and would keep the damaged side of the car facing away from the street. Before he got out, he had to search for his gun. It had flown off his lap during the accident. He could feel the seconds ticking away as he felt around the darkness for it. Finally, he found the SIG stuck between his seat and the door.

Adrenaline still pumping, he all but jumped out of the car. He had to force himself to walk, not run, around the front of the vehicle and onto the sidewalk.

The street was quiet. No one else was out. The only real noise was distant. Cars moving through the city as they did at all hours, a few horns. And sirens. More than on the average New York night. He tried to gauge their location and direction. None seemed to be heading toward him. Yet.

There was a Honda Prelude parked behind his Buick. He knew he'd have no problem getting in and getting it started. And its trunk would be large enough for the body of the Deputy Director.

Quinn walked over to the rear of his sedan, pulled out the key, and stuck it in the lock on the trunk. Only when he turned it, nothing happened. He tried pulling it open with his other

128

hand, but there was only the groan of the vehicle's springs.

The trunk lid wasn't going anywhere. It had gotten tweaked during the accident, and would take equipment and time he didn't have to open it.

He pulled out his phone and dialed Peter. 'It's Quinn,' he said.

'Where the hell are you?'

'You need to send someone for the car.' He gave Peter the address of the building closest to where he'd parked the Buick. 'You have to make it quick. The cops are looking for it now.'

'Jesus. I told you to park it in a — '

Quinn hung up, then began walking. It turned out he wouldn't need the Prelude after all.

# 10

By the time Quinn made it to the Marriott Marquis Hotel in Times Square, it was almost 3 a.m. Even then, there were dozens of people about. It was New York after all, where the night people replaced the day people, keeping the city in constant motion.

Escalators took him up several floors to the main lobby level. As he stepped off, his phone began to vibrate. He wasn't surprised by the name on the display. ORLANDO.

Instead of answering, he looked around, spotting her in seconds. She was across the lobby, standing against the wall. When their eyes met, she lowered her phone and smiled.

A moment later he spotted Nate standing several feet away from her. Quinn's apprentice was scanning the room, doing what he'd been trained to do in these exact kinds of situations.

'Took you long enough,' Orlando said once he reached her. Per standard procedure, she'd refrained from calling him after they split up.

He gave her a condensed version of what had happened. When he finished, he asked, 'Do you know if Peter got anyone to the car yet?'

'No,' she said, shaking her head. 'He's here, you know.'

'In New York?' Quinn asked, surprised.

'No. I mean here in this hotel.'

That gave Quinn a moment's pause. 'Where?' he said.

'He's got a room upstairs. He asked me to bring you up as soon as you got here.'

'He asked *you* to bring me up?'

'I didn't say I would. We can just leave if you want.'

Quinn paused. Orlando's suggestion was very intriguing, but after a few seconds he shook his head. 'Let's just get it over with.'

★ ★ ★

Peter's room was on the twenty-third floor. The door opened as they approached it. That wasn't surprising. Quinn had noticed several cameras placed discreetly along the corridor leading up to the door. Those inside had no desire to be surprised by unexpected guests.

Sean Cooper, one of Peter's men, stood just inside the room holding the door.

'Quinn,' Cooper said.

'Sean,' Quinn replied as he and the others stepped inside.

'Heard about the accident,' Cooper said. 'You all right?'

'I'm fine,' Quinn said.

The room had two double beds, a rust-colored couch next to the window, a small desk against the wall, and a television cabinet. Your standard tourist room.

There was a computer on the desk. The screen looked like it had been divided into

131

four images. Feeds from the cameras outside the room, Quinn guessed.

Peter was sitting on the couch, looking at them as they walked in. On a small round table in front of him was a tumbler filled with amber liquid and ice.

Quinn pulled out the desk chair and offered it to Orlando. But she shook her head and sat on the edge of the bed closest to the couch. Quinn took the chair for himself. Nate remained standing, taking up position a few feet behind Quinn.

A full minute passed before anyone said anything.

Peter finally shook his head and said, 'That didn't go as planned, did it?'

'Not exactly the way I would have wanted it,' Quinn agreed. 'Did you get to the car?'

Peter picked up a television remote sitting next to his glass and pointed it at the TV. There was a half-second delay before the television came to life. Quinn had to swivel the chair around so he could see. On the screen was a commercial for a car rental agency.

He looked back at Peter, his brow furrowed.

'Hold on,' Peter said, but offered no further information.

The commercial was followed by another for food storage bags, then an ad for a national chain of restaurants. Once the restaurant ad faded to black, there was a moment of nothing, then the screen filled with a graphic animation: *CNN Breaking News*. Accompanying the graphic was a quick, driving piece of music emphasizing the importance of what was to come.

When the image wiped away, it was replaced by a night view of a city street. A hundred feet from where the camera was positioned were dozens of parked police vehicles, most with lights flashing. For several seconds there was only the noise of the city, then a female voice broke in.

'You are looking at a live shot along West Twenty-seventh Street near Broadway in New York City, where the tragic end of what looks like a kidnapping has been discovered.'

The TV image split into two boxes. One continued to show the scene on the street, while the other contained a shot of one of the overnight anchors, a woman, her hair and makeup perfect. Her face was taut, unsmiling, in the universal news anchor look for 'this is serious.'

'I want to bring back CNN correspondent Daniel Costello, who has moved in as close as possible. He joins us via telephone.'

The shot of the anchor was replaced by a still image of a man in his mid-thirties. Under the picture the name Daniel Costello was printed in bold type.

'Dan, as I understand it, the police have still not made any official statements.'

'None so far, Connie,' Costello said, his voice distorted by the phone line. 'We've been told that a press briefing's been scheduled for ten a.m. Otherwise they're pretty much saying nothing.'

'What about the identity of the victim?'

'Nothing has been released yet. What we do know is that the body of a man was found in the trunk of a car parked on West Twenty-seventh Street. Through other sources, we have also learned that the victim was a prominent public figure.'

'But no name,' the anchor said.

'No. There's been some speculation here, but nothing concrete.'

'We've heard that the car in question was involved in some sort of incident earlier in the evening. Can you tell us what happened?'

'That's right, Connie. Apparently the NYPD had received a tip about the car several hours ago. Sometime after midnight, one of their patrol cars spotted the vehicle and began pursuit. During the chase the car was involved in an accident at the corner of West Thirty-third and Broadway, sending one man to the hospital. After the accident, the car continued for several blocks until the driver either could go no farther, or decided he would do better on foot. At that point, the police were in a full-scale search, so it wasn't long before the vehicle was discovered.'

'And that's when they found the victim in the trunk,' the anchor said.

'That's correct.'

'Is there any word on suspects?'

'The driver is reported to be male, mid-thirties, with short brown hair. At this time, the police have no one in custody. I've heard from sources that they should have a more accurate description by the time of the briefing later this morning.'

Peter switched the TV off.

'I told you to get someone there quick,' Quinn said.

'We did. But the police were already there.'

'Then you weren't quick enough.'

Orlando was staring at Quinn. 'They have a description of you,' she said.

'That was pretty generic,' he replied.

'It is now, but they obviously knew to look for us. Perhaps someone is feeding them a more accurate description right now.'

Quinn remained silent for a moment, then looked at Peter. 'You called me and warned me about the APB. How did the police know?'

'We're . . . not sure,' Peter said.

'Who knew we were going in the building?'

'Only me and my team,' Peter said, then looked toward the door where Cooper stood. 'Sean and Ida.' But Peter seemed to hesitate.

'Who else, Peter?'

'My client knew I was sending someone in, but he didn't know who.'

'Who the hell is your client?'

'Someone who would have very much wanted this to stay quiet.'

Nate cleared his throat, and everyone turned to him. Quinn could see his apprentice had something he wanted to say.

'What are you thinking?' Quinn asked.

'Isn't it possible that whoever killed the Deputy Director might have been keeping an eye on the building?' Nate asked. 'It's probably the same guy who planted the explosives, don't you think? Maybe we were just being watched.'

135

Quinn looked back at Peter. 'You're sure your client wouldn't have leaked this?'

'Absolutely.'

'Doesn't matter how they found out at the moment,' Orlando said. 'Pretty soon the whole city is going to be looking for you. We've got to get you out of town now.'

She was right. The search for Deputy Director Jackson's supposed killer would go nationwide, but it would be most intense there in New York.

Quinn stood up. 'We need a vehicle.'

Peter hesitated, then looked at Cooper. 'Get the stuff out of our car. They can take that.'

'No,' Quinn said. Cooper, who had already started for the door, stopped. 'Not out of the garage. Something on a nearby street. Something generic.'

There would be cameras in the garage of the Marriott Marquis, and maybe even security guards walking around who might take special notice of them. The less people who saw Quinn, the better.

Cooper looked at his boss, his eyebrows raised.

'Do it,' Peter said.

With a single nod, Cooper left.

Everyone was silent for several moments.

'You knew the DDNI would be in there, didn't you?' Quinn asked.

'No. I didn't,' Peter said, then paused. 'There was the possibility, yes. But I really didn't expect to find him there. Especially not dead.'

'Then what did you expect?'

Silence, nearly thirty seconds of it. Quinn

136

began to think Peter wasn't going to answer him at all. Then, 'I thought we might find a clue to where he'd been taken.'

'What do you mean?'

Again, Peter hesitated. This time, though, the silence lasted only a moment.

'Let me show you something,' he said.

He walked to the computer on the desk, pulled over the chair Quinn had vacated, then sat down. By the time Quinn, Orlando, and Nate had moved in behind him, he'd already minimized the surveillance images on the screen and replaced them with a spreadsheet. It was broken down into four columns. There were locations listed down the left-hand column, dates in the center two, and two- to four-digit numbers in the right.

'What is this?' Quinn asked.

'Inside the envelope you brought back from Ireland was a jump drive.' A tiny flash memory card able to hold multiple gigs of data. 'There were only four files on it. This was one of them.'

'Looks like an itinerary,' Orlando said.

'Yes,' Peter said.

'How the hell does this tie into what happened tonight?' Quinn asked.

Peter glanced at Quinn. 'The DDNI hired us a month ago for a special project. He'd been approached by a source claiming to have information about a potential terrorist operation.'

'Jesus, Peter. Every source says they have information about a potential terrorist operation,' Quinn said. 'It's the in thing.'

'That's why the DDNI hired us instead of

using his resources at CIA,' Peter said. 'He wanted to keep it quiet. Our job was to coordinate meetings with Primus, then check out the info he handed over.'

'I'm sorry. Who?'

'Primus. It's the code name for the DDNI's source,' Peter said. 'If it turned out the information was good, the DDNI would bring in his people at that point.'

Peter's story made sense. Much of Washington's behind-the-scenes work these days was outsourced to private companies. In this post-9/11 world, there just wasn't enough manpower to handle everything. Even wars were outsourced to companies like Blackwater and Halliburton.

'Are you saying the meeting in Ireland was with the DDNI's source?' Nate asked. 'Because if it was, he's dead. We all watched him get shot.'

A year ago, Quinn would have given his apprentice a look that would have told Nate to keep quiet. For the most part, that wasn't necessary anymore. Nate's questions now were more often than not the same questions Quinn would have asked.

Peter shook his head. 'The meeting concerned Primus, yes, but we never met with him directly. The men you saw killed were his go-betweens. Up until that point, the information Primus had been feeding us was pretty solid. Nothing big, just things meant to build trust. The package from Ireland was supposed to be the first about the specific operation Primus had told the DDNI about.' He nodded at the screen. 'This itinerary is the movements of one of the terrorist agents.'

'What have you learned from it?' Orlando asked.

'That this guy has made a lot of trips to a lot of different places. Mostly third world.'

'Who is he?'

'We don't know that yet.'

'Do you know what they're planning?' Quinn asked.

'No.'

Before Quinn could say anything else, Peter held up a hand, stopping him.

'Primus was supposed to feed us the rest of the information over two additional meetings. The first was to take place two nights ago. And the last, next Thursday.'

'Sounds like the one two nights ago didn't happen,' Quinn said.

'After Ireland, Primus got scared. He sent a message canceling both upcoming meets. But we knew we needed the information. It seemed like he might actually be onto something. So the DDNI sent a message back using an emergency contact system we had in place. He was able to convince Primus to meet with him personally, one-on-one. Nobody liked the idea, but it seemed like the only thing we could do.'

'You watched him, of course,' Orlando said.

'We did the best we could. The meeting took place here in New York. Grand Central Terminal. That was Primus's suggestion.'

Same type of location Quinn would have

suggested in similar circumstances. A large, public facility with plenty of nooks and crannies for a quick, private chat.

'We lost the DDNI there. That was three days ago.'

'Didn't he at least have a tracking bug on him?' Quinn asked.

'Of course he did,' Peter snapped. 'Sewn in the cuff of his pants. But it had been cut out and dropped in a trash can on Fifth Avenue.'

'So your valuable source kidnapped him? Was he setting him up the whole time?'

Peter took a breath, then said, 'We don't think he did it. Primus contacted us that night, wondering what the hell happened, why the DDNI hadn't shown up. He could have been just playing with us, but we don't think so. We think the same people who sent the assassin to Ireland are the ones who grabbed Deputy Director Jackson and killed him.'

The room became still.

'How does it tie in to the building today?' Orlando asked.

Peter turned back to the computer and opened another document. 'Primus sent us a list of locations in New York he thought might be of interest.'

The displayed list had at least two dozen places on it. Quinn spotted the address of the abandoned apartment building a little more than halfway down.

'How did he come up with this?' Quinn asked.

'We don't know.'

'Peter, for God's sake, you still trust this guy?

It sounds to me like he was in on it.'

'We're convinced otherwise,' Peter said. 'Our priority now is to get the rest of the information from him so we can judge if we have a credible threat on our hands or not.'

'The DDNI is dead,' Quinn said. 'You have a credible threat, all right. You've been talking to him.' He paused. 'And, you know what? Right now, shouldn't your number one priority be getting me out of trouble?'

'I have a question,' Nate said.

They all turned to him.

'Am I the only one wondering why Peter is telling us all this? I mean, no offense or anything, but usually you don't tell us anything. Am I wrong?'

Quinn could feel his gut clench. He would have noticed, too, if the evening's events hadn't pissed him off so much. He had come into Peter's room expecting to get answers, and answers he got. But now he realized why.

Peter must have seen it in Quinn's eyes. 'Number three,' he said.

'No,' Quinn said.

'Are you going back on the deal? No questions. You're the one who offered that condition. That means you take whatever I give you.'

Quinn could feel Orlando and Nate tense behind him, everyone realizing the fate they were about to receive.

'Here it is,' Peter said. 'Job number three. You help me get the information Primus knows, then help me stop it if necessary.'

141

'That's two jobs,' Quinn said, regretting more than ever the deal he'd made.

'It's one if I say it's one,' Peter said. 'The condition was no questions.'

There was a low, short hum followed by another a second later. Peter reached into his pocket and pulled out a cell phone. He flipped it open.

'Yes?' Peter said, then listened for a moment. 'All right. Stay there.' He closed the phone, then looked at Quinn. 'So what's it to be? Are you going to stand by your word? Or do I need to let people know you're unreliable?'

In Quinn's world, reputation was everything. He was pretty sure he could weather whatever negative PR Peter put out there, but it would still hurt. More important, though, Quinn considered himself a man of his word. If Peter wished to pervert a promise made out of necessity, there was nothing Quinn could do but go along with it.

'Fine,' he said.

'Good.' Peter smiled, then stood up. 'Sean found a car for you. It's on Forty-sixth, on the other side of Times Square, about halfway down the block. He's waiting.'

He pushed past them and headed across the room toward the door.

'Once you're out of the city, head north,' Peter said. 'I'll call you with instructions later.'

Peter let them out of the room. Quinn didn't even look at Peter as he stepped into the hallway, but he could sense the head of the Office lingering in the doorway.

142

'Quinn,' Peter said. 'The agent that was hurt tonight . . . '

Quinn stopped. 'What about her?'

'I thought you should know. It was Tasha.'

'Tasha?' Quinn said.

The name had also gotten Orlando's and Nate's attention. They had all crossed paths with Tasha the previous year in Singapore.

'Tasha Douglas?' Nate said.

Peter nodded.

'How is she?' Orlando asked.

'Not good, but she's holding on.'

'She working for you now?' Quinn asked.

'It was a . . . joint operation,' Peter said. 'With her out . . . see . . . that's why I need your help.'

Quinn stared at Peter, then said, 'This is the last one. And I'm not talking about just our deal, Peter. No more after this.'

Peter's jaw tensed, his words slipping through clenched teeth. 'I know.'

# 11

In only a week's time, fear had become such a dominant aspect of Marion Dupuis's life that she hardly even noticed it anymore. It had become her norm. Her friends would have picked up on it. Her family, too. But she had told none of them she had even returned from Africa.

The only people who knew she was no longer on the job were her boss at the UN who had approved her request for emergency leave — 'A family issue,' she had said — and the two trusted colleagues whose help she'd needed to leave Côte d'Ivoire.

The first thing she'd needed were papers to get out of the country. Not for herself, but for Iris. There was no way she was going to leave the child behind. One of her colleagues in Africa had assisted her with this. Noelle Broussard was the only one Marion had told the whole story to. Marion was afraid that if she didn't, the woman would have turned her in to the head of the mission instead of helping her to escape.

It must have worked, because ten hours later her friend showed up at her hotel room near the UN compound with a full set of backdated adoption documents, naming Marion as Iris's mother, and a Canadian passport for the girl.

And that wasn't all.

'Here,' the woman said, handing Marion a second packet.

Marion looked inside. There was another set of papers and two additional passports.

'What's this?' Marion asked.

'In case of emergencies.'

Marion pulled out one of the passports. The picture inside was hers, but the name was different. Niquette Fournier. Hometown: Gatineau. The second passport was for Iris, only her name was listed as Isabel Fournier.

'What am I supposed to do with these?' Marion asked, confused.

'Maybe nothing,' her friend said. She looked over at Iris. The girl was sitting on the bed, holding a doll, but she was watching the two women. The woman turned back to Marion. 'Someone came looking for you earlier today.'

Marion felt a chill go up her spine. 'What? Who?'

'A man. A European, I think.'

'Caucasian?'

'Yes. He asked about a woman with a child. An African child.'

'What did you tell him?' Marion asked.

'I didn't talk to him. But I heard about it later. Since no one else knows about the girl, they didn't know who he was talking about.'

'Did he say who he was?'

'No name, just said he worked for an NGO and needed to talk to . . . well, you, I guess.' She nodded at the document packet in Marion's hand. 'So hold on to those. If you don't want anyone to know where you are, they'll help. They're valid. No one will question you.'

Marion's initial thought had been that she and

145

Iris would be safe once they were out of the country. But would they be? Would she and the child need to disappear completely?

*You need to get her away . . . you need to disappear . . . don't let anyone know where you are.* Jan's words before Marion took Iris from the orphanage.

She put both sets of documents on the end of the bed and picked up Iris.

'Thank you,' she said to her friend.

The woman stood and walked to the door. 'Be safe,' she said, and then she was gone.

Marion hugged Iris tightly, feeling the child smile against her cheek. So innocent. So vulnerable, yet almost always happy. She would be childlike for life, thanks to a genetic misfire, but in a way Marion envied that. But it was also that misfire, that malformed chromosome giving the child Down syndrome, that had made her both unwanted in her own community yet desired by men with guns who tried to steal her in the night.

That's why Frau Roslyn had hidden the child at the first hint that her orphanage was going to be searched again. She had told Marion a few weeks earlier that there was a group on the lookout for discarded children of a certain type — those with traits that in the West would label them 'special needs.' Specifically those with either autism or Down syndrome. Other facilities had been searched, and word had spread among those who cared for the orphans in the city to be on their guard. Why someone wanted these children, Frau Roslyn had no idea. But whatever the answer was, she'd told Marion it could not have been good. And when Iris came into her possession, Roslyn had made Marion promise to do what she could to help keep the child safe. Only Marion hadn't realized at the time it would turn into this.

After what she and the child had been through, Marion knew she'd done the only thing she could have. And no matter how difficult, it had been the right thing. She was even starting to rethink her plan to find Iris a real home once they were safe. The child's home should be with her. How could it not be?

That was if Marion didn't get them killed first.

She brought Iris back to New York on the first flight another colleague, one who worked at the UN headquarters in Manhattan, could get her and Iris on. At JFK Airport, she had been tense as she approached passport control. She had chosen to go with the set of documents bearing her own name, but still worried about those Noelle had given her for the child. But Iris's papers had held up, and they were both allowed into the country without a second look.

Marion got a hotel room not far from Port Authority, but her sleep that night was counted in minutes, not hours. She told herself it was jet lag, though she knew that wasn't true. She'd been on edge for several days straight and now didn't know how to turn it off. She was up and out of the hotel with Iris before 7 a.m.

'They'll keep looking for her,' Frau Roslyn's cousin Jan had said. 'You need to get her away. Once you do, you need to disappear. Don't let anyone know where you are. These people will find you. And once they have the girl, they'll kill you.'

She knew she should get out of New York, but there was something she needed to do first.

She purchased an umbrella stroller for Iris from a Duane Reade drugstore on Fifth Avenue, then found a Kinkos.

Using one of the pay-by-the-minute computers, she searched for any news from Côte d'Ivoire about similar abductions, either attempted or successful. She needed to try to find out what was going on, knowing it might be the only way to save the child. But there was nothing; no news that even hinted at anything other than what could best be described as normal kidnappings and abductions. She almost quit there, telling herself she should be satisfied with the results, that the desire for Iris was an aberration, that Jan had just been overly cautious. And now that she and Iris were thousands of miles away, everything would be fine.

But she knew there was one more place she should check, a database that had more information than could be found in even the most ardent Internet searches.

She glanced around the computer room with the sudden feeling a thousand eyes were staring at her. But the two other customers and the attendant behind the desk were preoccupied with their own concerns, and none had a direct view of her computer screen.

She allowed her nerves to calm for a moment,

then typed an address into the Web browser. Using her own password, she logged on to the United Nations employee site. Her friend Noelle back in Côte d'Ivoire had promised not to process her leave of absence for several days, thus ensuring she would still have access to the site. Still, Marion held her breath until the home screen came up.

'Thank you,' she whispered.

It didn't take her long to navigate to the section she was looking for. Again, she had to use her password. Access to this area of the site was limited to those who worked in certain departments.

She selected the databases she was interested in, typed in her parameters: *kidnapping, children, Down syndrome, disabled, Côte d'Ivoire*. She hit Enter. Nothing came up. She decided to change up her search tags, changing *Côte d'Ivoire* to *western Africa* in case there were some reports from the surrounding area. This time the search took all of forty-five seconds to complete. When it was done, it presented her with a list of seventy-three potential matches. But while she'd been looking for additional cases in Côte d'Ivoire and the surrounding area, she'd actually found reports from countries spread across the globe: Guatemala, Rwanda, Kazakhstan, Afghanistan, Bangladesh, Cambodia, Malaysia, Mexico, and at least a half-dozen other developing nations.

Marion skimmed the list. She had seen similar reports before. Most would be secondhand observations from locals telling UN officials what they had seen. She eliminated those that were of no interest to her. When she was done, she was still left with forty-four items, many of them several pages long. Beside her, Iris stirred in the stroller. She'd be awake soon, wanting something to eat and some attention. Marion decided the best route was to print out the ten most promising reports and take them back to her hotel to read.

By the time she finished, Iris was fully awake, and sitting in her lap.

Iris made a fussy noise as if to say she wanted to be anywhere but here.

'Just one more,' Marion whispered in the child's ear.

She hit Print, then logged off the computer.

After collecting her printouts, she wheeled Iris up to the counter to check out.

'Cute girl,' the woman said as she handed Marion her change.

'Thanks,' Marion said.

'Is she yours?'

'Eh . . . no,' Marion said, taken aback by the question. Beside the fact that it was rude, Marion's sense of security kicked in. A Caucasian woman with an African baby would be remembered. 'I'm just babysitting for a friend.'

'Well, it looks like you're doing a pretty good job,' the woman said. 'What's her name?'

Another moment of panic. 'Emily,' Marion said, then immediately regretted it. Emily was her sister's name.

The attendant leaned over the counter. 'Hi, Emily. How are you?'

Iris smiled at the woman.

The look on the woman's face began changing from one of happiness to one of curiosity. Marion knew the woman had seen there was something different in the child's face — the epicanthic folds at the corner of the girl's eyes, her nose broad yet smaller than normal.

Before the woman could say anything, Marion wheeled Iris toward the door and out onto the street. As they headed away, she knew she could never return to this particular branch again.

She got them a room in a hotel just off Times Square. That evening, after Iris fell asleep on the bed, Marion was finally able to read through the reports. Some were only a paragraph, and some were several pages. A few had been investigated, but most had not. There was a note in the report from Bangladesh saying the story was probably fabricated, and that the people involved were most likely just trying to get some money out of the UN.

Marion would have believed it once. But not now.

The targets were always the same: unofficial orphanages where the parentless came to live because there was nowhere else. There was no set hour when the abductors would arrive. Sometimes it was during the day, sometimes night. But they always came for the same thing, for the special children, the ones like Iris. The children no one else wanted.

It was the report from Afghanistan that was most interesting. The details of the kidnapping

151

were pretty much the same. Several tough-looking men showed up at a building dozens of children called home. Once the men had what they wanted, they were gone. But it was the final paragraph that caught her attention.

A vehicle was stopped at a U.S. military checkpoint. Inside was a Caucasian male. He was accompanied by a driver and a bodyguard, both Afghanis. There was also a child in the car. The soldier couldn't say for sure, but he guessed the young boy was about six years old. Though the soldier had no way of knowing, the basic physical description he gave matched that of the boy kidnapped the previous day. The Caucasian man said he was a doctor, and that they were transporting the child to a facility in Kabul for treatment. He produced paperwork backing up his story. Seeing no threat, the soldier let them through. 'Our job isn't to look for doctors transporting disabled kids,' he told an investigator later.

The report surmised that the supposed kidnapping and the doctor with the child in the car were unrelated. Again, Marion might have believed that, too, at one time.

After she finished reading all the reports, a part of her wished she had stopped with her simple Internet search. Her mind might have been more at ease then. She would have assumed the incident involving Iris had been an isolated event. But now she knew that wasn't true. It wasn't even some localized event happening just in Côte d'Ivoire or even just West Africa. No, it was much bigger than that.

The next day she decided to collect as much information as she could. She wasn't sure who she would give it to, but someone had to know. And the more evidence she had, the better chance she had of someone listening. She found a coffeehouse with a couple of computers in back, and signed on to the UN site again. She got through the first portal fine, but when she attempted to navigate into the restricted area she'd been in the day before, her access was denied. A message popped up asking her to call the system administrator at her earliest convenience.

That was the moment she knew she'd made a serious mistake.

Immediately she logged off and left. She took Iris down into the subway system and randomly rode the trains as she tried to think what she should do. At Times Square she got off and found a pay phone.

She called the UN, but not the system administrator's office. She dialed the extension for the friend who had helped her with the airplane tickets, a Dutchman named Henrick Roos.

'It's Marion,' she said, before he could speak.

'Marion?' Roos said. 'Are . . . you all right?'

'I need you to check something for me,' she said. 'I seem to be locked out of everywhere but our main site. It was fine up until this morning. Is everyone having problems or is it just — '

'You should probably come in,' he cut her off.

She paused. 'Why?'

153

'There are some . . . questions that need to be answered.'

'What questions?'

'It would be best if you just came in. I'm sure it will all be fine.'

'Okay,' she said, trying not to let her fear seep into her voice. 'If you think that's best.'

'Yes. I do,' Roos said. 'When . . . can we expect you?' His words were unnatural, forced.

Marion took a deep breath, and did a quick calculation in her mind. 'I can be there in an hour and a half. Two tops,' she said.

'We'll see you then.'

He hung up without letting her say goodbye.

For a second the world seemed to pull away from her. She was standing in one of the busiest places on Earth, yet she felt like she was alone in the middle of a large clearing, visible for anyone to see her. A small cry reminded her that she was anything but alone. Marion reached down and pulled Iris out of the stroller.

'It's all right, sweetie,' Marion said, hugging the child. 'Everything's fine.'

Iris rested her cheek against Marion's shoulder.

'I won't let anyone hurt you,' Marion whispered.

*Two hours*, she thought. By then they'd realize she wasn't coming.

The only question was, how far away could she get by then?

# 12

Daylight invaded the room from somewhere. Quinn forced his eyes open, not really wanting to wake up, but knowing that it must be time. The light was coming from around the edges of the curtain covering the window on the far side of the room — the whiter light of midday, not the yellow of morning.

The room was as old and tired now as it had been when he'd entered it early that morning. The bedspread, the dresser, the nightstands, even the television, all relics of an older time. But as a place to sleep, it had done fine.

Quinn struggled for a moment to remember the name of the place. *The Murphy? Marsh? No, the Morgan Motel.* Just south of Albany, he remembered.

Quinn turned away from the window to reach for his watch when he realized he was alone in the bed.

'Orlando?' he called out.

No response. In fact, there was no other noise in the room at all.

Quinn rubbed his face with his palms, then, with an audible grunt, he sat up. He reached over to grab his watch off the nightstand, but instead managed to knock it to the ground. He decided the effort needed to pick it up was too much. Shower first.

In the bathroom, he got the water going as hot as he could stand it, then jumped in and stood beneath the stream for several minutes, unmoving. As the sleep that had been clinging to him began to recede, he rolled his head from side to side, stretched his back, then his shoulders.

When he walked out of the bathroom fifteen minutes later, clean and dry and awake, he found Orlando sitting on the bed, a paper sack and a plastic shopping bag beside her.

'Good morning,' he said.

'All right, we can go with morning, if that's what you'd like,' she replied.

He gave her a playful sneer, then removed a fresh set of clothes from his suitcase.

'I see you got breakfast,' he said as he pulled on his shirt.

'Lunch, actually. We missed breakfast,' she said. 'We've almost missed lunch, too.'

She tossed something at him. His watch. He caught it and looked at the display as he pulled it over his wrist. 3:41 p.m.

Once Orlando opened the paper bag the smell of burgers and fries wafted from inside. She handed one of the sandwiches to him.

'I also brought this.'

From the plastic bag she withdrew a newspaper, and held it up so he could see it.

It was the *Albany Times Union*. In bold print across the top was the headline:

# SPY CHIEF DEAD

Then below it in smaller type:

DEPUTY DIRECTOR OF
NATIONAL INTELLIGENCE
JACKSON MURDERED

But neither was what caught Quinn's eye, nor were they the reason Orlando was holding the paper up. It was the sketch above the fold that was of interest, an artist's rendition of the man police were looking for in connection with the crime.

'I don't think the guy could have done better if I'd posed for him,' Quinn said.

The image was definitely Quinn.

'Yeah,' Orlando said. 'I was thinking about cutting it out and framing it.'

'Were you?' He was trying to joke back, but funny was the last thing he felt at the moment.

He grabbed the paper from her so he could get a better look. The nose was off, and the eyes were too close together, but it was still a near enough match for someone to make the connection. The caption under the picture read:

WANTED FOR QUESTIONING. Composite sketch of man believed to have been driving the car containing the body of Deputy Director Jackson.

'Dammit,' Quinn said. He tossed the paper onto the bed.

'Hey, you're still free,' Orlando said. She reached into the plastic bag again, pulled out a box. 'Besides, you need a haircut anyway.' From inside she removed a pair of electric hair shears. 'I've also got some hair dye, and a few other things to change you up.'

He tried to smile.

'Food first, though,' she said.

The idea of food wasn't very appealing, but he knew he would need the energy.

While they ate, he flipped on the TV and turned it to CNN. Better to see what else was being reported than to ignore it. No surprise. All the news was focused on the death of Deputy Director Jackson. There was a background story on him, interviews with people he'd known and worked with over the years, a review of the events from the previous evening, and an update on the manhunt for the person who matched the police sketch, the image prominently displayed on the screen. Otherwise, there was nothing that was new.

'I miss the days when news wasn't so immediate,' Quinn said.

'I don't remember those days,' Orlando said.

'Go to hell, you're not that much younger than me.'

'But I am younger.'

Quinn glanced at his watch again: 3:52.

'Nate up yet?' Quinn asked.

'At least an hour. I sent him out to ditch the car and find us something new.'

On the TV, a *Breaking News* graphic cut across the screen. Quinn found the remote, then turned the volume up as the scene switched back to the two anchors on the news set.

'. . . by sources within the investigation,' the male anchor was saying. 'Police were apparently led to an abandoned apartment building by something discovered in the car the body had been found in. It was at this building the suspect was discovered.'

'There was nothing in the car that would lead them there,' Quinn said.

'What suspect?' Orlando asked.

They both leaned toward the television.

'To repeat. Sources inside the Deputy Director Jackson murder investigation report an arrest has been made. We have been told that while the person they've apprehended does not match the police drawing that has been circulated, he is suspected of being involved in the murder.'

'As we've heard time and time again,' his female counterpart said, 'the first forty-eight hours of a murder investigation are the most important. If they were able to make an arrest this quickly, that's a very good sign.'

Quinn lowered the TV volume again.

'Peter?' Orlando said.

'Must be,' Quinn answered.

Somehow Peter had managed to take some of the heat off. But —

'Would have been nice if he'd fixed it so it looked like the man in the drawing was caught.'

'He's staging it,' Orlando said.

She was right. It had been too late to control

the release of the initial description and composite sketch. So to guide the story, Peter would let a little bit out at a time, turning the direction of the story until the man in the drawing was forgotten. All fine and good for the long run, but in the immediate future Quinn would have to remain vigilant.

Orlando seemed to realize this, too. She reached down into the plastic shopping bag, pulled out two boxes.

'So, you prefer your hair black or blond?' she asked.

★　★　★

By 8:30 p.m. they were deep into upstate New York. Quinn — with blond hair and brown-framed glasses that looked over a decade old — was driving a Volkswagen Jetta Nate had assumed temporary ownership of several blocks from the hotel. Beside him, Orlando sat staring out the window. The only one who seemed to be making good use of the time was Nate. He was curled up in the back seat, sound asleep.

The call from Peter had come just before they left the Morgan Motel.

'Montreal,' he had said. 'As fast as you can.'

'And what are we supposed to do when we get there?' Quinn asked.

'Call me when you arrive, and I'll have further instructions.'

So they had continued on their northern route, only this time with a specific destination in mind.

Quinn glanced over at Orlando. She seemed to be focused on a constant point several car lengths ahead of them, and didn't acknowledge his gaze. He'd seen that look on her face before; she was working something in her mind, some problem she needed to solve. Whatever it was, he knew she'd share once she'd got it figured out.

He still had a hard time believing he and Orlando were together. For so many years it had been an unfulfilled dream with zero chance of ever happening. At least that's what he'd convinced himself.

Yet here she was, sitting next to him, the smooth, pale skin of her neck peeking out from beneath her black hair. And her smell — the familiar, comfortable, enfolding smell that was hers alone. God, how he missed that smell when they weren't together.

God, how he missed her.

But that wasn't going to be as much of an issue as it had been.

'I like the idea,' she'd whispered into his ear as he kissed her shoulder, then her neck before they'd fallen asleep at the motel earlier.

'What idea?' he said, then moved his lips down her shoulder toward her breasts.

'What are you doing?' she said. 'I thought you told me you were dead tir — ' Her words turned into a moan, and her breath stuttered as Quinn's tongue touched her nipple, then moved away, encircling it, teasing it. 'I wish you wouldn't do that.'

He stopped, and lifted his head an inch above her skin. 'Are you sure?'

Her fingers weaved themselves into his hair. 'No. I was lying.' She paused, but he remained frozen, his lips still hovering above the slope of her breast. 'Please.'

'I don't know. 'I wish you wouldn't do that' seems pretty definite to me,' he said.

'For God's sake don't listen to me.'

She pulled his head to her chest, and moaned again as he began tracing a line with the tip of his tongue that encircled her areola but didn't touch it. After a few moments, he began to spiral inward. When he reached the center, he caressed her nipple with his tongue, then began spiraling outward again, away from it.

He moved his hand down her waist, keeping his fingers hovering just above her skin so that they didn't touch her. She at first shivered, then sighed as his hand slipped between her legs. He lifted his head so that her lips met his.

When they had finished making love, she nestled into him, a sigh of comfort escaping her lips. Just when he felt she was about to fall asleep, he used his finger to retrace the movement his tongue had made earlier on her breast.

Her back arched. 'You keep doing that, we'll never get any rest.'

He laughed, then reluctantly moved his hand onto her back.

'You said something about liking an idea . . . ?'

For a moment he thought she'd fallen asleep, then she said, 'You getting a place in San Francisco. I like the idea.'

It took him a second to realize what she

meant. It was the conversation they'd been having in Boston before Peter had called. It had been less than twenty-four hours earlier, but with everything that had happened since, it could have been a month ago.

'Really?' he asked.

'I'm . . . thinking about getting rid of my place in Saigon,' she said. 'We've been spending more and more time over here, it doesn't make sense to keep it any longer.'

'But what about the relief agency?' he said. Orlando ran a small emergency organization called the Tri-Continent Relief Agency out of Ho Chi Minh City. It was a passion of hers, something she took very seriously.

'I'm not giving up the agency,' she said. 'I'll go back when I need to. But I'm going to open an office in San Francisco. It is the *Tri-Continent Relief Agency*.'

Quinn began to smile.

'Don't get too smug. It's not because of you,' she said. 'It's Garrett.'

Garrett, her son, was six years old. The product of a love affair with the man who had been Quinn's mentor. But that was over now. Permanently. Quinn liked the boy. He was smart and seemed to have a lot more traits from his mother than from his father.

She went on, 'He's been accepted to the French American International School in the city. He starts first grade in September. I . . . I think it will be easier for him over here.'

Quinn smiled. 'It *is* because of me,' he said. 'You want to be closer.'

163

'Don't be ridiculous.'

'Yes, you do. You can't stand being so far away.'

'You have a serious case of inflated sense of self-worth.' She tried to push away from him, but he wouldn't let go.

'Call it whatever you want, I know the truth.'

After several moments, she settled back into his arms. They stayed that way for a while, then Orlando yawned, and repositioned herself so that her chest was against his.

'Of course I am.' Her voice was soft and heavy with sleep.

'What?' he asked.

'Moving to be closer to you. Of course I am. That's why you were being ridiculous.' She paused. 'Stating the obvious.'

She was asleep a moment later.

Quinn continued to watch her for twenty minutes as she breathed in and out, her shoulders rising one second, then falling the next.

How in God's name had he gotten so lucky?

But he'd fallen asleep before he could come up with an answer.

# 13

'The last name's Dupuis,' Peter said. 'A woman, early thirties. First name unknown.'

Quinn had activated the speaker function on his phone so all three of them could hear. They were still in the car, the U.S.-Canadian border now ten minutes behind them, and Montreal about twenty ahead.

'That's not a lot to go on,' Quinn said.

'It's all I have,' Peter snapped.

'How's Tasha?' Orlando asked.

Peter took a moment before he answered, and when he did, he sounded calmer. 'Still unconscious. But she's made it twenty-four hours so far, so they tell me that's a good sign.'

'What are we supposed to do when we find this woman?' Quinn asked.

'That's a big if, I think,' Peter said. 'What I need you to do is find out as much as you can *about* her. Where she might go if she had reason to hide. Who might help her.'

'Does she live in Montreal?'

Peter paused again. 'The name came from Primus. He sent the information to the DDNI when they were negotiating the follow-up meeting after Ireland. An act of good faith, he'd said. It was an attached document with a single line of information. 'Dupuis. Female. Montreal. Unresolved.' That was it.'

'Unresolved? What does that mean?' Orlando asked.

'I'm open to suggestions,' Peter said.

No one spoke for a moment.

'Montreal. That doesn't necessarily mean she lives there,' Quinn said.

'Maybe she has family there. Or friends. I didn't say it was going to be easy.'

'So why are we looking for her?' Quinn asked.

Peter paused. 'It's the only lead we've got. And since she's apparently of interest to the other side, I think that's worth looking into, don't you?'

'She's part of them?'

'You have everything I know.'

Again silence.

'Peter,' Orlando said, 'any chance you can send me that itinerary you showed us?'

'Why?'

'Just something I was thinking about. Thought I could check it out.'

Quinn gave her a questioning look, but she only smiled.

'All right,' Peter said. 'I can do that.'

'Thanks,' she said. 'You said there were more documents, too. If you really want our help, you should probably send those to me, also.'

'Fine,' he said. 'Anything else?'

Quinn looked at Orlando. She shook her head. He then turned to Nate, who looked surprised by the attention.

'I got nothing,' Nate whispered.

'That's all for the moment,' Quinn said, then

disconnected the call.

Once they were back on the road, he said, 'Itinerary?'

'Something that was bothering me on the drive. I think there's a connection between all the destinations. But I need to see the list again to be sure.'

'What kind of connection?'

'Relax. Just let me take a look first.'

★　★　★

They got rooms at the Comfort Inn in Brossard just across the St. Lawrence River from the old city of Montreal. Nate used a localized jammer Orlando had brought along to neutralize the surveillance camera in the lobby when he made the arrangements for the rooms. Quinn had remained in the car, staying out of sight just in case.

By the time they were getting settled in their rooms — Nate in one, and Quinn and Orlando in another — it was 8:45 p.m. Outside, the sun had just sunk below the horizon.

While Quinn ran some cold water over his face in the bathroom, Orlando got out her laptop and checked to see if Peter had sent the documents.

'Nothing,' she called out.

'See what you can find out about the woman,' Quinn said. 'The sooner we get this done . . . '

Orlando nodded, then turned back to her screen and set to work.

167

After drying his face, Quinn checked the dresser and nightstand until he found what he was looking for. A phone book. Not just for Brossard and the South Shore, but the whole Montreal area.

He flipped through the pages until he came to the D's, then slowly turned a few more before stopping.

'Well, this isn't good,' he said.

'What?' Orlando asked, not looking up.

'I've got three dozen Dupuis right here. More than half are just initials. No first name. And you've got to believe there are at least as many other Dupuis unlisted.'

Quinn used the tips of his fingers to create a crease along the edge of the page near the binding, then tore it out of the book. He set it on the desk next to Orlando's computer.

'Here,' he said. 'In case you need to cross-reference.'

She glanced up at him. 'Why don't you get us some dinner?'

'Trying to get rid of me?'

'Yes.'

Quinn smiled, then nodded and started for the door.

As he was pulling it open, Orlando said, 'Wait.'

He looked back. Her attention was still on the computer, but she was waving him to return with her left hand.

'I think I found something,' she said.

Quinn walked back and leaned over her shoulder. She had the website for the *Montreal*

*Gazette* up on the screen. The specific page featured an article titled:

## FAMILY TRAGEDY
## NOT AN ACCIDENT

Before Quinn could read further, Orlando said, 'This is from two days ago. An elderly couple and their daughter, also an adult, died from a gas leak in their house. Went to sleep, never woke up. At first it was thought to be a faulty gas line, but now the police are saying the gas line might have been tampered with.'

'Don't tell me,' Quinn said. 'The family's name is Dupuis.'

'Yep.'

'Could be just a coincidence,' Quinn said.

'Could be,' Orlando said, but she didn't sound like she believed that.

'An adult daughter.'

'Yeah. Maybe that's who Peter was talking about.'

'Maybe,' Quinn said. 'Anything else on the family?'

'Hold on,' she said.

She brought up a search engine, then typed in the names of the three people who had died. Martin Dupuis, Rose Dupuis, Emily Dupuis, Husband, wife, daughter. A list of several links appeared, most associated with people other than those who had died. Orlando clicked through several of them before stopping on one.

'Here we go,' she said.

The website was for another newspaper, this time in French. *Le Journal de Montréal*. While Quinn was well versed in several languages, French was not one of his strongest. The same wasn't true for Orlando, though. She was fluent.

'What's it say?' Quinn asked.

'It's another article about the deaths, but it goes into more detail about the family. Martin Dupuis was a retired professor. Taught sociology at McGill University until two years ago. Rose was a teacher, too. Literature, but at a private high school. She was still working. Their daughter had apparently been living back at home following a recent divorce.' Orlando paused as she continued reading to herself. 'Interesting.'

'What?'

'There's another daughter. Younger than the one who died. Only says she no longer lives in Montreal. No name given.'

'Maybe they haven't been able to reach her yet,' Quinn said.

'Maybe she's the one who killed them,' Orlando suggested.

Quinn shrugged, then straightened up. There was no way to tell these were the Dupuises Peter wanted them to check out. Still, the potential was too large to ignore.

'Get an address,' Quinn said. 'Let's at least do a drive-by.'

'Already got it.'

★ ★ ★

170

They rousted Nate out of his room, then took the Jetta across the river into Montreal. They found the Dupuis house about forty minutes later on the northeast side of town. It was a neighborhood of single-family homes, on small economical lots that made it difficult for one neighbor not to know what the other was doing. Several had lights on in their windows, but many were already dark, the owners either settled in for the night or not home.

They passed the Dupuis home at a slow, steady pace. It was two stories tall, but narrow. Quinn guessed no more than twelve hundred square feet of living space. The windows were all dark, but a nearby streetlamp illuminated enough of the front to see a strip of yellow tape strung across the opening between two bushes that led to the front door. *Police tape.* There was also a makeshift memorial at the front of the lawn. Dozens of glass candle containers, half already burned out, and several bundles of flowers spilled over from the grass onto the sidewalk.

Other than that, it was just like any of the other houses on the street.

Quinn circled the block and came back down the road again. This time he pulled to the curb two houses before reaching the Dupuis', taking one of the few remaining parking spots on either side of the street. He stared out the window at the house the three members of the Dupuis family had died in, and tried to imagine the gas filling the house, pushing the oxygen out. But he was having a hard time believing it. From all

171

appearances the house looked well maintained. In fact it looked in better shape than most of those around it. Could it be possible that a family who took that good care of their home could be neglectful when it came to the maintenance of the house's inner workings? Quinn didn't think so.

'Are we going in?' Orlando asked.

Quinn thought for a moment, then nodded. 'Nate, you stay here.'

'Why me?'

'Someone needs to stay with the car, in case we have to get out in a hurry,' Quinn said.

'That doesn't answer my question,' Nate said.

Quinn's eyes narrowed. 'Because I told you to stay.'

'I can stay,' Orlando said.

'No,' Quinn said. 'You're coming with me.'

Orlando looked at Nate, but he shook his head and said, 'It's fine.'

Quinn opened the door and started to get out.

'Wait,' Orlando said. She reached into the small backpack she'd brought along, and pulled out three cloth packets. 'Radios. Just in case.'

She handed them around.

Once they were out of the car, Quinn and Orlando did a quick visual check up and down the block. There were no other pedestrians. Not surprising for 10 p.m. on a residential street.

Satisfied, Quinn started walking toward the Dupuis home, Orlando falling into step behind him.

'You could have handled that better,' she whispered.

'Not now,' he said. But she was right, and he'd known it the moment he'd told Nate to stay in the car. He was just trying to protect Nate, but everything he did made him look like an asshole.

A dog barked from across the street. Two yips, then nothing. A warning to not even think about crossing the road. In the house next door to the Dupuis', someone was watching a TV with the volume up much too loud. The blue flicker of the screen spilled through the second-floor window. The bedroom of an older resident, perhaps.

Quinn took one last look around before they reached the corner of the Dupuis' property. They still seemed to be the only people out. The memorial in the front yard was down to one burning candle that looked like it wouldn't last much longer.

'Let's do it,' Quinn said.

They turned up the short walkway like they lived there. At the end of the concrete path, a short two-step staircase led up to the door. But instead of ascending, they paused at the bottom. As Quinn had noted when they drove by, there was police tape across the walkway to the door. On the tape, bold black letters spelling out in both French and English:

BARRAGE DE POLICE PASSAGE INTERDIT • POLICE LINE DO NOT CROSS

Passage prohibited by the police. It was, after all, a potential crime scene now.

Quinn still wasn't sure if they should try and get inside, but he did know that using the front door was out of the question. The same streetlamp that had provided the good view of

173

the house when they drove by now lit their every move.

'Around the side,' he whispered.

Orlando nodded.

'Anything?' Nate asked.

'Nothing yet,' Quinn said.

As they moved down the side of the house, Quinn glanced more than once at the home next door where the TV blared upstairs. He wanted to be able to get the hell out of there if he saw someone staring back at him. But there was no one.

When they reached the rear corner of the house, they stopped. Quinn pulled out two pairs of disposable rubber gloves, and handed a set to Orlando. Once his were on, he retrieved his gun from under his jacket. He then peered around the edge, but pulled back immediately.

'What is it?' Orlando asked.

'Back door's open,' he said.

'I don't hear anything from inside. Do you?'

Quinn listened for a moment, then shook his head.

'Come on.'

He led them around the corner, and over to the door. Leaning forward, he listened again to see if he could hear anyone moving around. Still nothing. Then why was it open? Couldn't have been the cops. Quinn had been one himself before Durrie had recruited him to be a cleaner. He knew the training, and the precautions taken at crime scenes. Leaving doors open just wasn't done.

He moved his head a few inches so he could

look at the door itself. It had been swung open about halfway. The darkness made it hard to see anything for sure, but there were no obvious marks near the lock that would have indicated someone had broken in.

A friend with a spare key? A killer who picked up a key on his way out? Or maybe had one all along? A neighbor kid who did the yard work and knew where an emergency key was hidden? It was human nature, after all, to be drawn to the pain and the horror life sometimes served up.

But at the moment, it didn't matter who had left the door open. The question was, was anyone still inside?

Quinn looked back at Orlando.

'Anything?' she mouthed.

He shook his head, then indicated he was going in and wanted her to cover him. Once Orlando gave him a nod, Quinn leaned toward his mic and whispered, 'We're going in.'

'Copy that,' Nate said over the receiver.

Quinn put both hands on his gun, and aimed it like he'd been trained to do in dangerous situations as a rookie police cadet back in Phoenix. Behind him, he could sense Orlando moving into position.

He silently counted to three, then stepped around the edge of the building and into the open doorway, his gun moving left, right, down, up, looking for targets. But the room was empty.

It was a kitchen, lived in but neat. The semidarkness of the evening was cut only by the light filtering back from the lamps on the street, turning the interior into shades of gray.

Everything one would expect to be there was — refrigerator, dishwasher, sink. On the counter were several cookbooks, a toaster, a ceramic jar full of utensils, and a blender, all ready and waiting. And to the left, a small table was set against the wall wide enough only for one chair per each of the three remaining sides. One for Mrs. Dupuis and one for her husband, Quinn guessed. And the non-matching third chair that stuck out into the room? That had to be for the recently returned daughter.

The only thing that was unusual was the stand-alone stovetop range. It had been pulled away from the wall, and turned at an angle so someone could get behind it. One of the first places checked for the gas leak, Quinn guessed.

All in all, it could have been the kitchen of the house Quinn grew up in. All the similarities were there. Even the layout was basically the same. He stepped over the threshold, looking to his immediate left, then moved the door enough so he could look behind it and make sure no one was there.

'Clear,' he mouthed to Orlando.

He continued across the kitchen, and stopped just shy of the doorway that led into the rest of the house. There was a solitary creak behind him as Orlando stepped inside.

'Everything all right?' Nate asked.

'Fine,' Quinn whispered.

On the other side of the doorway was the dining room. An oval dining table surrounded by five chairs filled half the space. The chairs were all perfect matches to the orphan chair in the kitchen. Along the wall to Quinn's right was a wooden buffet cabinet. The bottom portion had two doors that would swing open to access whatever was stored inside. On the hutch above were three shelves. Instead of plates or other serving dishes, there were dozens of framed photos.

Enough light came in through the window for Quinn to make out the faces. A mixture of shots, but all had at least one of four people in them. The older man and woman had to be Martin and Rose Dupuis. That meant one of the younger women was their daughter, Emily. The third woman looked a few years younger than Emily, but bore a striking resemblance to the others.

*The missing daughter.*

'What's that?' Orlando whispered.

Quinn looked at her. She was in the doorway, but her eyes were focused on a point at the far end of the room, past where he was standing. So he turned to see what had caught her attention.

There was an item on the floor just a few feet beyond the dining room, in what Quinn guessed was the living room. It was a box, about the size law firms use to put files in. It was in the middle of the floor, definitely out of place. Quinn could see several items sticking out of the top — thin, flat, rectangular shapes.

He looked back at the hutch, scanning the pictures, concentrating on the placement of the frames instead of the pictures themselves. On the pattern.

He found what he was looking for toward the

right side on the second shelf. An obvious open spot that Quinn imagined the Dupuises would have never created. There was another spot, too, on the shelf above toward the center.

*What the hell?* Quinn thought.

He eased into the living room, his eyes taking in everything before he approached the box.

As he'd guessed, the items sticking out were pictures. But there were more than just two. Seven more by his quick count. But that wasn't all. There was a small wooden box, a stuffed bear, an old book, and what looked like a scarf or maybe a sweater under the pictures.

Quinn was leaning down to pick up one of the pictures when Nate's voice cut through the silence. 'Is that one of you?'

'What?' Quinn asked.

'Did one of you come outside?'

'No. We're both in the house.'

'Somebody just crossed the front lawn,' Nate said, his voice rushed. 'I think he came from around the side of the house. My angle's bad here, I didn't notice him until he was already a few feet into the yard.'

Quinn shot a glance at Orlando, then pointed toward the back door. He made a gesture for Orlando to go out and around to the left. With a single nod, she ran through the kitchen, Quinn only steps behind her.

'He's getting in a car parked out front,' Nate said. 'What do you want me to do?'

'Follow him,' Quinn said as he exited the house.

Instead of going to the left with Orlando, he

went right. At the back corner of the house, he slowed only enough to take the turn, almost slipping on the grass. The home next door with the blaring TV was silent now. The only thing Quinn could hear was the pounding of his own footsteps as he ran along the side yard.

'He's got it started,' Nate said.

'Where's he parked?' Quinn asked.

'Other side of the street. Almost directly across.'

Quinn reached the street side of the house a second before Orlando did. On the opposite side of the road a car was pulling out in a hurry. It was a small two-door sedan.

Quinn increased his speed as he weaved between two parked cars on the near side of the street, then raced across the asphalt toward the departing vehicle. He was able to come within a foot of the driver's side door before the car sped away. But it had been enough.

Back across the street, Nate made a quick U-turn from where he was parked, and took off in pursuit.

'Dammit,' Orlando said as she joined Quinn. 'Did you get a look at him?'

'Find us a ride,' Quinn said. 'But be discreet. I'm sure we've made more than enough noise to draw some attention.' He looked down the street to their left as the two cars disappeared around a corner. 'Meet me down there at the end of the block in five minutes.'

'Okay,' Orlando said. She turned, and soon disappeared in the shadows.

Quinn spent two of the allotted five minutes

finding a dark spot, then remained still, hoping to pick up on anyone who might be paying unnecessary attention to the Dupuis house. He saw the curtain of one window about five homes down on the other side of the street fall closed. Whoever had been holding it open seemed to have lost interest.

The street felt calm again, like it had returned to its normal evening self. He waited an extra minute just to be sure, then slipped from his hiding spot and made his way back into the Dupuis house.

In the dining room, he looked at the pictures again. The most recent one was a five-by-seven shot of the two daughters. Emily's smile seemed put on, but the one on the face of her younger sister seemed genuine.

Quinn grabbed the picture and started to turn toward the exit. But he didn't even make it a step before he stopped himself and looked back at the box still sitting on the floor of the living room.

He thought about it for less than a second, then walked over and grabbed it, adding the photo he'd just taken to the top. The photo of Emily and her sister — the same woman, not a man, who had been behind the wheel of the car Nate was now following.

# 14

Her parents were dead.

Her sister was dead.

And the only person who could be blamed for it was Marion herself. That's what she believed. How could there be any other answer?

She had taken Iris on the train north from Penn Station back to Marion's hometown of Montreal. She had used the false passports her friend in Côte d'Ivoire had given her when she purchased the tickets. She hoped it was enough to fool whoever was looking for her.

While the child was asleep, Marion would stare out the window, not sure what she was going to do, but knowing if anyone could help her, it would be her parents.

Sure, her sister was living back at home, and bringing a child into the house wasn't going to do a lot to help Emily's recovery. The divorce Emily had gone through had been wrenching. Marion couldn't imagine what it must have felt like when her sister found out her husband, who never wanted to have children, was having an affair with someone who was now pregnant. Of course, that had been over a year ago. The baby was born by now.

Marion knew her sister well. She knew Emily might not say anything, but she would feel humiliated, and think of herself as a freshly minted spinster too old to have children. It wasn't true, but that's the way Emily's mind worked. Poetic and tragic.

But Marion couldn't worry about her sister's feelings anymore. She'd been living with Emily's drama since the day she was born. It was time to stop getting pulled into it. The reason was stretched out in the seat next to her, not asleep at that moment, but content. Iris.

They arrived in her hometown that evening, then grabbed a taxi at the station. The cabbie took a second look at her and Iris, but said nothing.

Iris seemed very interested in the world outside the taxi as they drove through the streets. The smile on the child's face, the smile that was almost always there, seemed a fraction broader. Marion took this as a good sign.

As they turned onto the street where her parents lived, the anxiousness Marion had been feeling for so long began to subside. Soon she would be in the home she grew up in, eating her mother's food, sleeping in the room that had been hers, safe in the cocoon of family. But as they neared the house, she realized something wasn't right.

On the lawn in front of her house were dozens of flickering candles and bundles of flowers, and people, their heads bowed. The house itself, though, was dark.

'*Ici?*' the driver said, not hiding the surprise in his voice.

'No, no. Keep driving,' she told him in French. 'I must have the wrong street.'

The driver seemed relieved when she gave him

the name of the next street over.

'Horrible,' he said as he glanced over at her childhood home. 'Just horrible.'

She almost asked him what had happened. His words indicated he knew, but her own voice had left her. Someone had died in the house. There was no question about it. *But who? Why?* Water pooled in her eyes, but she held back her tears.

On the next street over she got out, paid the cabbie, then watched him drive away.

Ten minutes later, at a pay phone several blocks away, she called for another taxi.

'Where to?' the driver asked once she and Iris were in the back seat.

She had thought about this while she'd waited for him to arrive. She was afraid to use her false ID, thinking it might create a trail someone could pick up on. And there was no way she could use her real ID. She needed to find someplace anonymous.

'Saint Laurent,' she said, naming the borough on the west side of Montreal. 'Boulevard Marcel-Laurin.'

The cabbie eyed her in his rearview mirror. 'Do you have a specific location?'

She hadn't recalled the name of the motel, but knew basically where it was located. A sleazy place that she'd heard charged room rates by the hour. It worried her to take Iris there, but she at least knew they wouldn't ask for an ID.

'I'll tell you when we get there.'

'I'm sorry,' he said. 'I need to know now.'

She took a quick breath. She was on the edge of breaking down, but she forced herself to keep

183

it together. 'It's a motel, okay? I don't remember the name.'

The driver hesitated. 'Motel Monique?'

'Yes,' she said, realizing he was right. 'That's it.'

'Deposit,' he said.

'What?'

'I need a deposit first.'

'I'll pay you when we get there,' she said.

'Maybe you don't have the money.'

'I have the money.'

'Then pay me now. I'm not going to wait around while you say you're going inside to get the cash from one of your . . . customers.'

Marion stared at the man's eyes in the mirror, unable to believe what she was hearing.

'I'm not a . . . ' She paused. 'I've got a child with me! You think I'm a prostitute?'

'Wouldn't be the first hooker to have a kid, would you? Twenty dollars right now or no ride.'

She stared at him for another second, then broke eye contact and pulled a twenty-dollar bill out of her purse. She dropped it in the front seat, purposely avoiding his outstretched hand.

'Can we go now?' she said.

The driver shook his head a couple of times, like he'd seen it before and knew he would see it again. He dropped the taxi into drive and pulled out onto the street.

She spotted the Motel Monique a half a block before they arrived. It was a big dingy box of a building with a faded sign out front lit by a couple of floodlights. But most important, the neon sign that had been tacked on at the bottom said *Vacancy*.

The first thing she did after the cabbie dropped her and Iris off in front of the motel was to walk over to a group of newspaper dispensers in front of the liquor store next door. There were no more copies of *Le Devoir* left, so she was forced to buy a copy of the English paper, the *Gazette*.

It was right on front, the lead story.

## GAS LEAK ENDS IN FAMILY TRAGEDY

She stared at it, wanting to read more. But she knew if she did, she'd break down right there on the sidewalk. So she forced herself to fold the paper and stick it into her travel case.

Iris started to whimper against her shoulder. Marion repositioned her arm around the girl's back, then said, 'It's okay, sweetie. Everything's okay. You can lie down in a minute. Would you like that?'

The tone of Marion's voice carried an undercurrent of panic, but there was enough comfort to settle Iris. The whimpering ceased, and the little girl lay her head heavy against Marion's shoulder. A few seconds later her breathing was deep and even. Asleep now, no need for a bed.

Marion walked back to the Motel Monique clutching the child to her with one hand while pulling her suitcase behind her in the other.

From the moment she entered the motel's office, the clerk eyed her suspiciously. He was

185

sitting behind a poorly laminated counter with the very classy addition of a Plexiglas wall that extended from the counter's top all the way to the ceiling. There was a small circle cut into the see-through divider about a foot and a half above the counter, and another, half-moon shaped, where the plexi met the laminate. Like an old movie-house kiosk, only scummier. The plexi was scratched and worn, and at some point in the past several years it looked like someone had thrown liquid against the surface, and no one had gotten around to cleaning it yet. But it worked well with the rest of the office's décor: old, barely functional, and uncared for.

'Help you?' the clerk said as Marion approached the window. He was only slightly better than the room itself. At least it looked like he'd taken a shower in the last forty-eight hours.

'I need a room,' she said.

His gaze flicked to Iris, then back at Marion. 'For how long?'

'Just one night.'

'The whole night?'

'I just need a place to sleep. For me and my child.'

'That's your kid?' he asked, again with the suspicious eyes.

'Just tell me how much.'

'There's an EconoLodge not too far from here. You'll be more comfortable there.'

'Your sign outside says Vacancy. Are you telling me you don't have any rooms?' she said.

'Lady, you're not likely to get a lot of sleep here.'

She pulled out several bills. 'How much? Sixty dollars?'

A slight widening of his eyes told her sixty was more than the going rate, but she wanted to close the deal.

'Here,' she said. She put three twenties on the counter just her side of the half-moon opening. 'That should do it, right?'

He looked at the money for a moment, then reached under the counter and came up with a key.

'Third floor, in the front,' he said. 'You'll hear the street, but most of the other guests prefer rooms in the back.'

She understood what he was trying to tell her. 'Thank you,' she said.

She exchanged her money for the key.

'Elevator's out the door and to the right.'

★　★　★

The clerk had been right about the room. She *could* hear every car that passed on the street, but while there were the occasional voices from the far end of the motel corridor, there didn't seem to be anyone using the rooms nearby.

Iris didn't seem to mind any of it. She was fast asleep on the bed beside Marion. Something Marion wished she could also do. She had never felt this tired in her life.

*Bone weary.* It was a term she'd heard one of her American colleagues use. Now she knew what the woman had meant, for her exhaustion

187

went way beyond skin deep, touching every cell in her body.

But sleep wasn't coming. Not yet.

It wasn't that she was afraid she'd chosen the wrong place to stay. Far from it. The fact that the clerk hadn't even had her fill out any kind of registration card had confirmed she'd made the right choice.

It was the story in the newspaper. She had read it three times, then dropped the pages on the floor.

Her parents were dead.

Her sister was dead.

The paper had said it looked like an accident, a leak in a gas line that had filled the home while her family slept. But Marion knew that couldn't be possible. Her father had been meticulous in his care of the house. He'd had the entire gas system replaced only five years earlier. Far too soon for it to be experiencing any fatigue, and far too late for any installation mistakes to make themselves known. Besides, the new system had included leak detectors in each of the rooms where gas was used. The article had made no mention of detectors, and Marion found it impossible to think of a scenario where they all malfunctioned at once.

Her family was dead, and it was her fault. There was no other possible explanation. Whoever was looking for her had all the information they needed. For starters, they obviously had access to her UN file, and that would be more than enough. It would contain a history of anywhere she had lived, the names of places she had worked prior to the UN, her college transcripts, and the names and address of her family.

Maybe they thought she was in the house, too. At the very least, they'd thought the possibility she'd show in Montreal was high. Maybe they had tried getting her parents to tell them where she was. The article had made no mention of potential foul play, but could the police have been hiding that? Could her family have been tortured to see if they knew anything?

*Oh, God,* she thought, *I've killed them.*

Beside her, Iris smacked her lips in her sleep, then turned toward Marion, nuzzling against the woman's side before settling back down. Marion looked at the child, knowing she was the cause of what had happened but unable to blame the girl. It was Marion who had decided to safeguard her. She could have easily told her superiors in Côte d'Ivoire about the child. An appropriate place would have been found for Iris, and Marion's family would still be alive.

But that hadn't been the path she had chosen. She hadn't trusted her own people to keep Iris out of harm.

A thought occurred to her. Maybe everything would have still been all right if she hadn't started digging into similar cases. Maybe that was the trigger.

She closed her eyes. It was too much for her to think about, too much for her to consider. There was only one truth.

Her family was dead. And it was her fault.

★ ★ ★

The first light of morning woke her. She was still dressed, and propped up in the same position she had been in since she'd climbed into bed the previous evening.

Iris was asleep, lying comfortably on her back, her face slack and restful. The girl was amazing that way. She never seemed to have a problem sleeping. Maybe it was a kid thing, Marion thought. But she wasn't sure. She had seen plenty of children at the orphanages she visited, even at Frau Roslyn's, who woke up at least once or twice a night.

Marion eased herself off the bed so as not to disturb the child, and went into the bathroom. The shower looked questionable, but she knew she needed it, so she turned the water on as hot as she could stand it and got in. The stiffness she had felt upon waking began to loosen under the steaming water. Once she was done, she used one of the threadbare towels to dry off, then went back into the room.

She stopped after only a few feet and stared at the bed.

Iris was gone.

'Iris, where are you?'

She took a step to her right so she could look around one side of the bed, but the girl wasn't there.

'Iris?'

She shot a quick look at the door, but the security chain was still in place from when she'd locked up the night before.

'Iris?'

There was the crinkle of paper. It came from the other side of the bed.

Marion rushed over, then breathed a sigh of relief.

Iris sat on the floor grinning as she picked up one of the pages of the discarded newspaper and flapped it up and down. She let out a giggle as she noticed Marion.

'Having fun?' Marion asked. She picked the child up, hugging her tight.

'Why don't you stay on the bed while I get dressed, hmm?'

She set Iris down on the mattress, then retrieved the paper. She hesitated as she caught sight of the front page picture showing the house she'd grown up in. She almost put the paper back on the floor, but Iris was reaching out for it and making sounds like it was hers. Marion shook herself, then smiled and gave the newspaper to the girl.

Iris immediately began playing with it again. Marion suspected that most five-year-olds would pretend to read the paper or at least be interested in the pictures. But Iris wasn't at that point yet. She seemed caught up in the sheer joy of the sound the paper made as she moved it and hit it and rubbed it against itself.

There was a small TV bolted to a shelf against the wall. Marion couldn't locate a remote, so she walked over and turned it on, and was greeted with a scene of multiple naked bodies entwined in some kind of grotesque semblance of sex. The moans that came out of the speaker sounded more rehearsed than natural. Porno for the typical Motel Monique guest, she realized as she hastily changed the channel. She found a local morning news show, then got dressed as she watched, hoping to hear more about what had happened to her family.

The lead story of the six-thirty update concerned the kidnapping and murder of a prominent American official in New York City. There was even a police sketch of a possible suspect. Marion glanced up at it as she was pulling on her pants.

Then the story ended, and a new graphic appeared over the shoulder of the news anchor. It was a picture of her parents, and superimposed over them the word:

## Tragédie

Tragedy.

'Police now say the deaths two nights ago of a Montreal family while they slept might not have been an accident after all.' The anchor was a young woman looking far too put together for such an early hour. 'Francine Blanc is at the scene of the fast-breaking story.'

Marion sat down on the edge of the bed as the image on the TV switched to an outside shot across the street from her parents' house. There was a near clone of the anchor standing on the sidewalk facing the camera. She was holding a microphone in her hand.

'Francine, what can you tell us?' the anchor said.

'Nicole, police now think there is a very real possibility that this was not an accident. As you know, yesterday morning, the Dupuis family was found dead in their beds by a friend of the family who became concerned when Madame Dupuis failed to show up for work. At that time it appeared that the family had succumbed to a gas leak sometime during the previous night. While it is still believed that gas is what killed them, sources inside the police department are now saying the leak may have been caused by a deliberate act.'

They showed some video from the previous day, including an interview with the person who had found the bodies. It was Madame Devore from the school where Marion's mother taught.

'It's terrible,' Madame Devore said. There were tears streaming down her cheeks. 'They were just . . . please, I can't talk about this now. Excuse me. Please.'

There was a shot of one of the bodies being removed from the house. It was on a stretcher and covered with a sheet. Marion wondered who it was. Her mother? Father? Emily?

A new shot showed the candlelight vigil that had formed the night before, as the voice-over talked about a gathering of friends. Then the image of the reporter returned.

'It's clear that the Dupuis family had many people who loved them. Nicole.'

The image on the TV split, the reporter on the right, and the anchor on the left.

'We're hearing there might be another member of the family,' the anchor said. 'Is that correct?'

'Yes.' The reporter was nodding. 'Neighbors tell us there is a younger daughter who works in New York. One person told us she is with the UN, but I have not been able to confirm that yet. I can tell you that police have not been able to make contact with her, and think she might currently be on assignment overseas.'

'So she's not a suspect.'

'No. Not at this time.'

Marion stood up and turned the TV off. She stood there staring at the blank screen for several minutes.

Dead. Gone. No more.

No more reassuring smiles from her father. No more shopping trips with her mother. No more long talks with her sister. No more family Christmases. No more trips to the mountains. No more anything.

Perhaps she wasn't a suspect, but she was an unwilling accomplice.

A shout from Iris brought her back. The newspaper had fallen on the floor.

'Come on,' Marion said. 'It's time to get ready and go.'

They left the motel five minutes later.

Marion wanted to go back to the house. She wanted to get inside to see for herself. She knew it was stupid, but it was her family. She couldn't just leave.

She had another taxi drive her by just after 9 a.m. There were several police cars out front, and a crowd of the curious gathered on the sidewalk.

She made another try at 4 p.m. This time the police were gone, but some of the crowd remained. That was okay. It was still too early for her to try to get inside. In the daylight, she would be spotted in a second, and would be detained by the police, and no doubt forced to tell more than she was willing to.

She still had Iris to worry about. That had to be her first concern. But she wasn't going to leave Montreal without getting inside. She owed her family that much respect at least.

She felt like another taxi ride down the street would be one too many. Even if it happened after dark, someone might start to get suspicious. But her choices were limited. She couldn't rent a car, and she certainly couldn't get in touch with any of her friends and ask for help. God knows what would happen to them if she did.

Steal a car? Right. She'd seen it in movies, but suspected it was even harder than it looked. That was not even close to an option.

Her only choice was to walk in.

Her suitcase was a problem, though. She needed someplace to stash it. Her best solution was the same hotel they'd stayed in the night before. So it was back to the Motel Monique, where she arranged for a second night in the same room. The clerk didn't even question her this time. He simply took her money and handed over the key.

Suitcase dropped off, she and Iris headed back out. At a sporting goods store, she picked up a

195

hooded pullover sweatshirt. It was black, and would hide most of her features when the hood was up. She then found a diner, and waited there until dark.

At 9:15 p.m. she called another taxi. This time instead of driving down her street, she had the driver drop her and Iris several blocks away. They walked, avoiding any direct eye contact with the few people they passed. When they reached her parents' block, Marion slowed, eyeing everything in case there was someone waiting for her.

'No,' she said to herself as they neared the house, not hiding her frustration.

There were a dozen people out front again, and more candles. Another vigil. She wanted to be touched by the gesture, but all she could feel was anger at being denied access to the house yet again.

But when a few of the people began moving off, she realized the impromptu service was ending. She stopped one property away, and turned her head to Iris, to hide her face from those leaving the gathering.

A few of the people were talking as they walked by, and Marion was surprised to find she recognized one of the voices as a friend she hadn't seen in over a year. She wanted to turn and call out to her, to feel the warmth and sympathy of her friend's arms around her, but she remained where she was.

Once the steps began to recede, she chanced a look back toward her house. The only things left were a few dying candles. The crowd that had been there was gone.

Marion glanced up and down the street, making sure that there were no stragglers, then she started walking again.

As she got closer, she could hear the TV on in the Blair house. Mr. Blair was the only one who lived there anymore, his wife gone at least four years now. He'd been growing more and more deaf, and the volume of the TV had been getting increasingly louder every time Marion visited home. Her mother had joked that if they were watching the same channel, they could mute their own TV and still hear what was going on.

Marion slowed her pace as she moved in front of the house she had grown up in. When she reached the far corner of the property, she stopped again. She had noted the tape across the front entrance, but that was fine. The key she had worked on both the front and the back doors, and the latter was much preferable.

She glanced around again, saw no one at all, then took a deep breath.

'I need you to be quiet, okay?' she whispered needlessly to Iris. The child was one of the quietest she'd ever known.

Iris lifted her head up for a moment, then lay back against Marion's shoulder.

'Okay, then. Let's go.'

Marion turned and walked rapidly down the side of the house to the backyard. She had expected to find more tape across the rear door, but there was none. She slipped the key into the lock and turned it. Five seconds later, she was

197

standing in her mother's kitchen.

She walked through the first floor, looking at everything but touching nothing. It was like she was in her parents' house, but she wasn't. The familiarity was all there. The pictures. The dining table where she used to do her homework. The couch in the living room where she'd caught her sister making out with Peter from down the street. But even surrounded by all these things, it felt empty. *Soulless*, she thought. Home to no one.

In the living room, she hesitated at the base of the stairs before mounting them.

*This is why you're here*, she thought. *You wanted to see this.*

With a nod of self-confirmation, she climbed up to the second floor.

She didn't know what she expected to feel, but numbness was a surprise. She looked in her sister's room first. Someone had taken the time to put the duvet back in place. Not a perfectly made bed, but one that was hard to imagine had recently held her sister's body.

She moved to her parents' room. The duvet had been straightened here, too. Marion was about to turn and leave, when she spotted the picture on her mother's dresser. It was a family photo from a cousin's wedding two years earlier. It was the last formal photo the four of them had taken together. Marion walked over and leaned in for a closer look.

Her parents, happy and still very much in love. Her sister trying hard not to show the effects of her own deteriorating marriage. And Marion, proud of her parents, proud of her new job at the UN.

She reached out with her free hand and picked up the picture, knowing before she even touched it she wouldn't be putting it back. It was coming with her.

She carried Iris and the picture back into the hallway and walked over to the room at the front of the house. Her room. Like the others, the door was open wide, it, too, having been checked once the first body had been found.

Like the others, her bed was also made. Only instead of looking like a rush job, someone had taken the time to make it look good. Her mother. And the sheets underneath the duvet would be clean, waiting for Marion to come home for a visit.

*My God, what have I done?*

She slumped down onto her bed, and placed Iris beside her. The child's mouth was turned down, and her eyes were wide. It looked as if she was about to cry. She must have been sensing Marion's own desire to let the tears come.

'It's okay, sweetheart,' Marion said. 'We'll leave soon.'

Water began to pool at the base of the girl's eyes. It was the last thing Marion wanted. She tried to think of something to distract the child. Out of desperation she pulled the motel key out of her pocket and waved it in front of Iris. It was a regular metal key attached to a plastic rectangle with the name of the motel and the room number. Iris reached out for it, so Marion let her take it. But the child merely threw it

199

across the room, the key landing near the door.

As Marion got up to retrieve it, she happened to look at her old painted dresser near the door. On top was the stuffed bear her father had given her when she'd been a little girl. *Pauline.*

Marion smiled at all the memories Pauline represented. She grabbed the bear and handed it to Iris.

This time the distraction worked. The child's tears began to recede as she focused on her new stuffed animal. Pauline had a way of doing that, Marion remembered. The bear had always been good at pushing the tears back.

Marion realized there were several things she wanted to take with her, memories of her family, of her life. She had no idea how long she would have to stay away from home, from Montreal for that matter. Maybe they would continue to chase her, forcing her to be on the run for months, or maybe even for years. If that was the case, she needed something to give her strength. She needed the power of her memories.

While Iris played, Marion found an old box full of teen magazines in her closet. She pulled the periodicals out and set them in a neat stack where the box had been. At the door to her room, she realized the motel key was still on the floor. She picked it up and put it in the box, then walked through the house picking up items she felt the need to keep. A few more pictures, a scarf her mother had knitted for her, a copy of *A Wrinkle in Time* that her father had read with her so many years ago, a small wooden box that contained a gold-plated bracelet her sister had given to her for Christmas one year, even the grocery list her mother had started and pinned to the refrigerator with a magnet.

When she was done, she realized there was no way she was going to be able to carry the box and Iris at the same time.

*What a stupid idea*, she thought, knowing that the box was going to have to stay. She could put the scarf around her neck, and perhaps take one of the pictures out of its frame and stuff it in her pocket, but that was about it. The rest had been a waste of time.

But then she saw the key hanger next to the back door. There were three sets of keys, each on a separate hook. Her father and mother had never been big on driving, choosing instead to take public transportation or ride their bikes to where they wanted to go. So their keys were limited to those they needed for the house and, in her mother's case, work. But Emily's keys were different. She'd had a car. An old Saab, unless she'd sold it. The set of keys hanging from the hook on the left had a large key that could only be for a car. It was a duplicate, so there was no company name on it, but the vehicle had to be outside somewhere.

Marion grabbed her sister's keys, then sneaked a peak around the edge of the curtain in the living room. The only things she could see were a couple of cars parked directly in front of the house — neither familiar — and a third car driving by on the street. It was hard to tell, but it looked like the people inside the vehicle were gazing at her house. Probably curious about the

201

makeshift memorial in the front yard. All the same, she watched the car until it disappeared.

Once the vehicle was out of sight, she set the box down on the couch, then ran back upstairs. Iris, still happily occupied with the old bear, looked up when Marion hurried in.

'We're leaving in a moment,' Marion said.

She crossed the room to her window. It was a view she'd seen thousands of times before, tens of thousands even. The houses on the other side of the street had changed little. Some of the trees were larger, but that was about it. And like there had always been, cars lined either side of the street, waiting for their owners to wake and need them again.

She spotted Emily's car right away. The old silver two-door Saab was parked directly across the street. A lucky spot, they would have said. As Marion smiled, some of the tension left her body. Here was the break she needed, not just because she could take the box with them, but now they had transportation. Now they could drive to the other end of Canada if they wanted. It would free them, for a little while anyway.

'Come on, baby,' she said as she scooped up Iris and headed downstairs.

In the living room, she set Iris on the couch, then picked up the box to bring out to the car first. But Iris would have none of it. She reached out and grabbed Marion's leg.

'It'll just be for a minute,' Marion said.

But the child wouldn't let go.

'Fine. You first then.' She set the box down, then picked Iris up.

Marion knew it wasn't the best plan. But it would have to do. Iris would only be by herself in the car a few minutes at most. And it was doubtful anyone would notice her.

Marion carried the child out of the house and around the side. She was careful when she reached the front, checking twice to make sure it was quiet, then she scooted along the edge of the property to the sidewalk.

To be safe, she walked down half a block to avoid the light from one of the streetlamps before crossing the street. As she approached her sister's car, she half expected there to be another notice from the police, marking it as part of the crime scene. But there was nothing. Either they hadn't realized it belonged to her sister, or they didn't care.

She slipped the key into the lock and opened the door. Inside, the dome light came on. She leaned in and turned it off.

'Okay, you're going to stay here while I go get the box,' she said to Iris. 'I'll be right back, so you'll be fine.'

As she put the girl down on the small back seat, Iris's lower lip began to tremble.

'No, don't cry, sweetie. Just play with your bear.' Marion looked around. 'Where is it?'

But the bear wasn't there. They must have left it upstairs, she thought. That's why Iris hadn't wanted to be left on the couch.

'Dammit,' Marion said under her breath.

She glanced around to see if there was anything that could keep Iris occupied. The best she could come up with was a map of eastern

Canada, but it seemed to do the trick.

'I'll only be a minute,' she said, then shut the door and hurried back to the house.

Once inside, she went straight for the box in the living room. She started to pick it up, but then stopped. *Pauline.*

She first checked around the couch to make sure Iris hadn't dropped the bear there, then ran upstairs, her gaze focused on the steps to make sure it wasn't somewhere along the way.

She expected to see the bear sitting in the middle of the bed when she entered her bedroom, but it wasn't.

'Where the hell did you go?' she said, annoyed.

She got down on her knees and looked under the bed. Nothing.

She retraced her steps back into the hallway and down the stairs to the living room couch. It was nowhere. But that didn't make any sense. It had to be somewhere between the bed and couch. She knew she should just forget it and leave, but Iris had liked the bear, and it warmed Marion to think about the connection it gave the girl to Marion's father.

She headed back upstairs into the bedroom. She was almost at the point of wanting to tear the room apart when she spotted it wedged between the bed and her nightstand.

With a relieved laugh, she pulled it out and headed back downstairs. She put the bear in the box, then picked the container up and turned to leave. She made it halfway across the living room when she heard the noise.

It wasn't much. Just a subtle scrape at best,

but it had come from behind her, near the front door. She looked over her shoulder as she heard a second scrape. Not near the front door, just beyond it. Outside.

She froze, her gaze darting from one window to the other on either side of the front door. The curtains were drawn, but the light from the streetlamp made them glow. As she watched, a dark shadow of a man appeared in one window. He was heading from the front door toward the side of the house.

*It's them,* she thought. *They've found me.*

She set the box on the floor carefully so as not to make any noise, then tiptoed to the back door. She hesitated just inside it for only a second, then stepped through into the backyard. Unless the intruder had doubled back when she'd turned away, he'd be coming down the side to her right, so she moved across the yard to her left. When she turned the corner, she was relieved to see no one waiting for her.

She went only a few feet down the side, then stopped. She could hear steps. Faint, like someone was making an effort to be quiet. They were around the back side of the house now. Whoever it was had missed spotting her by seconds.

She waited, then heard a very light creak. Only someone who had lived in the house would have noticed it, and known what it meant. Someone had entered the kitchen. Then the creak came again. Not one person. Two.

Her breathing began to increase. She reached a shaky hand back and pulled the hood of her

205

sweatshirt over her head. She crept toward the front of the house, taking careful steps so as not to draw any attention. As she did, she listened for the progress of those inside, knowing the deeper they went, the better her chances of getting away.

She stopped a few feet before the front of the house, and waited until she was sure at least one of her pursuers was in the living room. That's when she made her move.

She rushed through her parents' front yard and across the street to the Saab in seconds. As she opened the door, she thought she could hear noise from the house. Had they heard her?

She was in near panic as she climbed into the car. The keys slipped in her fingers and nearly dropped on the floor. But she managed to get them in the ignition and get the car started.

'Hold on, baby,' she said to Iris, who was lying unsecured in the back seat. She knew the words would mean nothing, but was unable to do anything else at the moment.

Marion backed up as far as she could, then pulled out of the spot, just clearing the car in front of her. As she started to press down on the accelerator, movement outside to her left caught her attention.

She turned just in time to see a man approaching her car. His hair was short and blond, and the look on his face determined, like he would stop her at any cost. There was also something familiar about him. The hair was wrong, but she swore she had seen his face before.

And then he was gone, left behind as the

Saab's speed increased.

She worried that he might pull out a gun and shoot at her. But as she monitored him in her rearview mirror, he just stood there watching her drive away. Then it came to her. The news report that morning. The man who had killed the American official. The sketch. That's who this guy looked like.

But before she could process that thought further, she saw something else in her mirror.

A car making a fast U-turn and heading in her direction.

# 15

'Where are you?' Quinn asked. He had his phone to his ear. Nate was on the other end, his speakerphone switched on.

'How the hell do I know?' Nate said. 'I've never been here before.'

'You're still behind her, though,' Quinn said.

'Yes, I've still got . . . wait. Did you say *her*?'

'Her name is Marion Dupuis. She's the missing daughter.'

'You're sure?'

'I saw her as she drove off, and I've got a picture right here. Same person.'

Quinn was sitting in the passenger seat of a Lincoln Continental he and Orlando had stolen a block away from the house. In his lap was Marion's box. The contents seemed to be consistent with someone on the run, who wanted to take a few personal mementos along. Two items were of most interest. The first was a book. A French version of *A Wrinkle in Time*. Inside the cover, in the handwriting of a preteen, had been written: *Ce livre appartient à Marion Dupuis* — this book belongs to Marion Dupuis. That had given Quinn the woman's name.

The other curious item didn't fit with anything else in the box. A motel key for someplace called Motel Monique.

'Hold on,' Nate said. A moment later, 'Shit.'

'What?'

'Nothing. It's just a pain in the ass to follow someone who knows a city that I don't.'

'You lost her?'

'Of course not,' he said.

'Give us some street names. We'll see if we can find you.'

'I'm on . . . eh . . . Rue Drummond. It's one-way, but we just turned off a big street. Renee something.'

Quinn had found a map of Montreal in the glove compartment. It was old and worn, and had been buried deep under a stack of other papers. He looked down the street index for Drummond, got the coordinates, then found it on the map.

'Do you mean Boulevard René-Lévesque?' he asked.

'That sounds right.'

'Okay, I got you, then. Tell me when you change streets.'

'That'd be right now,' Nate said. 'Turning onto another big street. Dammit, where's the sign? I don't know the name.'

'Probably Rue Sherbrooke.'

'If you say so.'

'We're heading your way.' Quinn moved the phone from his ear and looked over at Orlando. 'Back the other way, then west. They're on the other side of the island.'

She nodded as she moved the car over to the left lane. At the next intersection she hung a U-turn.

Quinn switched his phone to speaker, then said, 'Still on Sherbrooke?'

'Yes,' Nate confirmed.

'Okay. You're basically heading north-northeast. For the moment it doesn't look like she is heading for any bridges, so she's still contained on the island.'

'Got it,' Nate said. 'She's behaving a little odd. She keeps looking back, but I don't think she's looking at me.'

'She knows you're following her?' Quinn said.

'Yes. Definitely.'

'Then maybe she *is* looking at you.'

'It just doesn't seem like it.'

Something nagged at Quinn's mind. A memory. A flash of when Marion Dupuis drove past him in the street. Movement elsewhere in the car. Maybe it was something moving around in the back. A bag, perhaps, or another box she had taken from the house. Whatever it was, Quinn couldn't see it clearly in his mind.

'Turning again,' Nate said. 'Right. Onto . . . Avenue Union.'

Quinn found the spot on the map. 'Got it.'

A moment later. 'Still on Avenue Union. Passing a big church on my right.' Then, 'Turning again. Rue Ste. Catherine. Left . . . dammit, here we go again. Left. Onto . . . I didn't get the name.'

Quinn guessed it must be Rue Aylmer, but he said nothing.

'She's really trying to lose me now,' Nate said. 'Left again.'

Over the speaker, Quinn could hear the tires of his apprentice's car screeching as Nate made a quick turn.

'She's a block ahead of me now, turning left again.' More screeching. 'We were on this road before, it's the one with the church.' Several seconds passed, then, 'Same turn as before. Onto Saint somebody. Can't remember the name.'

Quinn followed the action on the map, picturing the two cars racing down the streets.

'She's going to turn . . . no, wait . . . she's staying on this road for now. We didn't make the same turn again . . . Whoa!'

'What is it?' Quinn asked.

'A taxi just pulled in front of me. Trying to get around him, but he's slowing me down.'

'Do you still have a visual of her car?'

'Yeah, but she's almost a block and a half ahead of me now . . . she's turning! Right.'

Depending on how far they had gone, it was either Rue Ste. Alexandre or Rue de Bleury.

'She's out of my sight,' Nate said. 'Come on, faster, jerk!' The last words meant, no doubt, for the taxi that had gotten in front of him. 'Okay, he's going straight, I'm taking the turn. Ste. Alexandre.' The pause went on for several seconds. 'Ah, shit.'

'What?'

'She's gone. I . . . dammit . . . I lost her.'

'She's got to be around there somewhere. Maybe she parked along the curb.'

Quinn listened as Nate searched the street, but there was no sign of the woman. Marion Dupuis had gotten away.

'I'm sorry,' Nate said.

'Meet us back at the motel,' Quinn said.

'Give him a break,' Orlando whispered.

Quinn frowned, but knew she was right. Nate had done well under the circumstances.

'You did the best you could,' Quinn said. 'Don't worry about it. We'll find her some other way.'

'Thanks,' Nate said, a hint of relief in his voice. 'See you at the motel.'

The line went dead.

Quinn and Orlando drove in silence for several minutes.

'You're being too tough on him again,' she said.

Quinn glanced at her, then looked back at the road.

'I mean it,' she said. 'He's doing everything you tell him to.'

Several seconds passed before Quinn said, 'I know he is.'

'Then what's the problem?'

Quinn didn't answer right away. Instead, he looked out the side window. 'I . . . I'm not sure he's up to it.'

'You took him to Ireland. He did fine there.'

'He hurt like hell afterward,' Quinn said. 'He even limped a little bit when we moved the bodies to the boat.'

'He lost his *leg*. What do you expect?'

'I *expect* him to be ready in any kind of situation. I *expect* him to be able to function at a high level at all times. I *expect* him to do the job just like someone who still has both legs. It's a dangerous job, and I'm not going to put him out there if I think he's going to have problems.'

What he didn't add, what he was really feeling,

was that he was responsible for Nate's life. And if keeping his apprentice out of the way kept him from getting hurt, then Quinn had to do that. He had no choice.

'You're just as bad as Durrie,' she said, evoking the name of her former lover and Quinn's dead mentor.

Quinn whipped his head around, and started to open his mouth, but stopped himself. Why couldn't she understand what he was going through? Why couldn't she figure it out?

He spotted a Boni-Soir convenience store ahead. 'Pull over there,' he said, pointing.

'What are you? Hungry?'

'Just pull over.'

She did as he asked.

'I'll be right back,' he said.

He got out of the car and entered the store. Knowing the clerk would be more open to talking to him if Quinn bought something, he picked up a couple of bottles of water and a box of crackers, then headed to the counter.

'Six twenty-seven,' the man at the register said.

As Quinn was pulling out some money, he said, 'You don't happen to have a phone book I can look at, do you?'

'Pay phone in back,' the man said. 'It's got a book.'

The phone book was missing several pages, but the one he was looking for was still there. After he found what he wanted, he returned to the car, and handed Orlando a bottle of water.

'Thanks,' she said.

She put the car in drive and pulled back onto the street.

'We need to go in the other direction,' Quinn said.

'Thought we were going back to the motel.'

Quinn held up the key he had found in the box. 'Motel, yes. Just not ours.'

★  ★  ★

The Motel Monique turned out to be such a dump that Quinn wondered if the key was more a joke than a clue. Maybe stealing a key from the pay-by-the-hour place was something of a rite of passage, the key itself becoming a trophy Marion could have had for years. But it was something you'd leave behind, not take with you when you were fleeing.

'God, I feel like I need to take an hour-long shower just for stepping in here,' Orlando said as they walked down the hallway toward room 326.

Quinn knew what she meant. He'd stayed in worse places, but none he'd had to pay for. There was the permanent smell of mildew in the air, and something else Quinn decided was best not to dwell on. The lights were all too dim, the management trying to save a few bucks by using low-wattage bulbs.

From behind several of the doors, they could hear the grunts and groans of transactions in progress. A couple rooms ahead, a door opened and a man and woman stepped out. She looked done and anxious to leave, but he looked ready for more. When he saw Orlando, he lost all interest in the woman he was with.

'Where'd you find her?' the man asked as he walked by Quinn.

'Piss off,' Quinn told him.

'Fuck you, too,' the man said. 'Hey, babe, you got a number I can have?'

Orlando didn't look back, but she did flip him off.

'That ain't very ladylike,' he called out.

Quinn could sense Orlando tensing beside him. For a second he thought she was going to pull her gun on him.

'If he's still out here when we leave, you can shoot him,' Quinn whispered.

The hand that had begun moving upward relaxed back against her side.

'Ah, never mind. You're probably a pretty lousy fuck anyway,' the man said.

Quinn stopped, then turned back around. The man was twenty feet behind them, the woman he'd been with long gone.

'Hey, you're the one who wanted me to relax,' Orlando whispered.

'Excuse me,' Quinn said to the man. 'Not sure I heard you correctly.'

'Wasn't talking to you,' the man said.

Quinn took four casual steps forward, halving the distance between them.

'You think you're going to scare me?' the man asked. 'Turn around and go have your little fuck. I'll find her later when I'm ready.'

Orlando moved up beside Quinn. 'You sure I can't shoot him?' she asked.

'What's your name?' Quinn said.

215

'Mick Jagger. Who are you?'

'Inspector Barclay.'

The man laughed, though it wasn't as assured as his tone had been moments before. 'Inspector Barclay? That's funny. And who's she? Inspector Chan?'

'Please,' Orlando said. 'I'll just graze him. I swear.'

'You look kind of familiar,' the man said, squinting as he looked at Quinn. 'I know you, don't I?'

Quinn smiled at the man. Then in a single swift motion he pulled his gun out of the holster under his jacket. Orlando followed his lead and had her weapon out a second later.

'Shit. Oh, shit. Shit. Man, I didn't mean anything, okay? Shit.' He was backing rapidly down the hall. 'I'm sorry. I mean, I was just joking, okay? Shit.'

He reached the elevator and tapped the down button over and over until the car arrived. He jumped in and began his button routine inside.

Once the doors closed, Quinn slipped his gun back into its holster.

'You should have just let me pop him,' Orlando said as she stowed her weapon.

'Come on,' Quinn said, turning back in the direction they'd been headed before they'd been interrupted.

He had no concern that the man would come back. The guy had had all the earmarks of some office jerk out for a little action. Quinn thought it might be a long time before Orlando's would-be suitor would return to the Motel Monique.

216

At room 326, he slipped the key into the lock and gave it a turn. It worked. If it had been a trophy from years before, the motel didn't seem to care enough to change the locks.

Quinn drew his gun again, then pushed the door open and slipped inside. Once Orlando joined him, she shut the door.

The room was as worn and uninviting as the rest of the place. A bed with a spread from deep in the last century, a TV that couldn't have been much younger, and awful dark red paint on the walls.

'Are you sure she's staying here?' she asked. 'Doesn't look like anyone's used the room. I mean, you know, in the last twelve hours. I'm sure the room's had plenty of use otherwise.'

Quinn looked at her as she shivered in repulsion.

'She had the key for some reason,' he said.

Their search was a short one. The prize was lying flat on the floor, hidden behind the bed. A carry-on suitcase. Black like ninety-nine percent of the other carry-ons in the world.

Quinn picked it up and placed it on the bed.

'So she was planning on returning,' Orlando said. 'Maybe she's still coming back.'

'Perhaps,' Quinn said, but he didn't think so. The terror in her eyes had been genuine. And when she realized she'd left the key behind, Quinn didn't think there was any way she'd risk coming back no matter what was inside.

There was no lock, so Quinn unzipped the top and flopped it open.

Clothes mostly. Women's and —

'This is for a little girl,' Orlando said, holding up a small dress.

Quinn rooted around until he found something other than clothes. What he pulled out was a stack of passports. Four total. They were all Canadian. The first one was for Marion Dupuis. It was the most used of the bunch. There were several stamps inside, most recently from customs at JFK in New York, and a smeared one that he thought was from Côte d'Ivoire in Africa.

He handed it to Orlando, then opened the next one. A child stared out at him. According to her date of birth, she was five. Her name was listed as Iris Dupuis. The child was either from Africa or of African descent. And it was evident that there was something different about her. Her face was round and her features seemed closer together than normal. But it was her eyes that were the telltale sign.

'What do you think?' he said, showing Orlando the picture.

'Did you see a child with her?'

Quinn hesitated, then said, 'I saw something in the back seat. I wasn't sure what it was, but I think it might have been her.'

Orlando looked at the picture again. 'This girl has Down syndrome.'

Quinn had thought the same. There was no mistaking the look.

He looked at the remaining two passports. While the pictures were the same as in the other two, the names were different.

'False IDs,' Quinn told Orlando. 'She's on the run.'

Quinn put the two false passports back in the bag, but slipped the ones with the name Dupuis on them into his pocket.

Across the top flap of the bag was a cover secured by a couple of metal hooks. Quinn released the hooks and lifted the cover. Underneath was a single item. A manila envelope.

Orlando picked it up and unclasped the top. Inside was a stack of papers.

Before she could pull anything out, Quinn said, 'Let's not hang around here any longer. We can look at this back at our motel.'

Orlando nodded, then put the envelope back.

As Quinn closed the suitcase, he thought about the child. *Iris Dupuis*. Marion's child? If so, either her parents had disapproved or had not known. There had been no pictures of the girl in the house. Odd.

Even odder, though, was the false set of identification. A dozen questions came to him, one on top of the other. But he had no answers.

'Let's go,' he said.

★ ★ ★

Five rings, then voicemail again. A generic voice telling Quinn, 'Leave your message after the beep.' But he disconnected the call before the beep could sound.

'He's still not picking up,' Quinn said.

He'd been trying to reach Peter for the last ten minutes. He'd already left two messages on

219

Peter's mobile. A call to the Office's main line had been equally frustrating, the night operator simply telling Quinn the message would be passed on.

'I've got something here,' Orlando said.

She was sitting on their bed at the Comfort Inn, her computer in her lap. Beside her was the manila envelope from Marion's suitcase. The papers that had been inside now sat on top of the envelope in a neat stack.

Quinn walked over and sat beside Orlando.

'Is that Marion?'

She turned the screen so Quinn could see. On it was a photo of several people standing together, smiling for the camera. A posed shot that could have been taken almost anywhere. The background looked like it was the side of a building. The wall was dingy white, either stucco or plaster or something similar. There were five people total, four women and one man. Two of the women and the man were African. The other two were Caucasian. One was a lanky blonde, and the other a shorter brunette — Marion.

'What is this?' he asked.

Orlando hit the back arrow on her browser. A newspaper article appeared: *The Daily Telegraph*, from London, England. The photo was there, too, only smaller.

## U.N. SEEKS LOCAL HELP
## KEEPING CHILDREN SAFE

''Community leaders pose in front of a new children activities facility in Yamoussoukro, Côte d'Ivoire, with UN workers,'' Orlando read. 'This article says Marion Dupuis is part of the UN mission in Côte d'Ivoire. That explains where she got all those.' Orlando nodded at the stack of papers.

They had already established that the papers were printouts from a UN database. Before diving into them, Orlando wanted to see if she could establish what Marion Dupuis' connection to them might be. Turned out it didn't take her very long.

'I have contacts in New York who work there. I can verify her position fairly easily.'

'Do it.'

While Orlando composed an email to her contacts, Quinn stood up and walked over to the door and peeked through the eyehole. The fish-eye magnifier on the other end gave him a near 180-degree view of the hallway beyond, though only for a distance of about fifteen to twenty feet. The area he could see was empty.

*Where the hell is Nate?* he thought.

He had expected his apprentice to be waiting for them when they returned. But instead, they were the first to arrive.

Quinn wanted to call him, but that wasn't procedure.

'Maybe he got tired of waiting for us and went to get something to eat,' Orlando said, sensing, as she always did, what he was thinking.

Quinn grunted a response, then walked over to the TV and looked around for the remote.

'Please don't turn that on,' she said.

'Just thought I'd check the news.'

She looked up from her computer and stared at him for a moment. 'Even if something has happened to him, you're not going to find anything local right now. And I doubt he's made CNN yet.'

'I know,' he said. 'I just wanted to see if there was anything new about the Deputy Director's death.'

But his lie was a thin one, and she saw right through it. 'Just leave it off.'

He sat down on the chair next to the built-in desk, listening to Orlando's fingers tapping on her keyboard. He pulled a brochure about Montreal out of the desk drawer and tried to read through it, but got halfway before he realized he couldn't remember anything he'd just read.

A glance at his watch told him more than twenty minutes had passed since they had arrived. If it reached thirty, he was going to call Nate, to hell with procedure.

Quinn's phone rang at minute twenty-seven, Nate's name glowing on the touch screen.

'Don't be angry with him,' Orlando said as he was about to press Accept.

'Fine,' he muttered, then connected the call.

'Quinn?' Nate's voice was hushed.

Whatever Quinn had been feeling disappeared as he kicked into operation mode. 'What's going on?'

'We weren't the only ones interested in the woman,' Nate said.

Quinn wanted to ask what happened, but suppressed the urge and said, 'Do you need help?'

'I think I might need you to pick me up. I dumped the car and have been on foot for the last thirty minutes. Think I might have lost them, but I'm not sure. Heading into the metro now. I'll grab the first train and take it toward the end of the line . . . Hold on.' Quinn could hear the phone moving away from Nate's ear, and rubbing against something. 'Okay. I'll be on the Orange line, heading toward Henri-Bourassa. I'll plan on getting off a few stops ahead. Say . . . Sauvé.'

'Okay,' Quinn said. 'Do a check along the way.'

'I will,' Nate said. 'See you in a bit.'

'What is it?' Orlando asked as Quinn slipped the phone back in his pocket.

'Someone else was looking for Marion. When they spotted Nate, looks like they tried to find out who he was.'

'You're going to bring him in?'

Quinn nodded.

'You need me to come with you?'

'No. We'll be fine. You see if you can figure out what she was running from.'

★  ★  ★

They'd dumped the Lincoln several blocks from the Comfort Inn when they returned, thinking

223

they wouldn't need it anymore. Quinn considered using it again, but he wanted something less flashy.

He hiked ten minutes and found another motel with a large anonymous parking lot where he appropriated a three-year-old Toyota Camry for the night.

Soon he was back over the bridge into Montreal. He followed the Orange line aboveground as best he could until he reached Sauvé station.

There were two entrances, one on either side of Rue Sauvé, neither larger than a three-car garage. Each looked grimy and gray in the artificial illumination from the surrounding lighting. Quinn imagined they didn't look much better during the day.

He drove by, keeping a few miles an hour below the speed limit, his eyes on guard for someone emerging out of the shadows, but there was no one. He looped around the small grass-covered island in the middle of the block and headed in the opposite direction, taking him by the larger of the two structures.

He was almost past the end of the building when someone ran out toward him. His first instinct was to hit the gas, but he slowed to a stop when he saw the man's face. It was Nate.

Quinn reached across and opened the passenger door just as his apprentice arrived.

Before he even had the door closed, Nate said, 'I'm fine. Go.'

Quinn pressed down hard on the accelerator. 'Is someone back there?'

'I don't think so,' Nate said, breathing hard. 'But I heard another train pull in, so you never know. They could still be looking for me.'

Quinn spent several minutes driving randomly until he was sure they weren't being followed, then settled on a direction that would take them back toward their motel.

'Tell me,' he said.

Nate took a few more deep breaths. 'I was heading back to the motel. You know, like you told me to do. But after a few minutes I realized there was someone behind me. I made a few turns, normal stuff, nothing too fast, just to see if I was right. The guy stayed with me.'

'Did you recognize him from earlier?' Quinn asked, trying to put the pieces together.

'No. Like I said, I didn't pay attention when I was following the woman.'

'Her name's Marion.'

'What?'

'The woman in the Saab. Marion Dupuis,' Quinn said.

'Right,' Nate said.

'So you were being followed,' Quinn said, trying to get Nate back on track.

'Yeah. Once I knew for sure, I played it cool for a while, letting him get relaxed. Then, when I thought he was comfortable, I made a break for it. It worked great. I was able to get a little distance, enough that I could dump the car and head out on foot without them catching me.'

'Them?'

Nate nodded. 'There were two. Both guys, strong looking. One a little older, but I didn't get

225

much of a look at either of them. I tried, I swear. But that's all I got.'

'What happened next?'

'One of them got out of the car and chased me. But by then I had them beat. Lost them a few minutes later, then made my way to a metro station. That's when I called you.'

Quinn thought for a moment. 'Maybe they weren't following the girl. Maybe they were just interested in giving you a hard time.'

'I guess,' Nate said, his tone indicating he didn't believe it.

Quinn didn't believe it, either. It would have been too much of a coincidence. And Quinn just didn't believe in them. The easier answer, the more logical one, would be that they must have had some interest in Marion Dupuis. They had to have been staking out the Dupuis' house from farther down the street. But did that mean they had seen Quinn and Orlando go inside? What if there were more of them than just those in the car? Could they have followed Quinn and Orlando back to the Comfort Inn?

'Sorry,' Nate said.

'What?' Quinn said. 'No. You did fine. Better than fine. You got away.'

Nate was silent for a moment, then said, 'Thanks.'

Quinn pulled out his phone, intending to call Orlando, but his phone began to ring before he could dial. Peter. *Dammit*. Quinn hit Accept.

'Hold on, Peter,' Quinn said.

'Wait. What's going — '

'I said hold on.' Quinn put Peter's call on

hold, then punched Orlando's name on his quick-contact list.

'Hello?' she said.

'Everything all right there?' he asked.

'Fine,' she said. 'Why?'

'Serious. Are you okay?'

She paused. 'Hunky-dory,' she said, using their latest code to signify all was normal. 'What's going on?'

'We may have been followed, too.'

'From the Dupuis'?' she said. 'You would have noticed.'

It's true. He would have. He was excellent at the spotting-the-tail game, and he hadn't seen anyone suspicious on their way back to the motel. But if the others had the resources, there were ways to track a car without needing to keep visual contact.

'I still want you to get out,' Quinn said. 'We'll pick you up in twenty minutes.'

'All right,' she said, but she sounded annoyed.

Quinn clicked back over to Peter.

'What the hell are you doing putting me on hold?' Peter all but yelled.

Quinn ignored the comment. 'The Dupuis you wanted us to find. Is her name Marion?'

Peter took a moment, then said, 'I told you I don't have a first name.'

'Well, if it isn't, there's another Dupuis who's in a hell of a lot of trouble.' Quinn recounted the evening's events, up to and including the suitcase, what Orlando had learned online, and Nate's encounter with the men who had followed him.

'They weren't yours, were they?' Quinn asked.

'No. Not mine.'

'So is she who you wanted us to find?'

Silence.

'I . . . I don't know,' Peter finally said. 'It sounds like it, but . . . ' Peter went quiet again.

After several seconds, Quinn said, 'But what?'

Nothing.

'Peter?'

Quinn moved the phone away from his ear so he could see the display. The call was gone.

# 16

'Quinn?' Peter said. 'Goddammit. Quinn, are you there?'

The line was dead. The cause was right there on his display screen. No Sig — no signal.

He was on a private jet flying back to Washington, D.C., from New York. Usually the onboard equipment had no problem connecting his signal to the nearest ground station, but on occasion there were moments when it would fail.

Even as he was looking at his phone, the signal strength went from nothing to back to full. He started to redial Quinn, then stopped.

Quinn would want instructions on what to do next, but Peter wasn't sure. The woman sounded like a lead, but was it worth the extra effort to locate her again? Her connection could have been random, and the information she might have weak at best. Or maybe she was the missing link, the key to knowing what the terrorists had in mind. Hell, not only what, but who the sons of bitches were.

*Too many fucking unknowns*, Peter thought. Who? What? When? There were no answers to any of these questions. All he had was the word of Primus, and five dead men: the DDNI, Peter's two men, and Primus's team in Ireland.

At least Tasha was pulling out of it. The last report he'd heard, she'd regained consciousness for a few minutes. She'd been groggy, and in no

229

condition to talk. But she was alive.

The door in the front of the cabin opened. One of the officers stepped out from the cockpit and walked over to Peter.

'Sir. There's a sat-vid call for you,' he said. 'Would you like me to connect it?'

'I can get it,' Peter said.

'Yes, sir. It'll be on channel two.'

The officer returned to the cockpit, closing the door behind him.

In front of Peter's chair was a table connected to the wall of the plane. Rectangular, utilitarian, with a wide pedestal base that was as long as the table. On top was a recess hidden under a cover, unnoticeable if you didn't know it was there.

Peter touched the cover at exactly the right spot. It slid to the side, revealing a touch-screen interface underneath. With a tap in the center, the screen lit up. With another touch, a thirteen-inch flat screen monitor rose out of the table.

Peter selected channel two. There was a momentary pause before an image came onto the screen. A man sitting in what looked to be an office.

Chercover.

Peter wasn't surprised. He had assumed it would be either him or his minion Furuta. Both had been a pain in his ass since the DDNI had disappeared. They had stepped in once it was obvious Deputy Director Jackson was missing, and had wanted to be kept up-to-date on everything that was happening.

'Did you find the girl?' Chercover said.

'We know who she is.'

'So you don't have her yet.'

'It's not that easy, and you know it.'

Silence for several seconds. 'You're on this project not by my choice. Remember that.'

Peter tried to rein in his temper, but he knew he was less than successful. He could keep anger out of his voice if he really wanted to, but almost never off his face.

*Goddamn video phones.*

'We are making pro — ' he started to say.

'Who is the girl?' Chercover asked, cutting him off.

Peter took a moment to remember all that Quinn had told him. 'Her name is Marion Dupuis. Works for the UN, most recently in West Africa. Earlier this week her parents and her sister were killed by a gas leak in their home. We don't think the leak was an accident.'

'So our terrorist friends are after this Marion woman,' Chercover guessed.

'They at least want to send her a message,' Peter said.

'But you don't know where she is?'

Peter hesitated a mere half second. 'There was a possible sighting in Montreal. I have people there now investigating.'

Chercover stared through the monitor.

'She might be a dead end,' Chercover said. 'What we need to do is find out the rest of what Primus was going to tell us. That seems to me to be the most direct path, don't you agree?'

*And yet you're the fucker who told me to go after her in the first place*, Peter thought, but

231

only said, 'Of course.'

'Good. Forget about the woman. She isn't worth the effort.'

Peter could see Chercover's arm move, then the screen went black.

Peter touched the control panel again, and the monitor slipped back into its home beneath the surface of the table.

He placed his right hand across his forehead and tried to rub away the anger that threatened to consume him. On his list of top ten items he hated most, being micromanaged by a client was right at the top. And when the client was right, it was even more maddening.

Such was the case with Chercover. Of course the girl wasn't worth the trouble, not without more information. Peter could have Quinn search for her for weeks, but she might never be found. It was eye-on-the-prize time, and the prize was finding out the details Primus had yet to reveal.

Peter knew all this, but now whatever he did, it would seem like he was following Chercover's directions, not his own instincts.

He found his cell phone and dialed Quinn back.

The line rang but a single time, then, 'Peter?'

'Sorry,' Peter said. 'I lost signal there for a little bit.'

'What were you going to say before?' Quinn asked.

'I don't remember,' Peter said. He didn't, and whatever it was didn't matter anymore.

'We were talking about Marion Dupuis. You

said it was probably the woman we were looking for. But . . . But what?'

'Not important. We're going to drop her.'

'So you don't want us to find her?'

'No. I have something else in mind.'

Quinn took a moment before he spoke. 'I can hardly wait.'

'I'm going to have another go at our source. Try to set up a meeting to get all his information. It's the only way we'll find out what the hell is going on.' He paused. 'I want you to take the meeting.'

'Of course you do.'

Peter remained quiet, giving Quinn a moment.

'I have one provision,' Quinn said.

'What?'

'I want the meeting to take place at a location I'm familiar with.'

'That makes sense to me.'

'Someplace public. I'm guessing he'll want to meet me in New York. But that's not going to work for me, not with my face still plastered over all the papers.'

'That's getting cleared up,' Peter said. 'Another day or two and no one will even remember the drawing.'

'You'd better be right.'

'Trust me on this.'

'Fine. But New York is still out. D.C. wouldn't be good, either. Chicago would be better, or someplace like that.'

'I'll try,' Peter said. 'He might not go for it.'

'Then you take the meeting. Those are my terms.'

'Our deal was no questions,' Peter said.

'Our deal was not for open-ended jobs, either, Peter. You're taking advantage of my trust on this one. So we do the meeting my way, or you do it yourself.'

'Are you going to stay in Montreal?'

The only response was the line disconnecting.

★  ★  ★

Peter did not receive word back from Primus until noon the next day. He was afraid Primus had cut all communication links. The emergency cell phone number, a number that was only supposed to be used once, was no longer in service. The only thing Peter had left was an anonymous email address that he hoped Primus was still checking.

Thankfully, it appeared he was.

Peter's original message had read:

Request for meeting. Earliest possible.
The Field Museum. Chicago.

The response was equally brief:

Noon. Thursday.
Los Angeles, not Chicago. LACMA. Entrance.

Thursday was two days away. And the location would please Quinn. They were on.

# 17

They had almost got her. The people who had
wanted Iris, the people who had tried to trap her
in New York, the people who she was now one
hundred percent positive killed her family had
come within seconds of trapping her in her
parents' house. She had thought for a moment
that one of them, the man whose picture she'd
seen on the news, was going to try and pull her
out of her car as she drove away. But he had only
stared at her as she drove off. Then, thinking at
first she was free, a flash of lights swept across
her rearview mirror as a car pulled from the curb
and began following her.

'No! Leave us alone!' she had said as she
pressed the gas pedal down.

In the back, Iris first laughed, then screamed
in surprise as she slid along the upholstered seat.
Marion looked back, aware she had not secured
the child, but knowing she couldn't stop now to
do anything about it.

'Iris, sweetheart, give me your hand,' Marion
said. She stretched her right arm back toward
the girl, hoping Iris would understand. 'Come
on, please. Take my hand.'

After a moment, Iris reached out her small
five-year-old hand and put it in Marion's.
Marion closed her own around it and pulled the
child forward. Iris whimpered in fear, but
allowed Marion to move her toward the gap

between the front seats.

'All right, baby. Up here with me.'

She lifted Iris and tried to move her between the seats, but the girl's feet got caught and wouldn't come through.

'Lift your legs, honey.'

But Iris couldn't figure out what Marion wanted. She just smiled, her loving, simple eyes oblivious to the danger around them. Marion had no choice but to pull the girl through as much as she could, then lay her headfirst on the passenger seat while she freed the girl's legs.

Once she got Iris situated in the front seat, and the seatbelt fastened around the girl's tiny form as best as possible, she checked her mirror again. The car was still there.

As they drove onward, a streetlight illuminated the driver. A man. About her age or maybe even a little younger. He didn't look particularly menacing, but he did look determined, and that was all the danger she needed for motivation.

She remembered a church ahead. It was another four blocks down and off to the right. If she could somehow get to it while he was out of sight, she might have a chance. She turned a few blocks shy of the church and pushed the gas down hard. But he remained right with her.

Two blocks down, she went left, then left again, circling the block and hoping to get him off guard. Then she had her first bit of luck all week. A taxi pulled into the road behind her, and in front of her pursuer. It was driving slower and forced the man who had been following her to reduce his speed.

236

She went right at the next corner, going as fast as she dared. Half a block down on the left was the entrance to the church parking area. The tires of the Saab jammed up against the wheel well as she turned in to the lot. She doused the car's headlights but kept driving. Because there were few cars present, she was able to race across the parking lot and out the exit on the other side, onto the parallel road.

For the next hour she checked her mirror every few seconds, but there was no one there. She'd lost him. When she finally allowed herself to pull to the side of the road, she began to cry.

It was too much. She didn't know what to do. She didn't know if she should do anything. Maybe she should just give in to the inevitable, and wait for them to find her.

She heard sniffling to her right.

Iris.

The girl had been so quiet for the last fifteen minutes, Marion had almost forgotten she was there. But she wasn't quiet now. Her lower lip arced upward in the middle, quivering. Her eyes were full of water, some already spilling onto her cheeks, and her short, shaky intakes of air were punctuated by silent pauses. Her hands were against her chest, one holding the other.

'Oh, baby,' Marion said. She reached down, released the seatbelt, and lifted Iris into her arms. 'It's okay. It's okay.'

Together they cried, Marion's tears running down onto Iris's hair, and Iris's tears soaking Marion's shirt. The child, so innocent, so unknowing, scared of what was happening, scared because the woman who was protecting her was crying.

It was the jolt Marion needed, the reminder that giving up was not acceptable.

'We'll be fine, sweetie,' Marion said, her voice soft and comforting. 'Everything will be fine. I won't let anything happen. I'm here, okay? I'm here.'

After several minutes the young girl's sobs began to subside, and soon Marion could feel Iris's breath grow steady and deep. She had fallen asleep.

Marion returned her to the passenger seat, then tilted it back as far as it would go. She pulled the seatbelt over Iris's hips. It was loose, but would hold the child in place.

The one thing she knew was that they had to get out of town. She didn't know where, just away. As she drove toward the Motel Monique, she touched her pants pocket where she'd been keeping the key. Only it wasn't there.

'Oh, God,' she said aloud. *The key.*

She thought back to the last time she'd seen it, and remembered with horror putting it in the box, the box she'd left at her parents' house.

Their clothes, their passports, the documents she'd downloaded were all left at the motel. She took a deep breath and tried to calm down. *The night manager,* she thought. If she slipped him a little money, he'd give her another key. *All right. It's going to be okay. I'll just run in, grab the suitcase, and we can be —*

She cut herself off, her eyes growing wide. What if the others had found the box and the

238

key inside? What if they were headed to the Motel Monique, too? What if they showed up while she was there?

Ahead, she could see the motel. But instead of stopping she drove right by. The suitcase was lost now. She would have to forget about it, and concentrate solely on keeping Iris safe.

The one thing she had was her wallet. And inside that, an ATM card. She found the nearest ATM and took out as much money as she could.

She wasn't dumb. She'd seen plenty of movies and knew her transaction could be traced, but they already knew she was in Montreal, so since she was leaving town, it wouldn't matter. A calculated risk, at least that's what she told herself.

She wanted to get back into the States. She felt it would be much easier to get lost there. But without passports, driving into the country wouldn't be possible.

So instead of heading dead south for the nearest border crossing, she headed southwest toward Toronto, the largest city in the country. There had to be secret ways across the border there, someone who could help her.

Or so she hoped.

$\star$ $\star$ $\star$

She found an underground parking garage in downtown Toronto near the SkyDome, or as it was now officially known, the Rogers Centre, and took a spot on the third level, as far away from the stairs as possible. She then got into the back of the car, taking the still-sleeping Iris with her. Together they lay down on the cramped seat. The only good news was that it was a pleasant night. Cool, but not cold. The pullover sweatshirt she still wore would be enough to keep them both warm.

Exhausted, she thought she'd be asleep the minute she closed her eyes. But her mind still buzzed with the last drops of the adrenaline generated by her late-night escape. She gave in to it, knowing that fighting it would only push sleep further away. Her thoughts tumbled around, each taking center stage for a second, then being replaced by another.

Glimpses of Africa: the old shopkeeper with the Taser that didn't work, Frau Roslyn shutting the door to the secret room. New York: the Kinkos employee who had shown interest in Iris, the call to her friend at the UN. And finally Montreal: her parents, her sister, the awful motel with the pay-by-the-hour rates, the cabdriver who thought she was a hooker, and the man who had come running out of her house as she tried to drive away. His face, like a snapshot, hovered before her. She would not forget his face. The look of his eyes, the set of his mouth. This was the face of those who wanted her, who wanted Iris. And, she knew, this was the face of death. The news reports out of New York confirmed that.

She awoke to the sound of a car door slamming somewhere nearby. At first she had no idea where she was. She felt stiff and cramped. She glanced to her left and saw the back of the driver's seat, and remembered. The face that had stuck in her mind as she had fallen asleep came back to her again, but only for a brief second.

'Goah,' a soft voice said.

Marion felt Iris begin to move against her chest.

'Goah,' the girl repeated.

It was a sound Marion had come to understand. Iris was hungry.

'We'll go find something, okay?' Marion said.

Iris smiled like she understood.

Marion sat up, holding the child to her chest as she did. The lights in the garage gave no indication what time of day it was. But when Marion had driven in, she had passed no more than half a dozen other cars. Now the garage, at least on this level, was packed.

She glanced at her watch. Almost 9 a.m. No wonder Iris was hungry.

'What do you feel like eating?' Marion said, smiling. 'Pancakes?'

Iris smiled back.

'I could use some, too. And a cup of coffee.'

'Goah.'

'No coffee for you, sweetheart. Not for another few years, huh?'

Marion climbed out of the car first. Then as she reached in and started to pull Iris out, she heard several quick footsteps that stopped nearby. She pulled herself back out, knowing as she turned who she'd see. It would be him. The man from her house. The face of death.

But she was wrong.

There was a man there, yes. He was standing

241

near the back of her car, at the end of the gap between her Saab and the car parked next to her. But he was no one she had seen before. He was taller than the man at her house, stockier, and a few years older, too. He was wearing a suit, like he was on his way to work. That was it, she realized. Someone just passing by, and stopping to see if she needed any help.

'Miss Dupuis?' he said.

The relief that had begun flooding through her turned to ice.

She looked behind her, hoping there was some way out, but there was only the concrete wall her car was parked against. The man was blocking her only exit.

'Please, Miss Dupuis. You need to come with me.' He had an accent. Australian, maybe.

Marion's head whipped back and forth as she looked through the garage hoping to spot someone who could help her. But there was no one. *Nine a.m. and no one in the garage?*

The man smiled at her. 'I probably should tell you that the structure has been closed for a few minutes. An untimely gate malfunction. But don't worry. It'll be fixed soon.' He took a step closer. 'I guess what I'm trying to say is that there's no one around but you and me.'

Marion began to shake in fear. Iris, sensing something was up, started to cry.

'Goah. Goah,' she said between sobs.

'Help!' Marion screamed. 'Help me!'

Iris wailed, scared by the sudden outburst.

The smiling man walked toward Marion.

'Help!' she screamed again.

'That's not very cooperative,' the man said as he stopped only a few feet in front of her.

Before she even knew what was happening, one of his hands grabbed the back of her head while the other placed something over her mouth.

She struggled for a moment, but with Iris in her arms there was little she could do. Then she began to lose focus, her mind becoming heavy. It seemed to take everything she had to keep her eyes from closing, and then that wasn't even enough.

*No.* She wanted to scream it, but the only place the word was spoken was in her head.

She tried to open her eyelids one last time, frantic to stay conscious. And for a few seconds they obeyed.

Iris was there, her tear-filled eyes staring into Marion's.

'Goah,' she said, her lower lip jutting out the way it did when she was sad.

Marion's eyelids closed. She had no strength left.

*Please, God. Don't let them hurt Iris. Don't let them hurt . . . my . . . child . . .*

★  ★  ★

'The situation is secure,' the man Marion had first mistaken for a businessman said into his phone. To his colleagues he was known as Leo Tucker.

'What are their conditions?' Tucker's boss, Mr. Rose, asked.

'The woman's unconscious. The child seems fine, though she's scared. Naturally, I guess. What do you want us to do?'

The original plan had been to just remove Marion Dupuis and the child she'd stolen out from under them. Kill them and dump them someplace where it would be years before they were found. But Tucker knew things had changed the minute they realized in Montreal that someone else was also interested in the two targets. At least Marion Dupuis had been predictable enough to take her sister's car. The night Tucker and his men had arranged the 'accident' at Marion's family's house, he had also put a tracking device in her sister's car just in case. Preparation, that's what it was all about.

Unfortunately, what they hadn't been prepared for was someone else being there, too. Tucker would have been much happier if he knew who the man who'd followed Marion from her house had been, but whoever he was, he'd been able to lose Tucker's men. A problem, but not one Tucker could personally see to. He'd have to use one of his contacts to see if they could find out anything.

'Where's the plane?' Mr. Rose asked.

'Here. In Toronto.'

'Use it. Bring them here,' his boss said. 'We need to find out what she knows about the others. We can use the girl as motivation. And if the child is still alive after, we'll make her part of the program.'

'Consider us on our way.'

# 18

Quinn didn't even need to crack open his eyes to know where he was. He could sense it as his body began to wake. The feel of the sheets, the comfort of a known pillow, and the overall feeling that he belonged.

Home. He was in his house in the Hollywood Hills above the Los Angeles Basin. He smiled at the thought.

It had been almost three weeks since he'd last been here. First the job in Ireland, then the part job, part vacation in Boston, followed by all the fun in New York and Montreal. His work often kept him away for long periods of time, but for some reason it felt extra special this time to be back in his own bed.

When Peter told him the meeting was to take place in Los Angeles, Quinn almost didn't believe him. He made sure he, Orlando, and Nate were on the next flight west.

He opened his eyes and looked at the only thing that was out of place in his room. Orlando lay on the bed next to him, facing away. It wasn't that she'd never been here before, but those occurrences were few. Mainly he had either gone to see her in Vietnam or San Francisco, or they had met elsewhere. Hawaii, Bali once, Japan, and a very wonderful week in Switzerland.

But here she was now, her bare shoulder sticking out from under the sheet hinting at more bare skin below. Quinn moved over, spooning into her. He placed his arm over her side and rested his hand on her chest between and just above her breasts. She turned, moving into him, so that they could become as close as possible.

'Don't even think about it,' she whispered as his hand began to drift south. 'We don't have time.'

'The meeting's not until noon,' he said.

'That's only five hours away. We've got a lot to do before then.'

'I can be quick.'

'Then you can do it alone.'

There was a second of silence, then they both began to laugh. She turned to him, her face inches away from his. He started to move in for a kiss, but she pulled back.

'Morning breath,' she said.

'I love your morning breath.'

She snorted. 'That's the worst lie I think I've ever heard.'

'I don't care that you have morning breath. Better?'

She stared at him for a moment, then smiled. 'Better enough.'

She moved forward, her lips on his lips, her body on his body.

By the time they left the bedroom, there were only four hours left until the meeting.

★   ★   ★

They arrived at LACMA, the Los Angeles County Museum of Art, at 10:00 a.m., parking

Quinn's BMW on Sixth Street.

'We'll start on Wilshire and do a perimeter search,' Quinn said to Orlando. 'You go west and I'll go east.'

'Okay,' she said.

'And me?' Nate asked from the back seat.

Quinn handed Nate the bag of items he'd picked up at a 7-Eleven on the way. Inside were a couple bottles of water, an energy bar, and a newspaper.

'Find a table in the central court and relax,' Quinn said. 'That's where I'm supposed to meet him, so I want you to keep an eye on things. There's a chance he'll show up early to have a look around, too.'

'I can do the walk-around, one of you could sit and wait,' Nate said.

'We'll do it the way I said,' Quinn told him.

'You worried about my leg again? Jesus, haven't I shown you that it's not a problem? I helped you run down that guy in Ireland. I was *chased* in Montreal. I'm fine.'

'I don't care about your leg,' Quinn said. 'But if you want to walk, fine. Give the bag to Orlando.'

Nate didn't move. After a moment, he said, 'I'll do the court. Whatever you want. You're the boss.'

'Yes. I am.'

As soon as they got out of the car, Nate started to walk away.

'Wait,' Orlando said. 'You need this.'

Nate turned just in time to catch the small comm gear packet she had tossed at him.

He stuffed it in his pocket, then resumed walking away.

Once he was out of earshot, Orlando said, 'It was the leg, wasn't it?'

'I don't know,' Quinn said. 'I guess. Shit.'

'If you're not going to get past this, then release him. Set him up with someone else. Hell, I'll take him on. Make him an apprentice researcher. He can sit behind a desk all day, I'm sure he'll love that.'

'I . . . I don't know what to do,' he said, surprised by his own words. 'I want him to succeed, I do. But it's not as easy as that. I need to know he'll be ready for any kind of situation. I need to know he'll be able to function at a high level at all times. I need to know he'll do the job just like someone who still has both legs. Being a cleaner is a dangerous job, and I'm not going to put him out there if I think he's going to have problems. He could die. I can't have that.'

'Quinn, seriously.' She touched his arm, stopping him. 'Let it go. If he's not good enough, fine. Let him go. But you have to give him a chance to prove himself.'

Quinn looked at the ground near his feet for a moment, then, with a sigh, he tilted his head up. 'Come on.'

He wanted to let it go. He knew Nate would be a good cleaner. His skills continued to improve. But the leg. The leg that had been maimed while he was helping Quinn on that personal mission in Singapore when an LP operative had purposely smashed into it. Would it hold out in the worst of circumstances? Could

Quinn take that chance knowing he'd be responsible for whatever happened?

He gave her a faint smile, then started walking again.

★ ★ ★

Quinn's main concern was being set up. He was looking for any sign that this might be the case. Perhaps a couple of men waiting in a parked car around the perimeter of the museum, or maybe some tourist who didn't look the part.

He first walked by the Ahmanson Building and the old main entrance to the museum. LACMA was actually a collection of several buildings: the Ahmanson Building, the Bing Center, the Hammer Building, the Pavilion for Japanese Art, the old May Company building known now as LACMA West, and the newest building, the Broad Contemporary Art Museum.

The first four were clustered together near the center point of the museum grounds. In the middle of this group, beyond the entrance, was the central court where Nate would be sitting at one of the tables, reading the paper. There, in addition to a dozen or so tables and chairs, visitors would find the ticket booth, a café, and the museum store.

Quinn continued north along the sidewalk. Traffic on Wilshire was its usual midday busy, not bumper-to-bumper, but constant. Since rush hour was over, cars were again allowed to park along the street. Keeping his movements natural, Quinn checked each of the cars on either side of the street, making sure they were empty. So far, so good.

Past the last of the museum's buildings, the grounds continued for another whole block up to Curson Avenue. Here it was more of a park. Grass, trees, pathways, kids running around, people walking dogs, and, of course, four life-size mammoths and a small lake of black tar.

It was the centerpiece of the famous La Brea Tar Pits, a tar lake about the size of a football field. The mammoths had been added sometime in the past, no doubt to provide visitors an idea of what could happen at the pits — a single mammoth at that west end looked out over the lake, while at the east end a family of three was caught in a life-or-death struggle. One of the mammoths from the family was half-submerged in the black sticky grip of the tar as its mate and child looked on in horror from the shore several feet away.

Quinn turned north on Curson. Here no cars were allowed to park along the street, but there were several school buses. That explained all the children. Field trips.

He kept up a steady pace, assessing everyone he saw, and marking those in his mind that he felt might deserve a second look. Five minutes later he met up with Orlando on Sixth Street along the back side of the museum grounds.

'All clear?' he asked.

'As far as I can tell,' she said.

'Nate. Anything?' Quinn asked.

There was a pause, then the rattle of paper

250

before his apprentice's hushed voice came over his receiver. 'Quiet over here. The museum doesn't open until noon. Most of the people I've seen probably work here.'

'No one paying attention to you?'

'I know how to do the job,' Nate snapped.

'So that's a no?'

'That's a no.'

'Orlando and I are going to walk around the grounds, then I'll come over there and we'll switch.'

'Copy that,' Nate said. Then, after a slight pause, 'Sorry.'

'Don't be,' Quinn said, conceding without actually saying it that he might have pushed too much. He looked at Orlando. 'Let's go into the park, but switch. You take the east, and I'll go west.'

She was giving him her patented you're-an-idiot look, no doubt about the exchange with Nate, but she only said, 'Okay.'

After wandering through the park that surrounded the museums for another thirty minutes, noticing nothing unusual, Quinn decided it was time to get into position.

He'd almost reached the central court when Orlando said, 'I got something.'

Quinn stopped, instinctively turning east toward the part of the park she'd been in.

'Is it him?' he asked.

'Might be. I'm down near the east end of the lake, along that small walkway between the tar and the fence near Wilshire Boulevard. I have a good view here of the Curson gate.'

251

Quinn pictured the spot in his mind. 'All right.'

'Two men just entered. Not tourists. Casual suits. Looking very serious.'

Quinn thought about all the office buildings that were within a few blocks of the park. 'Could be a couple of businessmen trying to get some air.'

'Could be,' she said, 'but they have the look.'

He knew what she meant. Tough, focused, not letting anything escape their gaze. Quinn looked at his watch: 11:15, still forty-five minutes until the meeting was to occur. Advance men, maybe? Doing the same thing Quinn and his team were doing? Or another assassination team, like the one in Ireland, getting into place?

'This *is* L.A.,' Nate said. 'Maybe they're agents. You know, of the talent kind.'

Quinn was about to tell Nate to knock it off, but he stopped himself.

'Keep an eye on them,' Quinn said. 'Could be nothing.'

'Copy that,' Orlando said.

Instead of continuing toward the central court, Quinn headed down the path that ran along the back side of the Hammer Building, toward the tar lake.

'What are they doing?' he said.

'Hold on,' Orlando whispered.

Quinn picked up his pace as much as he could without drawing attention.

Five seconds passed. Then ten.

'What's going on?'

Nothing.

*Screw drawing attention.* He began to run, leaving the path when it veered to the left, and instead keeping to the grass that grew behind the Pavilion for Japanese Art. When he reached the end, he slowed again, then stopped behind some foliage that grew next to the building.

'Orlando?'

There was a single cough over the receiver. The message was clear. She was there, but she couldn't talk.

'I'm moving in to help,' Nate's voice broke in.

'No,' Quinn said. 'Hold your position.'

'But she might need — '

'Just hold your position.'

Quinn peeked through the bushes, trying to see what was happening. But Orlando was too far away, and the black wire mesh fence that surrounded the lake was between them.

He pulled out his phone, accessed the camera function, then activated maximum zoom and pointed the lens toward the lake. The image on the display screen jumped wildly as he moved the lens from right to left. There was a couple walking down the path, holding hands. Beyond them, a couple of kids were trying to throw rocks over the fence into the tar. Nothing for a while, then near the east end of the lake, a man in a suit leaning against the railing and looking through the wire mesh at the mammoth caught in its daily struggle for freedom. A hard man. A man with *the look*. And five feet farther on, also looking through the fence, Orlando.

Quinn continued scanning past her for a moment. She had said two men. But there was

253

only the one. Where had his friend gone?

'Nate,' Quinn said. 'Up and moving. Head toward the café, then take the ramp down into the park. One of the suits is next to Orlando's position. Don't worry about him, I'm on that. But I don't know where his partner is. Locate him. Do *not* intercept. Recon only at this point.'

'Copy that,' Nate said.

As he watched, Orlando pulled her camera phone out of her pocket and held it up to her eye, acting the part of tourist. She could pass, probably. But if the guy in the suit was a legitimate concern, something must have caused him to be interested in her.

'I think he's made you,' Quinn said. 'But you're too public there. Let's get him someplace we can deal with him. You think you can get him to follow you?'

A low, grunted 'Uh-huh.'

'Good.'

Quinn thought for a second. The problem with a public place was that there was too much public around. But he knew one place that might work.

'Head west, behind the museum. There's an observation pit of an old excavation area. It's covered by a cinderblock building, but there's an opening on the north side. When I was there a few minutes ago, no one was around. I'll wait inside.'

Another grunt of understanding.

Quinn watched through his camera as Orlando straightened up and began walking around the east end of the lake, then turned and headed west through the park. The man in the suit didn't move at first.

'Come on, you son of a bitch,' Quinn said.

After fifteen seconds, the man began to follow. Quinn waited to make sure it wasn't just a coincidence, then said, 'You've hooked him.'

'Great,' Orlando whispered, not sounding thrilled by the prospect.

Quinn slipped his phone back into his pocket and made his way to the observation pit.

The building was round, built with tan-colored cinder blocks, and encircled a small pit of tar that had long ago given up all its discoveries to the archaeologists who had worked it. Across the opening on the north side was an iron fence set several feet from the surrounding wall. It was painted burnt orange, and for as long as Quinn could remember, the gate had been closed and locked. This time was no exception. Beyond the gate a concrete pathway hugged the wall and spiraled down one level to a pit of tar. A short iron railing that matched the color of the gate lined the pathway to keep anyone from falling in.

Quinn retrieved his lock picks and set to work on the decades-old dead bolt that secured the gate in place. Once it was unlocked, he left it closed, then tucked himself into the small recess where the cinderblock wall met the fence.

'I'm just inside the opening,' he said. 'I don't think he'll follow you in, so just get him close to the entrance so I can get behind him.'

'Copy,' Orlando said. 'Should be there in one minute.'

Quinn counted off the seconds in his head. At forty-nine, Orlando spoke again.

'Okay, I'm almost to you,' she whispered. 'I'm going to give him a look to let him know I'm onto him.'

Quinn could hear her footsteps on the path outside. They passed by the entrance to the observation area, then stopped. A second later there was a second set of steps, quicker, heavier.

'Why are you following me?' Orlando said.

The other steps stopped, but the follower hadn't gone far enough. If Quinn popped out now, the man would see him for sure.

'Who are you?' she said.

'That's funny,' a male voice said. 'That was my question for you.'

'That's none of your business.'

'Not a big deal. I was only mildly curious anyway.'

There was a pause, then the all too familiar *thup* of a bullet passing through a suppressor.

# 19

Before Quinn could rush out of the structure, there was a second *thup*. Once out of his hiding place, the first thing he saw was Orlando.

She was on one knee, her back resting against the observation pit wall. Lying on the ground in front of her was the man, a bright red spot growing in the center of his chest.

'Are you okay?' Quinn asked Orlando.

She looked up. There was blood on her neck and left shoulder. She'd been hit at the point where her neck curved into her shoulder, but it looked like the bullet had passed through cleanly. Orlando had one of her hands over it, applying pressure.

'Check him,' she said.

'Don't have to,' Quinn said.

'Good.'

Quinn looked around. For the moment, no one seemed to have noticed them.

'We've got to get you out of here,' he said. 'Nate, where are you?'

'I was tailing the other guy like you wanted,' Nate said. 'He's heading over toward BCAM.' The Broad Contemporary Art Museum.

'I need you here now.'

'Copy.'

Quinn glanced at Orlando. 'Will you be okay for a minute? I need to move him.'

'Sure,' she said, her voice weak.

Quinn patted the man down, looking for anything that might ID him, but the man's pockets were all empty. Quinn then slipped his arms under the dead man's shoulders and pulled the corpse over to the observation pit and through the gate. The body left a nice trail of blood. Quinn went back and kicked as much dirt over it as he could. Before he finished, Nate arrived.

'Cover this up somehow,' Quinn said. 'Leaves, dirt, whatever.'

While Nate did that, Quinn checked on Orlando. He moved her hand to get a better look. Though the top of her shirt was soaked, the bleeding seemed to have slowed.

'I'll be fine,' she said.

'I know you will,' he told her. 'Hang on for just a few more minutes, okay?'

She nodded.

Quinn motioned for Nate to follow him into the observation area.

'You shoot him, or Orlando?' Nate asked.

'She did,' Quinn said. 'Grab his legs.'

'What's the plan?'

Quinn made a motion with his hand, mimicking moving the body over the top of the railing at the edge of the pathway and into the pit. They each grabbed an end of the corpse.

'This guy weighs a ton,' Nate said.

Quinn couldn't argue with that.

Once they got him on top of the railing, a simple push forward sent the body tumbling over the side. Their aim turned out pretty good. The body landed in the tar near the end closest to the pathway, and therefore out of sight from anyone who might take a peek through the fence. If they were lucky, it might be several days or even weeks before the body was found.

Once the gate was relocked, and Orlando had donned Nate's jacket to hide her wound, they headed back to the car. As Quinn helped Orlando into the front seat, Nate headed for the driver's door.

'You're in back,' Quinn said. 'I'll drive.'

But before Nate even moved, Orlando said, 'It's almost time for the meet.'

'It's canceled,' Quinn said.

'It's not, and you know it. Besides, that other guy I saw might be getting into position to kill Primus. You can't let that happen.'

'It's Peter's problem.'

'And we're working for Peter, so it's our problem. You're just concerned about me. If I was anyone else, the op would still go on.'

'Hell yes, I'm concerned about you!'

'Does Nate know where to take me?'

Before Quinn could say anything, Nate said, 'The Westwood facility?'

Quinn pressed his lips together, then nodded.

'Then I'll be fine,' Orlando said. 'But not if you keep arguing. I only have so much blood.'

Quinn stared at her, then took a step back, his hand still on the open passenger door. Orlando was pissing him off, but she was right. 'I'll call ahead.'

Orlando smiled as best as she could. 'Be careful.'

Quinn looked at Nate. 'Keep me informed.'

259

'I will,' his apprentice said, then climbed behind the wheel.

Quinn watched until they were out of sight before turning back and reentering the park.

★ ★ ★

Time was becoming his enemy more than anything else. The meet was only ten minutes away, and he still hadn't found the second man.

Maybe he'd seen his partner go down, and had decided the situation was too hot to hang around. But for a professional, the loss of a team member shouldn't have mattered. The mission would take precedence. And given the circumstances, it was best to assume the guy was a pro.

Quinn checked his watch once more. Eight minutes to go. Just enough time to check the central court again. He headed toward the ramp at the west end of the lake leading up to the central court level, but he slowed before he got there.

There was another way up from this side, one few members of the public used. To the right of the ramp was an asphalt path lined by grass and bushes, and squeezed between the lower level of the Bing Building on the left and the lower level of the Japanese art pavilion on the right. It only went about one hundred feet in, then stopped. And there, surrounded by tall bushes, was the alternate route up, a metal staircase that curved around itself until it reached the central court.

Quinn veered down the path, ready to pull out his gun at the first sign of trouble.

There were windows along the ground level of the Bing Building. Most were covered with shades, but a few were uncovered enough to see the offices beyond. As he neared the end of the pathway, he noticed a chain strung across the staircase. There was a sign mounted on a metal stand posted in front of it. The intent was clear enough. The stairway was closed.

He progressed only a few feet farther when he heard a door to his left open. Instinctively his hand moved under his sports coat, his fingers wrapping around the butt of his pistol. But he didn't pull the weapon out, holding position until he could assess the threat.

A security guard emerged from the building and started walking toward him.

'Excuse me, sir,' the man said. 'Can I help you?'

'I was just going to take the stairs up,' Quinn said as he returned his hand to his side.

'I'm sorry, sir. The stairs aren't open to the public today. If you'll just return the way you came and take the ramp up, that's the quickest way from here.'

'It used to be open, though, didn't it?' Quinn asked. 'I remember taking it in the past.'

'It's closed today, sir.'

Quinn smiled. 'Sorry to have bothered you.'

'No problem. Have a good day.'

The guard stayed where he was as Quinn turned and began retracing his steps along the pathway. That was a good thing. In fact it was very possible it had been the only thing that kept Quinn alive. For in the bushes near the base of the stairs, Quinn had seen him. The man in the suit.

He had somehow gotten past the security guard's gaze, and was lying in wait. All he would need to do was to slip under the chain barrier and climb up the stairs at the appropriate time to catch Quinn and Primus together.

Only now Quinn knew he was there. And the suit had to assume the same.

Quinn walked rapidly back into the central court, then glanced at his watch. 11:57 a.m.

He only had three minutes until the meet time, and he had failed to neutralize the suit. Not good.

There was a tiny voice in the back of his mind that said maybe the men in the suits had been with Primus. His protection team. *Maybe*. But it seemed even more probable to Quinn that, like the assassin in Ireland, they had been sent to derail the meeting and permanently remove Primus.

Quinn would just be collateral damage. A necessary hit, but a nameless body representing those Primus was working with. It would be Primus who was the big prize. With him gone, the pipeline of information would be sealed.

Quinn ran into the central court. Unlike the sparse crowd Nate had described earlier, there were several dozen people there now, many in line to buy tickets, while others milled around waiting for the museum doors to open at noon. Most of the tables were also occupied. People having early lunches or drinking cups of coffee. Some in groups chatting, others alone reading the paper or sipping their drinks. A few children were even running around.

Quinn scanned those close by, but no one matched what he was looking for. Dark salmon polo shirt and jeans. That had been all the description Primus had given Peter.

Quinn moved farther into the crowd, knowing he had to find Primus immediately, before the remaining assassin could get to them.

Dark salmon polo shirt.

He glanced over at the ticket lines. There seemed to be an equal mix of men and women, most older, retirement age. Noon on a weekday, most of the younger set was too busy working toward their first heart attacks to visit a museum.

Dark salmon.

*Goddammit!*

There were several polo shirts, but the majority were either blue or black or white. None salmon colored.

His gaze moved toward the Ahmanson Building, scanning toward the right.

Dark salmon polo —

There.

His gaze zeroed in on the back of a man at the far end of the central court. A polo shirt that looked almost brown but could pass for dark salmon. The guy's black hair was trimmed short and had more than a hint of silver running along the sides and across the back. And on the top there was very little hair at all. Fifties, maybe, or a youthful sixty.

He was headed toward the northwest exit. *Primus?*

Quinn glanced over his shoulder to see if he could spot the suit, but there was no sign of the potential assassin. Ahead, polo shirt had picked up his pace and was nearing the path between the buildings that would take him out of sight.

Quinn weaved through the growing crowd, his own pace a step below a jog.

'Sorry,' he said as he sidestepped a couple who'd moved into his way.

Primus was only a few steps away from disappearing around the corner. Quinn started running, acting as though he was trying to catch up with a friend. It seemed to work. People moved out of his way, but few even gave him a second glance.

As the gap closed, the man must have heard Quinn, for he glanced over his shoulder, the look on his face a mixture of anger and worry.

'Hey,' Quinn said, sounding like a friend. 'Glad I caught you. It's been a long time.'

Primus slowed, allowing Quinn to catch up.

'Peter sent me,' Quinn said in a low voice.

'I know who you are,' Primus said through unmoving lips. 'But the meet's off.'

Quinn had a flash of Orlando kneeling next to the dead man by the observation pit, her shirt soaking with her own blood.

'I don't think so,' he said.

Primus's eyes narrowed. 'You come rushing in, not caring who notices you. You could have gotten us both killed. We're through here.'

'No,' Quinn said as he clamped his hand on Primus's arm. 'We're not.'

The man tried to pull it back, but Quinn was

264

in much better shape. In fact, Quinn would have wagered that the man hadn't been in a gym in thirty years. He was carrying a spare tire around his waist that, at the very least, would get a small car to the next gas station.

'Stop it,' the man said. 'Let go of me.'

Quinn ignored the suggestion. Gripping tightly just above Primus's left elbow, he pulled the man around so they were walking back into the central court area.

'What the hell do you think you're doing? I said let go of me.'

Quinn glanced at the man, then returned his gaze to the crowd, scanning for trouble.

'I'm trying to save your life,' Quinn said. 'So I would appreciate it if you would shut the hell up.'

# 20

Primus seemed intelligent enough to know when to speak and when to follow directions. He allowed Quinn to lead him through the central court area and down the walkway that led out to the sidewalk along Wilshire Boulevard.

If this had been New York, in no time they'd have been sitting in the back of a cab heading safely away. But this was L.A., where if you wanted a taxi you had to call for one, then wait at least twenty minutes until it arrived. So they were on foot until Quinn could secure a ride.

There was a crosswalk to the left of the LACMA entrance. A small group of people were already waiting at the curb, several leaning forward, anticipating the changing of the traffic light on Wilshire. A second later the pedestrians got their green light to cross the street.

'Come on,' Quinn said.

He yanked the man toward the street. The red palm that meant wait started blinking in the crosswalk signal just as they stepped off the curb.

'Faster.'

Primus complied, matching Quinn stride for stride.

They had already passed the divider in the middle of the road and were halfway across the two eastbound lanes when something whizzed through the air several feet to the left of Quinn's head.

'What the fuck was that?' Primus said, his step faltering.

Quinn knew exactly what it was, but this wasn't the time for talk. Instead, he pushed Primus to the right. Another bullet flew behind them, and a woman's voice cried out in pain. And then screams everywhere.

Quinn pulled Primus to the right, altering their path again, before reaching the curb.

'Jesus,' Primus said. 'Someone's shooting at us!'

Quinn held on tight, willing the man to remain calm. Just beyond the sidewalk was one of the older parking lots used by LACMA.

'Follow me,' Quinn said.

He guided Primus between the parked cars, then pulled Primus behind a Ford SUV and stopped. Quinn peered through the vehicle's windows toward the museum. There was no one on the street. The pedestrians had scattered when the attack began.

Since the bullets had come at a downward angle, Quinn scanned the roofline of the Bing Building looking for the other suit. He spotted him almost at once. The man was hidden behind one of the small concrete blocks that decorated the roofline. But either he was a lousy shot, or he'd just reached the roof as Quinn and Primus began crossing the street and was rushed.

'That was meant for me, wasn't it?' Primus said.

Quinn glanced over, then followed Primus's gaze back toward the street.

The woman who had been hit was leaning

267

against the back side of a large metal utility box near the corner. It was just big enough to shield her and the man with her from the shooter. The man, her husband perhaps, was talking to her as he pressed his hand down on her wound. She seemed to still be conscious, but she would need medical attention very soon.

'I think it might have been meant for both of us,' Quinn said.

He looked back at the roof where the assassin had been, but he was gone.

Sirens, dozens of them, wailed their way toward LACMA. The assassin would have heard them sooner up where he had been, and realized it was time to cut out.

'Let's go,' Quinn said. He started to turn, but Primus stopped him.

'We're going to get shot!' he said.

'He's gone,' Quinn told him.

'Gone?' Primus glanced at the building, then back at Quinn. 'How can you be sure?'

'You hear the sirens?'

The man nodded.

'He's gone. Now come on.'

'What if you're wrong?'

'I was right about getting you the hell out of there, wasn't I?' Quinn said.

Primus looked at Quinn for a moment, then nodded.

★　★　★

Fearing the whole museum complex, including the parking lots across the street, would go into lockdown the moment the police arrived, Quinn led Primus into the neighborhood farther south of Wilshire, then over to Olympic before heading west toward Fairfax.

He found what he was looking for near the intersection with San Vicente Boulevard. Another parking lot, this one serving a Shakey's Pizza at one end and a Starbucks Coffee at the other. There was enough room for maybe forty cars, not huge but big enough.

Quinn concentrated on the cars behind the pizza parlor. The restaurant had no windows along the back, so he could work unobserved. And since it was only a little after noon, most of the car owners would most likely be in the middle of their meals and not returning soon.

It took him under a minute to find a car that was open.

'Get in,' he said to Primus.

'You're going to steal a car?' the man asked like it was the crime of the year.

'Get in,' Quinn said. His tone left no room for further conversation.

Primus climbed in through the driver's door, then maneuvered himself over the center console and into the passenger seat. Quinn followed him in and closed the door.

'Belt up,' he said as soon as he got the engine running.

'You've done this before,' the man said.

'Once or twice.'

Quinn dropped the transmission into reverse, and looked out the rear window as he began to back up. Their new ride was only halfway out of its space when two men came around the corner of the building. Young guys, in slacks and dress shirts. They came to a dead stop at the sight of the car pulling out of the space.

'Shit,' Quinn said.

'What?'

Quinn didn't have time to answer. He hit the accelerator, whipping the car the rest of the way out of the space, just missing the passenger van parked in the next spot. There was a moment's pause as Quinn shoved the car into drive, and the two men continued to stare at them. Then they all began to move at once, the car and the two men.

The men were able to pull level with the rear fender as Quinn reached the exit, but that was as close as they got. Quinn swung to the right and sped off down an apartment-lined street. In his rearview mirror, he could see the men give up running.

*But not the chase*, Quinn thought as he saw one of them pull out a cell phone.

Quinn zigzagged through the streets, moving south, then west, then south until they reached Venice Boulevard. He headed west, keeping pace with other cars and blending in. Soon they would be in Culver City, an independent city with its own police force. A stolen car from Los Angeles would not be high on the priority list of the Culver City PD.

He glanced over at his passenger. Primus had sweat beading on his brow and balding dome. His right hand was rubbing the spot on his left arm Quinn had been holding on to, a grimace of pain on his face.

'You all right?' Quinn asked.

'Fine,' the man said.

'Good. We agree on that,' Quinn said, knowing Primus would have been dead without him.

He slipped his hand into the interior pocket of his jacket and retrieved a square piece of plastic, half the length of a business card, and a quarter-inch thick.

'What's that?' the man asked.

Quinn glanced over again, but said nothing.

The answer to the question was, 'A digital recorder,' but if Primus was too stupid to figure it out on his own, Quinn wasn't going to enlighten him.

There were a couple of buttons along the top. Quinn pushed one of them, then wedged the square into the partially opened, unused ashtray, mic facing out.

'Time to talk,' Quinn said.

'I told you the meet is off.' The man looked out the window. 'In fact, you can just drop me off here.'

Quinn whipped the car to the right, ignoring the honks from the car he cut in front of, then brought them to a sudden stop at the curb. He reached over and turned off the digital recorder, then pulled his gun out of his shoulder holster and rested it in his lap below window level. One pull of the trigger and Primus would be looking for a new way to digest his food.

The sudden stop must have surprised Primus, for he hadn't moved an inch.

'You want out? Fine,' Quinn said. 'But the step you take onto the curb will be your last.'

'W-What?'

'Who are you?'

The man's gaze flicked from Quinn's eyes to the gun and back. 'You shoot me and you'll lose everything that I know.' The words came out slow, as if the man were trying them out as he spoke.

'True,' Quinn said, the gun unmoving. 'But at the moment it would be pretty damn satisfying.'

Quinn continued to stare at the man, daring him to give a reason to pull the trigger. After only a few seconds, the man turned away.

'So, are you leaving or are you staying?' Quinn asked.

The man mumbled something.

'What?'

'Staying.'

Quinn stared at him for a few seconds longer, then pulled the car back out into traffic, aiming the gun away from his passenger only after they were in the flow with the other cars.

He reached over and turned the recorder back on.

'Let's start with a simple one,' Quinn said. 'Who are you?'

'No,' the man said. 'That's not part of the deal. It has nothing to do with what I know.'

'It'll tell us how serious to take it.'

Quinn could feel the man tense beside him. 'That gunman back at the museum should have told you that.'

'You could have set it up,' Quinn said. 'To convince us.'

'You think I'd — ' He stopped himself.

For half a minute neither of them spoke. Then the man said, 'My name isn't going to tell you if the information is any good.'

'Then tell me something that will.'

Again, silence.

'I know who you are,' the man said.

'Don't count on it.'

The man let out a small laugh. 'You're that cleaner.'

Quinn kept his eyes forward and his left hand lying across the grip of his pistol, his outward demeanor as cool as ever.

'Quinn,' Primus said. 'Jonathan Quinn.'

Quinn did nothing to confirm or deny.

'You were in Singapore last September. Right?'

Quinn remained quiet.

'You had an unfortunate encounter with an assassin. I believe she killed a friend of yours.'

'Who the hell are you?'

'Me?' the man said. 'I'm one of the ones she worked for.'

273

# 21

How he kept from pulling the trigger of his SIG,
Quinn never knew. He wanted to. He wanted to
so much that his index finger ached from desire.
He wanted to see the expression on Primus's
face as one of Quinn's bullets shredded the
man's insides.

If he was who he said he was . . . if he was in
charge of the assassin who had killed Quinn's
friend Steven Markoff the year before in a quest
to do the same to a U.S. congressman, then he
was right. The only thing keeping him alive was
the information in his head.

And if he was who he said he was, it meant
one other thing, too.

He was a member of the LP.

Only why would the LP be trying to work *with*
the DDNI and Peter?

A year before, Quinn hadn't even heard of the
group, and now here they were again. While his
knowledge of the organization had grown in the
last year, it was still limited. That first time he'd
crossed them, Peter had told him all he knew:
that the LP was a shadow organization working
from both within and without the U.S.
government, that they had their own agenda, a
desire to use the government for their own gains,
taking an active hand in ensuring that their
investments would flourish. Conveniently, those
investments seemed to be wrapped up in the

274

defense and security industries. So the LP's main tools for keeping those industries flourishing was destabilization and the occasional bout of chaos.

After his encounter with the LP in Singapore, Quinn had wanted to learn more. So with Orlando's help, he began subtly nosing around. It wasn't long before they both suspected the LP's financial angle was a means, not the end, and that the desire for power, real political power, was the main objective. And to achieve this, they'd inject a bit of chaos and instability throughout the world whenever they felt it necessary.

Though Orlando couldn't prove it with facts, she'd uncovered enough to know the LP played a large role in the Asian market crisis of the late 1990s. And that was only the beginning. It had only been a test for what both she and Quinn now suspected was a grander scheme, one that began the previous year. Soaring gas prices, an American mortgage crisis, then the collapse of Fannie Mae and Freddie Mac — the publicly traded, federal mortgage organizations that had a hand in trillions of dollars of American home loans, both bought out mid-crisis by the U.S. government. And it didn't end there. Financial institutions, near self-implosion, sold to other institutions for bargain-basement prices. Countrywide, Lehman Brothers, Merrill Lynch. A consolidation of power, and chaos for the everyday man.

The only question was, what was their endgame? Because it certainly seemed like they were moving toward something. But neither Quinn nor Orlando could come up with an answer. So Quinn had turned over what they'd learned to Peter, then moved on.

According to Peter, he'd been unable to connect any more dots. He needed someone who had knowledge of the details. Someone who knew the LP, was maybe even a part of it. But no one had ever officially been identified as a member of the organization, so there had been no one to interrogate. Worse yet, most high-level government members didn't even believe the LP existed.

DDNI Jackson had been one of the few believers. And the revelation of Primus's connection to the LP at least cleared up in Quinn's mind why the DDNI had been so actively involved. The DDNI would have had to proceed with caution, but here was a potential source *within* the organization itself, someone who could shed light on the true mission of the LP.

Quinn glanced at the man, his eyes hard and angry. 'Name,' he said.

'I told you, you don't need my name.'

Quinn adjusted the gun in his hand, making sure his movement was broad enough to draw the attention of his passenger. Since he was keeping his eyes on the road, he didn't see the man look at the weapon, but he did feel Primus shift in his seat, his sense of superiority come down a notch.

'I will kill you,' Quinn said. 'I don't give a shit about whatever information you have. If you

276

don't answer my questions, I will kill you. Is that clear?'

A hesitation, then, 'Your boss at the Office won't be too happy if you did.'

'I don't care. I will *kill* you. Right where you're sitting. Do. You. Understand. Me?'

'Yes.'

'Then answer the question.'

He could hear the man take a deep breath, then let it out.

'Hardwick,' the man said. 'My . . . my name is James Hardwick.'

A tickle in the back of Quinn's mind. He had heard the name before.

As if in confirmation, Hardwick said, 'We've met before, you know.'

Quinn didn't respond, but he knew. It wasn't recently. Hell, not even in the last ten years. It was back when Quinn was still an apprentice for his mentor, Durrie.

A stuffy room . . . in Jordan . . . Amman.

The target had been an arms dealer who had crossed the wrong people. Durrie and Quinn weren't there to remove the body. Their client wanted the body found. They were there to remove any evidence that might have been left by those who had done the killing.

Hardwick had been in that room. He'd sat in the corner as others did the briefing. Only once did he speak. He'd been asked to elaborate on something one of his colleagues had said. He spoke for maybe thirty seconds, then went silent again. Quinn had the clear impression at the time that the man was a desk jockey, not an operative, brought along as an information source only.

Until that afternoon, those thirty seconds in Jordan were the last words Quinn had heard the man speak. Hardwick had been thinner then, with a lot more hair. He had also been CIA. So how long had he been splitting his loyalty between the Agency and the LP?

'You remember, don't you?' Hardwick said.

Quinn pulled into the center turn lane, then made a left onto the small road that ran along the east side of the old Helms Bakery Building. He only stayed on it for a moment before turning left into a small parking lot next to an art gallery. There were half a dozen open spots along the Venice Boulevard side. He chose one in the middle of the group, pulling in as close to the car on the right side as he could so it would be impossible for Hardwick to open his door and flee.

As he turned to Hardwick, he switched the gun from his left to his right hand, the barrel never moving from its target. With his free hand, he reached over to the digital recorder. He pulled it out of its resting place, then took a quick glance at the display screen to make sure it was still running. Satisfied, he shoved it back into the ashtray.

'Okay. What is it?' Quinn asked.

Hardwick's brow creased, a question on his face.

'The information you have for us. What is it?'

Hardwick nodded, then leaned back against the passenger door like he was trying to put as

278

much room between himself and the gun as possible. 'All right.' He paused. 'At first we weren't sure what was happening.'

'We?' Quinn asked. 'The CIA?'

'I'm not CIA anymore. I haven't been with the Agency for over six years. NSA now.'

'Sorry. I haven't been keeping up with your career.'

'You'll check me out anyway and find out soon enough. I work directly with the National Security Advisor.'

'You still haven't answered my question. I don't think 'we' was in reference to the NSA, or am I wrong?'

Hardwick stared at Quinn for a moment. 'You know you're not wrong.'

'Then say it.'

'What? That the information I have has been developed by . . . an outside organization?'

Quinn stared at Hardwick.

'Do you want what I have to tell you or not?'

Quinn said nothing.

'Then I can continue?'

A single nod.

'At first we didn't know what was happening. In fact, we still don't know everything. But something bad is about to go down. That is, unless your people do something to stop it.'

'Why haven't you tried to stop whatever it is?' Quinn said.

'We are not . . . equipped in that way.'

'You could have used your NSA resources. Gotten word to the right people.'

'Better to keep this separate,' Hardwick said.

Quinn snorted, but motioned for Hardwick to continue.

'I chose Los Angeles to meet for a reason,' Hardwick said. 'Enough time has been wasted, but this is the last time I do any of the work for you.'

'I'm sure we can arrange a medal for you later,' Quinn said.

A perfunctory smile from Hardwick. 'North-east of here there is a facility. It used to be military, but that was decades ago. Though the facility was transferred to civilian use, it has remained very hush-hush. Even the locals don't know about it. Not that there are really that many locals around. The government called it Yellowhammer.'

'Where exactly is it?'

'You can figure that out yourself,' Hardwick said. 'Shall I go on?'

Quinn held his tongue and nodded.

'The lease has recently been transferred to a corporation out of Portland, Oregon, called Cameron-Kadash Industries. I give you the name only because you will undoubtedly want to check what I'm going to tell you. There is no such organization in Portland, or anywhere else for that matter. It does not exist. Not as an actual company, that is. The facility *has* been occupied. And there is something going on there. I don't know what specifically, but its purpose seems pretty clear.'

When Hardwick didn't go on, Quinn said, 'What purpose?'

Hardwick seemed to think for a moment, then

said, 'I should back up a step. Last fall we were approached by a group who thought we might be interested in helping them with a project they had. As you might expect, we get these kind of offers from time to time.'

'I'm sure.'

Another smile. 'This particular idea would affect multiple nations.'

'In what way?'

'Fear, panic, maybe a little chaos, too.'

'All things you at the LP love.'

'Don't think for one minute you understand us,' Hardwick snapped. 'What you know is so little that it's the same as knowing nothing. You are in *no* position to make judgments about us. You have no idea what we are really about.'

'Then tell me what you're really about. I'd be more than happy to listen.'

'That's not what this meeting's about.'

'Of course not,' Quinn said, not hiding his contempt.

Hardwick ignored the response, and picked up where he left off. 'We strung them along for a little while, enough to learn a little more about what they were planning. But when they realized we weren't serious, they broke off contact. I felt it was necessary to keep tabs on them. If they were really going to move forward, it would serve my group well to have advance warning.'

'The LP ready to take advantage of the situation. That's nice,' Quinn said.

'Despite what you think, we have the best interests of the country at the front of every decision we make. I *am* the one bringing this to

281

your attention. Don't forget that.'

'And do your friends know you're doing this?' Quinn asked.

Hardwick paused, then shook his head. 'No.'

Quinn could see that Hardwick wanted to tell him more, but he remained silent.

'All right,' Quinn said. 'So you're acting on your own. We can go with that for the moment. But you still haven't told me anything useful.'

Hardwick glanced at the gun. 'Do you mind? I keep thinking your finger might slip.'

'If this goes off, it won't be because my finger slipped.' But Quinn moved the end of the barrel a few inches to the left so that it was aimed at the door instead of Hardwick's midsection.

'I don't find that ver — '

He was cut off by a low hum.

'What's that?' he asked.

Double-buzz-pause-double-buzz.

It was Quinn's phone, the pattern indicating Nate was on the other end. Quinn knew he should ignore it, but it would be about Orlando, and he had to know she was okay.

'Don't move or say anything,' Quinn said.

Hardwick shrugged, then nodded.

Quinn retrieved his phone and touched the Accept button.

'Yes?' he said.

'Is everything all right?' Nate asked.

'As best as can be expected.'

'The news is broadcasting a report that police have the museum area cordoned off and are looking for at least one man with a gun. Are you still there?'

'No.'

'What about the meet?'

'It's . . . ongoing.'

'He's there with you?'

'Yes,' Quinn said. 'What about . . . ?'

'Orlando?' Nate said, guessing what Quinn meant. 'She's pissed and has a raging headache, but the doctor gave her something that should deal with the pain. Told us it should kick in soon. He also said the wound was more of a graze than anything too serious. She's not going to be able to turn her head for a little while, but other than that, he thinks she'll be okay.'

Some of the tension left Quinn's face. 'Excellent.'

'The doctor wants her to stay overnight.'

'She must love that.'

'It wasn't quite what she wanted to hear,' Nate said. 'Where are you?'

'Not too far away,' Quinn said.

'I'm not sure where I'd find that on a map.'

Once again, Nate was acting in the exact way Quinn had trained him. Covering his partner whether he wanted him to or not. It was more proof that Nate was going to make it hard for Quinn not to keep him on. If Orlando had been around, she wouldn't have said 'I told you so' out loud, but the look on her face would have conveyed it just the same.

'Look, I'll call you soon,' Quinn said. His words told Nate to call him every ten minutes until Quinn gave him the all-clear code.

'Problems?' Hardwick asked.

'I believe you were about to give me some hard information.'

Hardwick smiled. 'Who were you talking to? That kid who helps you? Or was it your woman friend?'

Quinn's anger spiked. In less than two seconds his right hand was wrapped around Hardwick's neck, squeezing tightly.

'Please,' Hardwick said, his voice a low croak. 'I can't breathe.'

'That's a lie, Mr. Hardwick. If you couldn't breathe, you couldn't talk.'

'Please,' Hardwick repeated.

Quinn held on until he was sure Hardwick couldn't get any air into his lungs, then he let go.

Hardwick gasped, then coughed as he rubbed a hand over his throat. 'Jesus Christ.' His voice was raspy and strained. 'I'm doing you a fucking favor! You know what? Forget it. We're done here. Done.'

He started to open the door, but stopped when he realized he could only open it a few inches.

'We're done after you finish telling me what you need to tell me,' Quinn said.

'Fuck you,' Hardwick said.

The skin on his brow turned red in anger, and his eyes looked like they were on fire. But when he didn't make any move, Quinn knew he wasn't going to do anything stupid. At least, not too stupid.

'Talk,' Quinn said.

Hardwick breathed deeply, his shoulders moving up and down each time air passed over his lips. After several seconds the rhythm slowed, and the color of his skin mellowed.

'Fine. I'll tell you,' he said. 'Then you'll let me out of this car, and you and your boss will never hear from me again.'

'You forget, I know where you work.'

'That's what you think,' Hardwick said.

'What does that mean?'

But Hardwick only stared back at Quinn.

'All right, then talk,' Quinn said. 'You can start with who this group is that approached you.'

'As far as I know, they don't have a name, just a plan of action.'

'What kind of plan?'

'I'm afraid I can't help you with that, either. Until we signed on in full, they weren't going to tell us everything. And since we didn't sign on . . . '

'Convenient.'

'I do have a name for you.'

Quinn looked at him, waiting.

'I passed an itinerary of one of their agents on to the DDNI. His travel schedule is very intense, and his destinations . . . unusual. Again, what he was doing we were unable to discover. I was hoping the DDNI, or I guess your friend at the Office now, would have been able to figure something out from it already.'

'Couldn't you have done that with your own resources?'

'Perhaps. But this isn't our number one priority.'

'Care to tell me what priority number one is for the LP right now?'

285

'Maybe some other time.'

'You said you had a name,' Quinn said.

'Yes. A freelancer. He's been around a few years. Our guess is he's handling security for the group. We suspect he's only doing this for money.'

'So not the name of one of the principals, then.'

'No,' Hardwick said. 'That I don't have. But this person might be a way in.'

'The name?'

'Tucker.'

Quinn could feel the hair on his forearms begin to rise. 'Do you have a first name?'

'Leonard. Goes by Leo.'

*Son of a goddamn bitch*, Quinn thought.

Tucker was someone he knew. Someone who had no right to be walking around. By all rights, Quinn should have killed him in Berlin a year and a half earlier. He'd had a hand in the kidnapping of Orlando's son. But they had made a deal, the boy's location for his life.

'You know him?' Hardwick asked.

Quinn ignored the question. 'Yellowhammer? Leo Tucker? And, what? That's it? Just hearsay from a member of the LP about some nameless group and an operation you have no details on? That's all you can give me? Is this what got your men killed in Ireland? And DDNI Jackson. He's dead because of this, too.'

'Jackson's death didn't have anything to do with what we uncovered. I'm sure he had a lot of people who wanted him dead. Somebody got to him and stuffed him into the trunk of their car.'

286

'Jackson died in the tunnel below one of the apartment buildings on your list in New York.'

'What are you talking about?' If Hardwick was red before, he was all white now. Quinn's revelation was apparently news to him, bad news.

'I found him myself in an old equipment room off a tunnel that ran below the building. The rats got to him first.'

Hardwick's right hand began to shake. 'Jesus.'

'What's wrong? Hitting a little too close to home? I think you need to tell me everything. Might be your only chance to stop them from coming after you.'

'I've . . . I've told you everything. I swear. If there was more, I would give it to you.'

'Is Yellowhammer where this supposed attack is going to take place? Or just a staging location?'

'I don't know.'

'What are they planning?'

'I don't know.'

'What's the target?'

'I . . . ' There was something in Hardwick's eyes.

'You know what it is.' As Quinn spoke, his phone began to vibrate in his pocket. This time he ignored it.

'No . . . I don't. I don't know.'

Quinn raised his gun a few inches. 'Tell me.'

'I . . . I . . . ' Hardwick shifted uncomfortably in his seat. 'This is only a guess. No one has told me *anything*.'

'Then tell me your guess.'

'Can I show you?'

Quinn's eyes narrowed. 'How?'

Hardwick reached into his front pants pocket and pulled out a folded piece of white paper. He hesitated for a second, then handed it to Quinn.

'The timing and proximity seem . . . advantageous.'

Quinn unfolded the paper. It was a news article printed from the Internet. And at the top, the headline:

## G-8 SUMMIT BEGINS SATURDAY CALIFORNIA'S HEARST CASTLE READY TO PLAY HOST

# 22

The son of a bitch kicked Hardwick out of the car right there in the parking lot, then drove off. Hardwick almost dug out his cell phone and called the cops to tell them he'd spotted a car he suspected was stolen. But that would have been counterproductive. Hardwick needed everything to stay on course. Quinn, Mr. Rose, the Office, Chercover, they all had parts still to play, and he had to make sure they performed as he'd planned.

The reason why was simple. The LP's main directive counted on it, the reason why they were in existence at all. His manipulation of events would bring the goal of the organization that much closer to reality. It wouldn't be long now, Hardwick knew that much. And God willing, he would be one of the lucky ones who'd still be around when the LP's ultimate objective was realized.

It was all because a couple of intelligent patriots — what else could you call them? — foresaw a future where America's power would begin to slip, where its position at the top of the economic ladder would no longer be secure. They knew they couldn't let this happen, realizing even then that democracy wasn't as important as two cars in the garage, a refrigerator full of food, and a yearly vacation at the beach. One only needed to look at China's resurgence to see how well that was working.

So they recruited like-minded intellectuals and formed what would one day become known as the LP. They spent years drafting their plan, then doing everything they could to make it a reality. And now, a half-century later, the LP's figurehead was in place, and already making a name for himself. In a few years, when he announced the creation of a serious third-party challenge to the status quo, the country would be ready, and would beg him to take command. The years the LP had spent fueling the polarization between the Democrats and the Republicans would finally pay off. That, combined with the softening of the electorate toward the acceptance of a third party that the LP had been fostering since before the Nixon administration, would create an atmosphere ripe for political revolt. In electing the LP's man, the public would feel like they'd accomplished something for once, when in reality all they would have done is exactly what they were manipulated into doing.

After the LP's candidate took the oath of office, suddenly the nations that had taken a hard line against the U.S. but were really under the control of the LP would start falling in line. Then the economic roller coaster the Western world had been stuck in would level off thanks to the LP's grip on the financial institutions it had had a hand in re-creating during the great banking consolidation in 2008.

And once all that had occurred, the country wouldn't even blink an eye when presidential term limits were repealed. It was just a matter of time now. Time that could be measured in years, not decades. Soon the LP would achieve the goals its founders had set out at the beginning: not only controlling the United States of America, but also nearly twenty percent of the rest of the world.

The realization that they were so close calmed Hardwick. He pulled out his phone, but not to call the cops on Quinn.

'It's me,' he said when his boss picked up the other end.

'How did it go?' Chairman Kidd said.

'I don't think he was happy to learn who I worked for,' Hardwick said.

'Do you think it was a mistake?'

'No. He needed to know. It'll help him believe later.'

'Maybe. But I'm not so sure.'

'Doesn't matter now.'

'No, I guess not,' Chairman Kidd said. There was a pause. 'Do you think he'll follow through?'

'He'll tell the Office. He has to. And they'll tell their clients. Chercover won't let it drop. He may not have cared about us before, but Deputy Director Jackson was his protégé.'

'Killing him was an inspired idea,' the Chairman said.

'Thank you,' Hardwick said.

The finding of Jackson's body had gone near perfect to how Hardwick had envisioned it. As had the killings in Ireland, and the staged shooting at the museum less than an hour earlier. All had been designed to increase

Chercover's and the Office's belief in the information Hardwick had been passing to them. Now there was only one last thing he had to do, and that would depend on what happened with Yellowhammer.

'Do you think it's almost time to blackball the Office?' Chairman Kidd asked.

'Let's wait and see what Quinn does,' Hardwick said. Forcing the Office out of business was just another step in Hardwick's plan. They'd proved to be a problem for the LP, so using this opportunity to stop them was a no-brainer. 'Once it looks like they've taken our bait, and send him to Yellowhammer, we move. Chercover first, though. Then we blackball the Office.'

'I'm looking forward to it.'

'After that I think it's time for us to go into quiet mode,' Hardwick said.

There was a pause, then Chairman Kidd said, 'Agreed. I'll make sure everyone knows.'

'One other thing,' Hardwick said. 'I've retired as of this moment. Do you think you can arrange things for me?'

'Of course. It's time you became a member of the council anyway.'

Hardwick smiled. Plans within plans, all coming together. 'I would be honored.'

'I'm glad,' the Chairman said. 'I'll be waiting for your final call.'

'The morning after tomorrow. If everything sticks to schedule it should be around 12:30 p.m. your time.'

'Remember, there can be no loose ends.'

'There won't be.'

'Great, a vacation when you're done, then,' Mr. Kidd said. 'Someplace warm.'

'It's like you read my mind.'

'Be careful, James. I'll talk to you soon.'

Hardwick slipped the phone back into his pocket. A vacation did sound like a good idea. But he had to see this through first. And even before that, he needed to find a ride back to his hotel.

*Goddamn Quinn.*

★   ★   ★

Marion awoke to darkness.

At first she thought there might be something covering her eyes. But as her fingers touched her face, she realized nothing was there. *Blind?* No, of course not, she told herself. It was just dark, darker even than the tiny space in the wall of Frau Roslyn's orphanage.

'Iris.' The name slipped from her mouth.

She reached around her bed in the dark trying to find the girl. Not a bed, really. Not even a mattress, more a thick piece of foam. There was no sheet. No blanket.

No Iris.

Marion began working her way across the floor, feeling every inch of the cold concrete surface.

'Iris!' She clung to the hope the child had just wandered off and fallen asleep, but the desperation in her harsh whisper betrayed what she really believed.

Her fingers touched the far wall a half-second before her head did. A spike of white-hot pain lanced her skull, forcing her into a near blackout before she was able to regain control.

She reached out and touched it again, but this time using it as a crutch to help her stand. Her head was still pounding from the blow, but she fought through it, willing herself to push the pain as far away as she could.

'Iris?' she said again.

She finished her search of the floor by shuffling her feet forward. The room wasn't that big. She figured no more than eight feet by ten. She found a door along the wall near the foot of the mattress. It was made of metal, solid, cold, and flush to the floor. There was absolutely no light seeping around the edges.

But other than the door and the mattress and the cold walls, there was nothing else.

Her memories of the last hours — days, maybe? — were sketchy at best. The parking garage she remembered. The man with the accent. But after that nothing was clear. Lights, darkness, a constant hum, someone helping her to walk, then another hum, louder this time, more powerful. Then . . .

Then nothing until now.

She felt around the walls, looking for a window. Maybe there was one that was covered. Or if she *had* gone blind, maybe it was filling the room with light she could not see. Either way, it was a possible route of escape. But there was no window. Nothing but solid wall.

And a door.

And a mattress.

She wanted to lie back down, curl up, and let the tears that were screaming to pour out stream down her face. But she couldn't let herself, she just couldn't.

*Iris.*

Iris needed her. God knows what they had done to the child. If anything happened to Iris, it would be Marion's fault. There was no other way for her to spin it. Iris's life was Marion's to care for, Marion's responsibility. That was what Frau Roslyn expected.

Marion worked her way back to the door and felt for the knob, her palms moving frantically over the surface where it should have been. But there was no knob. She moved her hand along the edges of the door. No hinges, either. It must open outward, she realized.

So she did the only thing she could. She began pounding on the door.

'Help!' she yelled. 'Help!'

Maybe she had been abandoned somewhere. Perhaps no one knew she was there.

'Help!' she screamed again.

Light. Faint, and seeping around the edges of the door. One second it hadn't been there, then the next it was, like someone had flipped a switch.

'Let me out! Please, anyone. Let me out!'

Something banged against the door from the other side, loud and sharp, shocking her into silence.

'Step back,' a muffled voice said. It was male, and not sympathetic.

She shuffled backward and almost tripped over the mattress.

There were several clicks along the right edge of the door, then the distinct sound of a latch opening. Light streamed into the room, stinging Marion's eyes and forcing her to cover them with her hands.

She heard steps, more than she could count, enter the room and approach her. She blinked again and peeked between her fingers. The light coming from behind her visitors was still too bright to make out anything more than several silhouettes. Three? Four?

She never saw the hand that slapped her cheek. It rocked her to the left. Her foot caught on the mattress and she went down to her knees. One of her hands grazed the wall as she tried to stop her fall, but she only bruised her palm and scraped the flesh at the base of her thumb.

Someone reached down, grabbed her, and pulled her to her feet. She tried to cover her face with her hands, not wanting to be slapped again, but her hands were shoved away.

She could see them now. Three, not four. All men. The two nearest her were big and unsmiling and unfamiliar. But the one behind them she had no trouble recognizing. It was the man from the parking garage, the one who had taken her.

He stared at her for a moment, then looked at the man nearest him. 'Let's go,' he said.

The two larger men grabbed Marion by the arms and pulled her toward the door.

'What do you want with me?' she said, voice

trembling. 'What are you going to do?'

No one even looked at her.

'Where's Iris?'

She'd aimed her words at the man from the parking garage, but he remained silent.

'Where is she?'

She tried to plant her feet just short of the doorway, not wanting to go anywhere with them until they answered her questions. But it took only a halfhearted shove from the guy on her left to keep her moving across the threshold and into a narrow hallway.

The corridor was only wide enough for one man to walk beside her, so one of the brutes moved behind her, while the garage man took the lead. There were two light fixtures hanging from the ceiling, metal reflectors with dome wire cages on the bottom. Above them several pipes ran the length of the hallway, covering most of the actual ceiling. As they walked, she kept being bumped into the wall. It was hard and cold like the door of her cell. Metal, she realized.

The garage man opened the door at the end of the hallway, then stepped through. Marion and her escort followed.

They were in another corridor, this one considerably wider. Its walls were also gray and made of metal. *A ship? Maybe military?* There was no sensation of movement, so if it was a ship, they didn't appear to be out at sea. Only something wasn't right.

The doorways, that was it. *Don't navy ships have those doors that sealed shut in case of an emergency?* There were no such doors here. But if she wasn't on a ship, then where was she?

A door ahead opened and two men dressed in military fatigues and armed with rifles stepped out. As Marion and her escort neared, the men moved to the side of the hall, and nodded at the garage man like he was someone important.

Farther down the corridor, another soldier appeared, then another behind him.

Marion could feel her hands and feet go cold.

Whatever hope of escape she'd been clinging to slipped away like it had never been there at all.

★ ★ ★

'Who have you told?' Mr. Rose asked again.

The Dupuis woman was crying now. Tears poured down her cheeks as she wordlessly pleaded with Tucker's boss to stop.

'Who have you told?'

She sobbed. Tucker could see she was trying to get words out, but nothing was coming. Mr. Rose nodded at him.

Tucker turned to one of his men, Linden. 'Give her another.'

Linden touched the controller, and sent another jolt of electricity down the wires attached to the woman. She grew rigid as her muscles contracted, the restraints the only things keeping her from falling to the floor.

When the sequence ended, she slumped in the chair.

'Who have you told?' Mr. Rose asked again.

'Just Henrick Roos,' she said, naming her friend at the UN.

'Who else?'

'Noelle. Noelle Broussard in Côte d'Ivoire. That's all.'

'I don't believe you, Ms. Dupuis. Someone else knows. Someone else has been trying to help you. Who are they?'

She tried to look at him, her eyebrows furrowed. 'I . . . I don't know . . . who you mean. I've been alone. No one has . . . '

Her last words were lost as her head fell forward.

'Who have you told?' Mr. Rose said.

Her shoulders began moving up and down as her tears returned.

'More?' Tucker asked.

Mr. Rose stared at the woman. His face was scarred and wrinkled, his slicked-back hair pure white. On bad days his hands shook so much he had to drink from a straw. But his eyes were always like laser beams, cutting into whatever he was focused on. And his voice, that was the clincher. Strong, manipulative, and unrelenting.

'Who have you told?'

But Marion Dupuis seemed unable to respond.

The laser eyes turned to Tucker. 'Again.'

The woman looked up, her eyes growing wide in fear.

'No. No. I'll — ' But the renewed current cut her off.

This time when the cycle ended, she fell forward against the restraints, unconscious.

'Goddammit,' Mr. Rose said.

Tucker moved in and checked the woman's

pulse. She still had one, which was almost a surprise. They'd been at this for a while now. He'd seen others who hadn't lasted as long, needing to leave in a body bag instead of on their own feet.

And with all they'd given her, she hadn't broken. Whoever the others at her house in Montreal had been, she wasn't telling. The only ones she had given up were her two colleagues at the UN, people who had been easy to trace through other means so were no real revelation. Neither of them had lasted as long as Marion when Tucker had interrogated them.

It was the people in Montreal. If she *did* know who they were, Mr. Rose would find out. And if she didn't, it wouldn't matter anyway. Either result would end in her death. That was the only given here.

'You want me to wake her?' Tucker asked.

Mr. Rose looked at his watch. 'Take her back to her room.'

Tucker nodded at Linden and his partner, Petersen. Both men stepped forward and picked the woman up.

As soon as they were gone, Mr. Rose said, 'I need to get down to the lab to supervise the final preparations.'

'All right,' Tucker said. 'When do you want her back here?'

'Walk with me.'

'Of course,' Tucker said.

Mr. Rose was one of those people who got annoyed if you didn't read his mind, and got even more upset if he changed his mind about a task and you hadn't anticipated it. Tucker didn't like it, but he'd grown used to it. It was the pay that kept him around. Nothing else.

Tucker followed Mr. Rose out of the interrogation room, through a short maze of hallways, then back into the main corridor. The lab of the underground facility was one level below, so Mr. Rose turned left toward the elevator.

'These people you saw in Montreal, do you think there is any chance they might have followed you here?' Mr. Rose asked.

Tucker felt a little like the woman. It wasn't the first time Mr. Rose had asked him the question. It wasn't even the second or the third.

'No way.'

'They concern me.'

'We searched her. Everything she had, everything she was wearing. We even ran her through the scanner. Nothing. No tracking device. No hidden radio transmitter. Nothing.'

Mr. Rose thought about this for a moment. 'You're sure?'

'One hundred percent.'

When they reached the elevator, Tucker pressed the down button to call for a car.

'And the child?' Mr. Rose asked.

'What about her?'

'You did the same with her? Check her clothes? Scanned her?'

This was a new question, but the answer was the same.

'Yes.'

The elevator door opened and Mr. Rose

301

stepped inside. As Tucker stepped in to join him, Mr. Rose said, 'I can't have a loose end like this.'

'I understand.'

Tucker reached out and pushed the button marked R3, the lab level.

'Do you? Do you really understand?' Mr. Rose's laser eyes kept Tucker from answering. 'It's a loose end. A distraction. We don't want or need distractions at this point.' He paused. 'There are people who want to stop me. Your job is to make sure that doesn't happen.'

'I'm well aware of that.'

'That woman,' Mr. Rose said, more to himself than to Tucker. 'She could ruin everything. That . . . that *bitch*!'

Tucker tried to contain his surprise. He'd never seen Mr. Rose react like that before.

'I think I'll use the woman's brat as the trigger.' As Mr. Rose said this, a smile grew on his face. 'Yes, I think that will be an excellent idea.'

The elevator door opened, and Mr. Rose stepped out. Tucker knew to stay where he was.

'Find out who those people in Montreal are,' Mr. Rose said, looking back. 'And make sure they won't be a problem.'

'Yes, sir,' Tucker said.

Mr. Rose turned and walked away.

Alone in the elevator on the ride back up, Tucker wondered if the people in Montreal had let Marion Dupuis run so she could act as bait. It was something he would do.

But even if they had, they wouldn't have

been able to find her now. They would have lost her the minute Tucker's plane left Toronto. Had they kept looking? Or had they just given up?

That's what Tucker needed to find out.

# 23

It took Quinn just over ten minutes to get to the private hospital facility from the old Helms Bakery lot where he'd left Hardwick. It was in Westwood, only a few blocks from the UCLA campus and the famed UCLA Medical Center.

The building itself looked like any of half a dozen other typical medical office buildings in the area. Five stories and bland. Brick on the first floor and concrete the rest of the way up, the whole structure in need of a new coat of paint. There were silver letters across the front. THE LUNDGREN MEDICAL BUILDING.

Quinn circled the block and entered the parking garage behind the building. A sign with an arrow pointing toward a gate at the base of the up ramp read Public Parking, but Quinn bypassed it, instead heading for a different gate at the top of the down ramp. Unlike the public gate that was made of wood and pivoted upward when open, this one was a wire fence that closed off the entire entrance like a see-through curtain. The sign above it read Employees Only.

To the side was a box mounted on a pole at driver's eye level, which housed a keypad and a speaker. Quinn punched in an access code he kept stored in his phone.

'Yes?' a voice said. Male, businesslike.

'Dr. Paul to see Dr. Yamata,' Quinn said, using the code phrase.

'What time is your appointment?'

'My patient's already here.'

'Hold one moment, please.'

The delay lasted fifteen seconds while they no doubt compared his security camera image to the one they had on file, then the gate began to open.

'Please park in spot number seventy-two,' the voice said.

Spot 72 was on lower level three, the same level as the entrance to the facility. As Quinn got out of the stolen car, he saw his BMW parked nearby in spot number 67.

The door to the facility was not marked. Most who saw it wouldn't have given it a second glance. It was painted the same off-white as the rest of the garage.

As Quinn approached it, he felt his cell phone vibrate twice, then stop. A message. He then remembered the call that he had ignored when he'd been with Hardwick. He pulled out his phone and listened to his message.

'Jake, it's Liz. I thought you were going to visit Mom and Dad. I talked to Mom a few minutes ago, and she said you hadn't been there yet. I'm not sure what's keeping you so busy, but could you at least do me a favor and not tell Mom you'll be coming then don't show up?'

Quinn stood in the parking lot for a moment, his eyes closed and his hand rubbing his brow. He had never told his mother when he'd be coming, just that he would be coming soon. The events of the last couple of days had obviously delayed the trip. He should have called her. He made a promise to himself to do it as soon as he had a moment. Liz he wouldn't bother with. She'd never understand anyway.

As he neared the door, he heard a faint click. He turned the knob and stepped into a long hallway that stretched from the garage to the lower level of the Lundgren Building.

A similar door and a similar click greeted him at the other end. Again, he wasted no time passing through it.

Not a hallway this time. A twelve-foot-square room. The off-white was gone, too, replaced by light green walls. If there had been chairs, it would have looked like a waiting room.

A man stood in front of a second door across the room. Broad shouldered, but about Quinn's height. He was wearing a gray suit, jacket unbuttoned. Medical facility or not, the bulge under the man's jacket was not a stethoscope.

'Mr. Quinn,' the man said.

'Yes.'

'You're here about your team member.'

'Yes.'

The man turned and opened the door behind him. 'This way please.'

The facility occupied the three basement levels of the Lundgren Building. It billed itself as a high-end plastic surgery operation. Very private, very discreet. All of which was true. They made plenty of money that way, for sure. But there was another side of the business, a secret side that very few of their employees knew about.

The facility was a medical sanctuary for those whose injuries were best not reported to the local authorities. No unnecessary questions asked, no damaging information given. There were only two conditions for using the facility: one, patients had to come with a recommendation from someone the facility had previously cleared, and two, because their services were anything but cheap, they had to have the ability to pay.

Quinn had long ago been cleared after a recommendation from Peter. In turn, he had later secured access for both Orlando and Nate just in case.

Quinn's guide led him to an open elevator, then pressed the button marked B2.

'How is she?' Quinn asked.

'You'll have to ask the doctor,' the man said.

The car stopped one level up, but the doors didn't open.

The man looked up at a security camera mounted in the corner of the car. Quinn did the same. A second later there was a ding followed by the door sliding open.

'Welcome to Lundgren,' the man said as he let Quinn pass through first.

He led Quinn down several more corridors before stopping in front of a door marked 403.

'She's inside,' the man said, then walked away.

What Quinn found beyond the door was better than he hoped.

Nate was sitting in a chair near the bed, his eyes glued to the TV mounted on the opposite wall. On the screen was an overhead image of LACMA and the La Brea Tar Pits.

'We made it on TV again,' Nate said when he

307

noticed Quinn. 'And by 'us,' I mean you.'

'You really know how to keep a low profile,' Orlando said. She was propped up in the bed. A large bandage covered her neck and shoulder, but she was smiling, so that was a good sign. 'This isn't going to do us much good at getting future work.'

'Well, maybe if you hadn't let yourself get shot, things would have gone smoother,' Quinn said as he stepped over to the bed.

'Now it's *my* fault?'

Quinn shrugged. 'You set the tone.'

They stared at each other for a moment. Then Orlando started to laugh, but stopped suddenly, wincing in pain.

'So humor's not exactly a good idea?' Quinn asked.

'Not at the moment,' she said, her voice tight with pain. 'Are you okay?'

'Me?' he asked. 'I'm fine. You're the one in the bed.'

'I mean the meeting, with Primus. Nate said you were with him when he called.'

'Yeah,' Quinn said.

He glanced at the TV. Orlando followed his gaze.

'What are they saying happened?' Quinn asked Nate.

'Some lunatic with a gun,' Nate said. 'Two people injured.'

'Two?'

'A woman on the street, and a guard inside one of the buildings.'

Quinn nodded. The security officer probably

308

got in the way of the assassin's route to the roof.

'The woman's doing okay, but the guard's in critical.'

'They catch the gunman?' Quinn asked.

'Nope, unless they're not saying.'

Quinn turned back to Orlando. 'How you doing?'

'I'm fine.'

Quinn raised an eyebrow. 'Really?'

'I'm fine,' she said.

Quinn turned to Nate. 'What did the doctor say?'

Nate tore his gaze from the TV. 'That she was lucky it didn't shatter her spine.'

'So what got hit?' Quinn asked.

'Muscle mainly.'

'You said the doctor wants to keep her overnight?'

'Hold on,' Orlando said. 'I'm not staying. You're taking me to your place.'

'She said the same thing to the doctor,' Nate said.

'I mean it. I'm not staying.'

'I think it might be better,' Quinn said.

'I know how to take care of myself,' she said. 'I've gotten hurt a lot worse and not seen anyone. Get me some pain pills and antibiotics and I'll be fine.'

Quinn looked down at the floor. Sleeping here or sleeping at his place wasn't going to make that much difference. If there were any problems, he could get her back here fast enough.

He was about to say as much, when she said, 'Quinn, goddammit, I'm not staying here.'

'Okay,' he said.

'I'm serious.'

'I know you are. I said okay.'

She narrowed her eyes. 'Okay you're going to get me out? Or okay you're listening but you're not going to do anything?'

'Okay I'll take you home.'

She stared at him a moment longer like she wasn't sure she should believe him or not. After several seconds she said, 'Tell us about the meeting.'

Quinn hesitated. It was possible there was no bug in the room; in fact, Quinn thought that very likely. The facility was supposed to be neutral ground, a safe house where no one asked what your business was. If word ever got out that that trust was compromised, then business would disappear. Worse, really. Someone would eventually show up to deal with the double-cross. Still, Quinn wasn't interested in taking the chance.

'Not here,' he said.

'Then get me the hell out.'

★　★　★

Before leaving the medical center, they made arrangements with the head of security to dump the stolen car someplace it wouldn't be found for a few days. By the time they headed back to Quinn's place in his BMW, the sun was starting to set.

On the drive, Quinn told Orlando and Nate about his meeting with Hardwick. There was one thing he did leave out, though. It had been a

310

spur-of-the-moment decision, his thinking that given Orlando's current condition, she didn't need any more stress. She could learn about Leo Tucker's involvement later.

'Yellowhammer?' Orlando said. Her voice was low and sleepy.

'That's what he said.'

'He didn't tell you where it was?'

'Here in California somewhere. Said we should be able to find it easy enough.'

'Does the name mean anything to you?'

Quinn shook his head. 'You?'

'No.' She paused.

There was a momentary lull.

'I'll check it out when we get to your place,' Orlando said.

Quinn gave her a quick sideways glance. She was leaning against the passenger door, her eyes half-closed.

'Nate can do it,' Quinn said. 'You're going to bed.'

'That's sweet, Quinn. But I don't think I'm going to be in the mood.' Even in her near-semiconscious state, she was able to crack a smile.

'Oh, God,' Nate said. 'My ears. I didn't really need to hear that.'

★   ★   ★

Quinn's house was built against one of the many slopes of the Hollywood Hills. The top floor was at street level and contained the living room, dining room, and kitchen in an open format that

311

made it feel almost like one room. The floor below, following the incline of the hill, contained the bedrooms and a gym.

As soon as he got Orlando settled in the master bedroom, he returned upstairs. Nate sat at the kitchen table using Quinn's laptop to try and get a line on Yellowhammer. Quinn didn't want to disturb his progress, so he grabbed his phone and walked to the other end of the living room.

He stood in front of the plate glass window that made up the whole rear wall of this level, and looked out on the city. The L.A. basin glowed white with millions of individual lights, some moving, some stationary, but all adding to the visual mix of the city.

He took a deep breath, then looked down at his phone and called Peter.

'I expected to hear from you hours ago,' Peter said, irritated.

'I had a man down.'

'Jesus,' Peter said. 'I saw the news. The shooting at the museum. Who?'

'Orlando.'

Silence. 'Is . . . is she okay?'

'She'll be sore for a while, but she'll live.'

'What happened?'

Quinn gave him the rundown of the fun at the museum. 'I'm willing to bet it was the same people who hired the assassin in Ireland.'

'I think you're right,' Peter said. 'Tell me about the meeting.'

'You mean the meeting with the guy from the *LP*?' Quinn said with no attempt to hide his anger. 'The goddamn *LP*, Peter. I thought you were working against them, not using them as an information asset.'

More dead air.

'How long have you known?' Quinn asked.

Still no response.

'Peter, how the hell long have you known?'

A chair in the kitchen screeched against the floor. Quinn glanced over and caught Nate looking at him before his apprentice could look away. Nate grabbed an apple off the counter and returned to the laptop.

'Not long,' Peter said.

'That's a bullshit answer.'

'After Ireland, all right?'

Quinn stared out into the night. 'The assassin,' he said.

'Yes,' Peter said. 'Once we ID'd him we realized he was on an LP watch list. We didn't know if he worked for them for sure, but we knew it was a possibility.'

'What happened? He break when you questioned him?'

'He didn't break.'

'Losing your touch?'

'He didn't break because someone got to him before he gave anything up.'

'Someone *got* to him?' Quinn couldn't believe it.

'He wasn't under our control. We handed him over to the DDNI as soon as the plane landed. One of my men worked up the ID kit on the plane. Fingerprints, hair and saliva samples, photos. But by the time we were able to figure out who he was, he was already dead. The Agency stuck him in a supposedly secure safe house, but he didn't even last that first night. A suicide pill slipped to him by one of the agents in the facility. The agent left before anyone knew what happened and hasn't been seen since. The DDNI was furious, but there was nothing he could do. When I confronted him with what I'd found out, he was reluctant at first, but I think he realized he had to close ranks and use only his most trusted assets. Apparently I was one of those.'

'Help me out, Peter,' Quinn said. 'The DDNI was getting information from someone in the LP, and the LP was also trying to kill his messenger and yours? How does that make sense?'

A pause.

'The contact was anonymous. He used some back channels to reach DDNI Jackson directly. Based on who you say Primus is, he could have just walked into the Deputy Director's office and left a package on his desk.'

'Is that how it was done?'

'No. Emails, and a letter to Jackson's home. Primus provided information on some small things at first. A planned kidnapping of a Russian official's daughter by the Chechens in Odessa. DDNI Jackson passed that information on to his counterpart in Moscow. The kidnappers were caught, and the plan was exposed. And you remember what happened to Anton Likharev?'

'The arms dealer?' Quinn said. 'Sure.'

Likharev, known in many places as the

Merchant of Death, was a former Soviet officer turned gunrunner. Only he was distributing weapons on a scale no one had ever done before. He'd been captured in Southeast Asia, then deported back to the States to go on trial. A trial, as far as Quinn knew, that still hadn't happened.

'Primus told the DDNI about a meeting Likharev was attending in Bangkok. Jackson gave it to the station chief at the embassy, and the next day Thai police had Likharev in custody.'

'Wait a minute,' Quinn said. 'How long has he been passing on this kind of stuff? That was almost a year and a half ago.'

'It started just before that.'

'So when did the Deputy Director find out that Primus was LP?'

'Only two months ago.'

'And he didn't break off contact immediately?' Quinn said.

'The information Primus passed on had all been good. Very reliable.'

'So fucking what?' Quinn said. 'These are the same people who have been trying to dictate the way the country is run, to hell with what the rest of us think. At least that's what you've told me. Didn't any of you think maybe he was trying to get you to do the LP's dirty work for them? Maybe they benefited from having Likharev out of the picture. Maybe everything Primus passed along helped their situation. Maybe he was using the Deputy Director. For God's sake, Peter, didn't anyone think of that?'

'Calm down,' Peter said, his own tone becoming angry. 'First, I didn't find out about it until just a week ago. Second, I had the same reaction as you. I confronted the DDNI with the ID of the assassin. I told him I thought the LP might be trying to stop Primus from passing along information. That's when he told me Primus *was* LP. Jackson told me everything then. He said Primus had become disillusioned with the movement. But he also knew he couldn't just get out. That's not the way the LP works. So instead he started passing information he came across. Doing what he could to balance his personal scales, I guess.'

'When I met with him, he sounded like he was still very much part of the organization.'

'But he did tell you he was working on his own. You told me that.'

'It all sounds like bullshit to me.'

'Jackson didn't believe him at first, either,' Peter said. 'But Primus gained his trust with more good information.'

'Why did he tell Jackson at all?'

Peter took a breath. 'He told Jackson pretty much the same thing he told you. That a group had approached the LP with a potential project, but that the LP had declined. But the project troubled him enough to keep tabs on it. Primus realized that something needed to be done, but that LP wasn't going to make a move. He had already established a relationship with the DDNI, so decided to give him the info. But to convince the DDNI that what he was going to pass on was credible, he knew he had to come clean about who he worked for. He also knew the risk of exposure to his own people would increase, so he took steps to cover his tracks.'

If Ireland and what had happened at LACMA that afternoon were any indication, he hadn't done a very good job.

'A turncoat in the LP,' Quinn said under his breath. It didn't seem possible. These were the same people who had killed a friend of his. Hell, the same people who had destroyed Nate's leg and forced him to use a prosthetic the rest of his life. 'You believe he's not just using us?'

'I'm not one hundred percent. I know caution is in order. But goddammit, Quinn, something's going on. Something that people are trying to stop us from finding out. And if it has anything to do with the G8 meetings . . . they start the day after tomorrow, for Christ's sake. We can't just sit around and see if something happens.'

Quinn frowned. 'Hold on,' he said.

He moved the phone away from his ear and tried to let his mind go blank for a second. He needed to clear away all the conflicting thoughts that were ramming against one another. Only then would he be able to truly assess the situation.

In the distance he could see a police helicopter circling above the Beverly Center. It wasn't much more than a point of light, but he watched it go round and round several times before he brought the phone back up to his ear.

'Here's what's going to happen. You will tell me everything you know,' Quinn said. 'You will send me copies of any information you have. And you'll do it right now.'

'So you'll stay on it?' Peter asked.

'That was our deal, wasn't it?' Quinn said. 'But you need to know moving forward, whether my team and I continue is going to be a minute-to-minute decision.'

'Okay . . . okay. I can live with that. I . . . appreciate it.'

In the distance, the helicopter had moved off in search of trouble elsewhere.

'Talk,' Quinn said.

# 24

Peter was true to his word, and as soon as he had finished briefing Quinn on the phone, he uploaded everything he had to a secure FTP site. Quinn booted Nate off the laptop for a few moments so he could download and print out all the documents. Stack of paper in hand, he got out of Nate's way and moved over to the kitchen counter.

Peter had done the same thing to Deputy Director Jackson that Quinn was doing to him, demanding everything the DDNI had from and about Primus. There was almost two years' worth of material. Most was information passed on before Hardwick had revealed his LP ties. The information on the Odessa kidnapping was there, as was the tip about the arms dealer's trip to Thailand. There were other things, too. Guerrilla cells in South America, money transfers between terrorist organizations, two potential assassination attempts.

Good stuff all, and a treasure trove that would make whoever possessed it look like a superstar. But from all Quinn could tell, the DDNI didn't use any of his newly obtained knowledge to improve his position. Instead he acted on it, often passing tips to appropriate governments anonymously. No personal gain, just doing the job he was hired to do.

Quinn opened the refrigerator to grab a beer

before diving into the stuff that was most relevant, the information concerning the group who had approached the LP.

'Can I have one of those?' Nate asked, looking up from the laptop.

'Depends. You get anything yet?' Quinn asked, already reaching for the second bottle.

'I think so,' Nate said. 'At first I did all the basic searches. Public sites and that kind of stuff.'

Quinn set the bottles on the counter and popped the tops, letting Nate go over his process uninterrupted. It was the way Quinn had taught him to operate if time permitted. Quinn had said it was so that he'd be able to evaluate Nate's progress. That had been true at first. But Quinn had come more and more to trust Nate's abilities, so now it was just habit.

'I got a couple hits,' Nate went on. 'But they were mostly about the state bird of Alabama. But I did find a Yellowhammer Lake in California.'

'That sounds promising,' Quinn said as he handed Nate a beer.

'Thanks,' Nate said. They both took a drink. 'I thought so at first, too. But it's remote. Yosemite area. You have to hike into it. So I thought I should keep digging.'

'Let me guess,' Quinn said. 'Couldn't find anything.'

'Close, but you'd be wrong. I came across a few odd entries that mentioned an actual place called Yellowhammer, and it didn't seem like they were talking about a lake. The first was so random I thought someone must have mistyped it.'

'I'm guessing there's a 'but' here.'

'Right,' Nate said. 'The second one. It was on a blog that posts wartime letters. Some of them from as far back as the Revolution. I found another mention in one of the letters. It was dated near the end of World War II. Some guy writing home to his wife saying he'd been assigned to a place called Yellowhammer.' Nate turned to the computer. 'I'll read it to you.'

He clicked one of the tabs in his browser, then skimmed the text on the screen with his finger.

' 'They're sending me to Yellowhammer until my time's up. I finally get to go to California, I guess, but it's so far from you. At least it's only four months and then I'll be home. I do wish I was there now.' Goes on for a little while longer, but that's the important part.'

'That could be anything,' Quinn said. 'The military loves code names. Might not even be a place at all, but an operation.'

'I had the same thought.'

'Another 'but'?'

Nate smiled. 'Orlando's been giving me tips for accessing some less public sources.'

'Skip the rundown, and tell me what you found.'

'There was a government facility, here in California, called Yellowhammer. The last mention of it was in the early sixties, a few months after the Cuban Missile Crisis. It was apparently decommissioned then.'

'Where exactly is it?'

'See, that's the funny thing. I've found nothing on that anywhere. I found the name. I know it existed. I'm just trying to pinpoint it now.'

Quinn stared down at the laptop, not really looking at the words on the screen. A secret facility? A secret *decommissioned* facility? That didn't make Quinn feel very good. But it jibed with Hardwick's story.

'All right,' Quinn said. 'Keep at it. Also send what you've found to Peter. Maybe he can use his resources to dig something up.'

'Yeah,' Nate said. 'I was going to suggest that.'

'Were you?' Quinn said.

Nate brought up a window on the laptop that had been hidden. 'I've got the email ready to go.'

Quinn was impressed, but kept his face blank. Once again, he had taken to underestimating Nate.

'Send it,' he said. 'I'm going to go check on Orlando.' He picked up the papers from where he'd left them on the counter. 'Don't stay up all night. I have a feeling we're going to be on the move tomorrow.' He paused as he was about to walk out. 'Nate. Good work.'

Downstairs he found Orlando in the same position she'd been in when he'd watched her fall asleep. She didn't even twitch as he sat beside her and checked her pulse. Steady and strong. By all accounts she was doing fine.

It should have made him happy, but he was pissed that she was in this condition at all. The LP had taken the leg of his apprentice the year before, and they had come within inches of

322

paralyzing the woman he loved. Whether it was the LP behind the shootings or not didn't really matter. They were *involved*, and that was enough. Those sons of bitches had screwed with Quinn too much. He only wished there was something he could do about it.

He took his beer and the papers out onto the small balcony off the back of his bedroom. There was a chair, and a table, with a light plugged in to a socket at the base of the wall. Often a gentle breeze would move through the hills, but tonight the air was still.

He took another swig of his beer, then dove in. Though there were dozens of pages, most were painfully short on details. The first half-dozen items had been email exchanges, each no more than two lines long. The final one arranged for a meeting where Primus promised to hand over tangible information. Looking at the log Peter had sent along, this meeting took place in Philadelphia three weeks before the Ireland disaster.

The tangible info turned out to be an initial tracking report on someone identified at the time simply as Alpha, but who Hardwick claimed was Leo Tucker. The document was very similar to the one Peter had passed on to Orlando while they were still back east, only a little lighter on details. There was also a note from Primus.

Director Jackson,

For some time now I have trusted you with data I thought could be useful to you. From what I've been able to learn, you have used that information to avoid many potential incidents that could have been damaging to both our country and our friends. You have on numerous occasions asked me to tell you how I have been able to know what I know. To this point I have resisted, thinking that the information I've already given you should be proof that I have the country's best interests at heart.

But I find now I must answer your question, and trust that your reaction will not negatively affect our working relationship. I tell you this thing so you know that I have sources that are unavailable to you through any other channel, but can be very useful to you. And I tell you this because I now find myself at odds with the very reason I have access to those sources.

I am well aware of your personal fight against an organization known as the LP. I know this because I am a member of that organization. Now before you send your people in search of me, let me say that you will never find me. You will never discover who I am. And if I sense there is an attempt to find out my identity and/or take me into custody, you will never hear from me again. I'm sure this is not a condition you would welcome.

The information I have been giving you has been accurate and excellent. And the information I want to pass on to you now is the same.

It is your choice. Consider the accompanying data as an act of good faith. The person
identified at this point as Alpha is an agent for
an organization that has been in contact with
the LP. They wanted our help, but we have
declined. Still, they are pressing on. I feel it is
vitally important that they are not allowed to
succeed. I'm sure you will feel the same. If you
choose to continue our relationship, I will spell
out why I'm telling you who I work for, and
why Alpha is important to you.

Please send your response via the new email
address I've listed below.

Primus

Quinn read the letter twice. Peter had been right.
The DDNI hadn't known about Hardwick's LP
affiliation for more than a couple months.
According to the log, the DDNI hired the Office
two days later.

Made sense. While Deputy Director Jackson
might have wanted to continue his relationship
with Primus, he wasn't stupid. He knew he'd
need help, but because of his previous
experience with the LP, he didn't know who he
could be sure of in his own organization. Tasha
Douglas, of course, but beyond that he would be
taking risks. The Office had been an obvious
choice. Peter had proven his trustworthiness.

And when Peter suggested using Quinn to
keep tabs on the next meeting, a meeting that for
safety reasons was to take place outside the
States in Ireland, it would have made sense to
the DDNI. Quinn, after all, had been the one to

stop the LP's assassination attempt in Singapore the previous year.

The picture that emerged from the rest of the documents was nothing more than hints mixed with scant usable data. It was maddening. But not just to Quinn. He could see the DDNI's own frustration in emails he'd sent to Primus.

This is moving too slow. You need to tell me everything instead of just giving it to me in bits.

But Hardwick wasn't biting:

You can accept my information or we can stop now. But this will be by my timetable, not yours. If it gives you any comfort, I believe three more face-to-face meetings with my couriers should be sufficient.

The first of those three was the Ireland meeting. Then the DDNI had been killed, and the next two hadn't happened.

Quinn read through everything again, then set it all on the table and reached over and turned the light off. He sipped his beer as the night washed over him. Though it was a few minutes before 2 a.m., he could still hear the distant rumble of traffic.

He leaned back, resting the bottle against his chest, and let all he'd absorbed drift through his mind. He didn't force any connections, just let things simmer.

He didn't remember closing his eyes, but he did remember the last image that passed through his thoughts before he fell asleep.

Marion Dupuis in an old, beat-up Saab, looking out her window at him, her eyes wide. And in the back seat, movement. A body now, coming into focus. Small.

A child. A child . . .

* * *

Quinn woke at first light with the realization that he had yet to call his mother. He also realized that he'd spent the entire night in the chair on his balcony. Carefully he sat up and retrieved his phone. Given the two-hour time difference, he knew his mother would be up, so he dialed her number. But the answering machine picked up. He left a lame message, promising to be there as soon as he could.

'Shit,' he said to himself after he hung up. He felt like an idiot, but it wasn't like he could call back and rerecord it.

He stood up, every muscle in his body aching, and made his way back upstairs to the kitchen.

Nate was already there.

'Peter came through,' Nate said.

'Did you sleep?' Quinn asked.

'Enough.'

He handed Quinn a printout of an email.

Yellowhammer. Naval test facility loosely associated with the old Naval Ordnance Testing Station, later the Naval Weapons Center, at China Lake. Actual location just north of the city of Lone Pine,

327

near site of Manzanar Japanese internment camp. (Map attached.)

Decommissioned in December 1964. Security of facility had been maintained by government contractor Colstar until last year, when contract was picked up by Cameron-Kadash Industries. I've included the blueprints of the facility, but note that they are over fifty years old.

Might be their ops center. Find out.

Keep me updated.

Peter

'Did you print out the blueprints?' Quinn said.

Nate pushed himself out of his chair and stood up. The sight of Nate's bare stump surprised Quinn. Since his apprentice had received his new prosthetic, Quinn had never seen him without it on. It had seemed like Nate wanted Quinn to forget the real leg was even missing. But now, as he hopped over to the printer hidden in a cabinet along the wall, Quinn couldn't help but remember the pain Nate had been in, and the months of therapy and training he had gone through to get himself back in shape.

'What?' Nate said as he hopped back, holding a few pieces of paper in his hands.

'Nothing.'

'I just haven't put it on yet,' Nate said, his tone defensive. 'I wanted to check if we heard from Peter first. Is that all right?'

'It's fine.'

'You don't look like it's fine.'

'Sorry,' Quinn said. 'It's just been a while . . . you know . . . since I've seen you without it.'

'I see it that way every day,' Nate said. 'It's the way it is. It's not growing back.'

'I know.'

'Do you? Then accept it. And accept the fact that I'm still good enough to do this.' He shoved the papers at Quinn, not waiting for a response. 'Here.'

Quinn took them, then said, 'I'm getting there.'

'Yeah, well. I guess we'll see, won't we?' Nate stared at him for a moment, then sat back down. 'The first two are the Yellowhammer blueprints. The last is the map.'

Quinn, not knowing what else to say, looked at the printouts. The facility was built underground at the base of the Sierra Nevada. There were two levels, each containing several rooms connected by corridors. There were limited living quarters inside, and barracks for two hundred additional workers located aboveground. But a note on the blueprint indicated that the ground-level quarters had been removed at the time of decommissioning.

Now the only aboveground signs of the facility were four air vents, and a structure that hid the main entrance. There was an additional way in, an emergency entrance. But it was hidden in a rock crevice wide enough for only one person to pass through at a time.

This didn't shed any light on what the current inhabitants might be up to, but it did give Quinn their location.

'This looks like it's going to be fun,' Nate said, his earlier defensive tone gone.

329

'Loads,' Quinn agreed.

He rolled his shoulders back, trying to loosen the muscles in his back that hadn't expected to spend the night sitting in a chair outside. He took a closer look at the second page. It was the lower level of the complex, designated R2.

'I think this is some kind of laboratory,' he said.

'Maybe seventy years ago,' Nate said. 'Who knows what they're using it for now?'

'True. They could be just using the main level.'

'The main level of what?' The voice had come from behind them.

Quinn and Nate turned.

Orlando was standing at the edge of the kitchen. She was dressed and, except for the large white bandage covering her wound, looked almost normal.

Quinn pulled out one of the kitchen chairs, then took a few steps toward her.

'You shouldn't be walking around,' he said.

'It's not my leg that got hurt,' she said, then looked at Nate. 'No offense.'

'Hey, I get it,' he said. 'No worries.'

She walked over to the table and looked down at the blueprints. 'What are those?'

'Blueprints,' Quinn said.

'No kidding,' she said, all but calling him an idiot. 'Of what?'

'Yellowhammer,' Nate said.

'So this is where they are,' she said.

'So it would seem,' Quinn said.

They were all silent for several moments.

'What are we waiting for?' Orlando asked.

'Nate and I were just leaving,' Quinn said.

'We were?' Nate asked.

Quinn ignored him and looked at Orlando. 'You, though, are staying here.'

'The hell I am.'

'You need rest, not a four-hour ride in the car.'

'I'm going,' she said.

'We can do this without you.'

'If I were anyone else, you'd expect me to continue on the project.'

Her eyes narrowed, daring him to contradict her. But Quinn couldn't.

'Put me in the back seat,' she said, her tone softening a notch. 'Nate, grab me a pillow.'

Nate pushed himself out of the chair. 'Thick or thin?'

'Thin, please.'

'Hold on,' Quinn said.

'What?' Orlando asked. 'It's all settled.'

'Nothing's settled,' Quinn told her.

'It's settled.'

Quinn started to open his mouth, but stopped. Why the hell was everyone arguing with him this morning? He felt like going back to bed and forgetting the whole thing. Unfortunately, that wasn't an option.

And as far as Orlando going along, like she said, it was settled.

# 25

Before leaving the city, they filled the trunk of Quinn's BMW with gear they thought they might need. Ropes, clamps, gloves, and carabiners they picked up at a mountaineering store on Pico Boulevard. Crowbars, listening gear, explosive charges, and other specialized items they got out of Quinn's storage facility near Venice Beach.

Once they were finished, they headed north, taking first the 405 freeway, then Highway 14 into the upper Mojave Desert.

About two and a half hours into the trip, a desert valley opened up off to their right.

'According to the map, that should be China Lake,' Nate said, then paused for a moment. 'Everything's so . . . tan. Summers here must be killers.'

'I think there's a certain beauty to it,' Orlando said.

'Sure. Okay, if you say so,' Nate said. 'Anyway, when the government controlled Yellowhammer, the navy station at China Lake had administrative jurisdiction.'

They fell silent again as they transitioned onto Highway 395 and left the desert for the higher-elevation scrubland that would be with them the rest of the way. Outside, the temperature dropped a few degrees every twenty minutes. At this time of year it wasn't a drastic difference, but Quinn knew that unlike the desert they'd just passed through, this area would be touched by snow a few times every winter. Perhaps not a lot, but enough. And with the new valley being so narrow, Quinn could imagine winds whipping between the mountain ranges, making life miserable.

It took another hour before they passed a sign indicating they were a few miles from the town of Lone Pine. That got everyone moving. Lone Pine was the gateway to the Alabama Hills and would serve as their base.

Here the Sierra Nevada felt like an impenetrable rock wall miles high, its jagged skyline daring anyone to try and cross it. One of the peaks, Quinn wasn't sure which, was Mount Whitney, the tallest mountain in the lower forty-eight states. It was rugged country, and, on that aspect alone, the perfect place to build a facility you didn't want anyone to know about.

To Quinn it looked just like what it was, a sleepy town of around two thousand, living off the tourists who came to see the mountains or were passing through on their way to the Mammoth Mountain Ski Resort another two hours farther north. The highway acted as Main Street, and played host to most of the businesses Lone Pine had to offer. A grocery store, a few bars, some restaurants, a couple of gas stations.

'There's the motel,' Nate said, pointing ahead and to the right.

Quinn saw it. The Dow Villa Motel. Nate had made reservations before they left L.A.

Quinn parked near the motel's office, then waited in the car with Orlando while Nate went inside to check in. While the sketch of Quinn from New York hadn't been in the news for the last twenty-four hours, he still felt the need to keep a low profile.

'How you feeling?' he asked Orlando.

She hesitated, then said, 'I'm fine.'

'You're cute when you lie,' he said.

'I'm fine, really,' she said. 'You want to know if it hurts? Of course it does. But I'm fine.'

They were silent for a few moments.

'I assume you want to do a recon,' she said.

'Yeah.'

'Then we can just drop off our bags and go.'

'You're staying here,' Quinn said.

'I said I was fine.'

'I know you did. But you could use some rest. You look exhausted.'

'I don't want to argue with you about this,' she said.

'I don't want to argue, either. But this first trip out, we're just going to do a scout. That I don't need you for.'

The look on her face was far from happy. 'I can stay in the car. Monitor communications. Something might go wrong. You'll need me there.'

'No,' Quinn said. 'We won't. We're not going to get close enough for anything to go wrong.'

She leaned back into her seat, her lips pressed together and her eyes drilling a hole in the center of Quinn's forehead.

'Come on. Don't be stupid. You don't have all your strength back yet. You know that. I *will* need you, and when I do I'll need you fully rested.

Going out now with us will drain you, and that I *don't* need.'

'Fine,' she said, her tone indicating it was anything but.

'You know I'm right.'

Before she could respond, the car door opened and Nate climbed back in.

'Our rooms are toward the back,' Nate said, holding up two key cards. 'Rooms 4 and 5. The guy inside said there's parking right in front of them.'

Before Quinn could turn around to restart the car, Orlando snatched one of the keys from Nate, then looked at Quinn.

'I'll take this room,' she said. 'You can stay with Nate.'

★ ★ ★

The terrain north of Lone Pine was similar to that which they had just been driving through for the past hour, except for one large exception. To the left, between the highway and the Sierras, were the Alabama Hills, a rolling pile of granite and volcanic rocks. To Quinn it looked like a dump of surplus material someone decided wasn't needed to make the mountains.

According to the information Nate had dug up, most of the hills were under the protection of the Bureau of Land Management, and were set aside for public use. But there was an area toward the north end that had been claimed by the military, and cordoned off decades ago.

*Yellowhammer*, Quinn thought.

335

'That's it, isn't it?' Nate said, pointing across the highway at a dirt road leading off into the hills.

Quinn glanced at his odometer. They were 4.7 miles north of Lone Pine. 'Mileage is right.'

The map Peter had sent them indicated that the road they had just passed was the only direct approach to the facility's entrance. Chances were good that whoever was running it now had security in place to warn them the minute someone headed their way.

They went a couple miles farther up the divided road, then looped back using a dirt access road between the two strips of asphalt. Besides the main entrance to Yellowhammer, the map highlighted several other roads that led into the hills.

There was one that came within a half mile of the Yellowhammer road before turning back north. Quinn pulled to the side of the highway, a few car lengths away from where it met the highway. He could see that the dirt road cut a straight line across the barren expanse between the highway and where the hills jutted upward, where it then disappeared into a gap between some boulders.

Nate reached into the rear seat, and retrieved the electronics sniffer from his backpack. It looked a little like a palm-size TV remote, and was able to detect electrical signals up to a hundred feet away.

'Be right back,' he said.

He got out, then jogged over to where the dirt road began. Quinn thought he detected a bit of a

336

limp. But maybe it was just Nate's new gait.

*Dammit, you've got to let this go,* Quinn thought. *He's going to be fine.*

Nate disappeared behind the downward slope just beyond the shoulder, then reappeared two minutes later. Again, there was the limp as he ran back to the car.

'It's clear,' he said as he climbed in. 'No trip wires. Didn't pick up any signals, either.'

'Good,' Quinn said as he put the BMW back in drive.

Up until the dirt road entered the rocky hills, it was a smooth ride. But the moment they passed between the boulders they had seen from the highway, things changed.

Ruts and erosion had deteriorated the surface of the road to the point where Quinn had to take it down to a near crawl. Even then, several times the BMW's tires smacked the top of the wheel wells. The rocks that lined the way were also a danger. They undulated in a random pattern, often coming within inches of banging into the side of Quinn's car.

The road bent to the south for several minutes, but then, two and a half miles in, it turned east for a couple hundred feet before swinging back to the north.

'Shit,' Nate said. 'I think that was it.'

'Think, or it was?' Quinn asked, stopping the car.

Nate looked at the map for a moment, then said, 'Yes, that was it. This will just take us farther and farther away.'

Quinn backed the BMW down a gap between

the rocks, following its contour as it curved around one of the hills. Once he was sure the car could not be seen from the road, he stopped.

Quinn popped the trunk, then they both got out and met at the rear of the BMW. From a case in the back, they each chose a firearm — Quinn taking his SIG, and Nate grabbing the Glock.

'Comm gear?' Nate asked.

'Yes,' Quinn said.

Nate tossed a set to Quinn.

'Thanks,' Quinn said.

As soon as he had his earpiece in and mic secured, Quinn pulled out his own equipment backpack and donned it.

He stopped before he closed the trunk and looked up at the sky. While it was still afternoon, their proximity to the mountains meant the sun would pass out of sight in the next hour or so, putting this part of the valley into a deep shadow. That could be helpful while they did their recon, but it might also make getting back to the car difficult.

He reached back in and moved a couple of the boxes out of the way until he found what he was looking for. It was a black hard-plastic container not much bigger than an old-fashioned cigarette case. Inside were four plastic squares stacked together. They were each about the size of a business card cut in half, and an eighth of an inch thick. To their right was a small panel built into the box housing a single button. It was a homing device. All the squares were linked to the device and, when on, would guide the bearer back to the box. Quinn removed two of the squares, then touched the button on the panel, shut the box, and placed it back in the trunk.

'Here,' he said, tossing one of the squares to Nate. 'It's going to be dark soon. We may need a little help getting back.'

Nate pocketed the remote, then they headed out across the hills toward the road that led to Yellowhammer.

'I doubt they'll have audio sensors, but we should keep conversation to a minimum just in case,' Quinn said after they'd been walking for several minutes.

'Copy that,' Nate said.

The hike wasn't an easy one. Everywhere there were rocks, most the size of small cars, some the size of a house. Red and gray, vertical and horizontal, stable and loose, it was like the set for an alien planet out of some sixties sci-fi show. *Star Trek*, maybe. Or *Lost in Space*. Boulders balanced on top of boulders, others jetted upward and leaned against each other like books on a shelf. Where enough rocks gathered together, they formed the hills.

Quinn tried to lead them through the lower passes, but at times they were forced to go higher on the hillsides to find the easier route.

After fifteen minutes, Nate took over the lead. Quinn kept an eye on him, looking for signs of fatigue or struggle, but his apprentice pressed on as if both his legs were whole.

'I see the road,' Nate said a few minutes later.

He was about thirty feet ahead of Quinn. He had crouched down near the top of the next hill.

'Empty?' Quinn asked.

'Seems so,' Nate said.

'Any sign of sensors?'

'Hold on,' Nate said.

Nate pulled out the sniffer.

'I'm not picking up anything,' Nate said. 'But the road's just at the edge of this thing's range.'

He set the sniffer down and removed a pair of small but high-powered binoculars out of his pack. Quinn watched as Nate moved his head from right to left, then returned to a spot just off center and stayed there for a moment.

'There's something down there that might be a motion sensor,' Nate said. 'Come take a look.'

Quinn climbed up beside him and pulled out his own binoculars.

'Where?' he asked.

'See that rock that's leaning about twenty degrees to the left?'

'Yes.'

'All right,' Nate said. 'Now go another ten feet to the right, and closer to the road, maybe three feet from the edge. Mounted on top of a small rock.'

Small was relative out here. The small rock Nate was talking about was the size of a recliner. There was a bump on it that seemed out of place. Quinn adjusted his zoom to get a better look. It was hard to tell, but there was no question that it was man-made. A square box with a little rounded dome on top. He retrieved his camera and shot off several images so they could take another look at it back at the motel, then match it up to a specific product.

'This is about as close to the road as we should get. If we go down there, they'll know it right away.' Quinn looked back behind them. 'We can parallel it from over here.'

'Okay.'

'Keep the sniffer on.'

'I guess this means we're at the right place, at least,' Nate said.

'Doesn't mean anything yet.'

They started out again, this time heading toward the Sierras, always keeping a mound of rocks between them and the Yellowhammer road. Every five minutes they would check the road again, and each time they spotted more of the sensors.

'That one looks brand new,' Nate said at one stop.

The sensor he was referring to was only a dozen yards away, at the base of the hill they were perched on top of.

Quinn held his hand out, and Nate gave him his binoculars. One look at the device confirmed Nate's assessment.

'Probably we can rule out that they were left by somebody else,' Nate said.

Quinn wasn't surprised. It was the assumption he'd been working under since they'd seen the first one. Still, it would have been nice to discover that the sensors had been no more than junk left by a previous occupant. But nothing was ever that easy.

'Come on,' Quinn said as he pushed back from the edge.

Distance was hard to tell out here. Their route

341

was far from straight. Instead it wound through the boulder graveyard. But after another ten minutes, Quinn figured they were about three miles from the highway.

'The map shows an obstruction crossing the road,' Quinn said. 'If I'm right, we're less than a quarter mile from it. It's got to be a fence. My bet is it goes around the entire perimeter of the facility. Keep an eye out. We don't want to get too close.'

Nate was a good twenty feet ahead of him. He made no physical indication that he had been listening, but his voice came through Quinn's earpiece loud and clear. 'Copy.'

Two minutes further on Nate cut to the left for another road check.

'I've got movement,' Nate said. His voice was hushed but urgent. 'A man.'

Quinn stopped at the bottom of the slope. 'Did he see you?'

'No,' Nate said.

'What's he doing?' Quinn asked.

'I only have a partial visual,' Nate whispered. 'Waist and above. He's walking down the road. East, in our direction. He's armed. M16. And he's wearing fatigues. Brown camouflage. Army . . . wait, he stopped.'

'He's alone?'

'I don't see anyone else,' Nate said. 'He's turning around and heading back the way he came. Looks like guard duty to me.' Nate said nothing for several moments, then, 'Okay, he's moving out of sight . . . and . . . gone.'

Quinn waited for Nate to crawl back down,

then said, 'I think we need to put a little more distance between us and the road. Just to be safe.'

'Safe sounds good.'

The sun slipped behind the ridge of the Sierras five minutes later engulfing Quinn and Nate in a dark shadow, and almost instantly dropping the temperature several degrees.

'Tighten up,' Quinn said into his mic. 'It's going to get dark quick. Let's keep each other in sight.'

'Do you hear that?' Nate asked.

'You hear someone?'

'Not someone. It's constant, low. I can almost feel it more than hear it.'

'Hold your position.'

Quinn jogged ahead until he was standing next to Nate.

'I don't hear anything,' he said.

'My ears are younger than yours.'

'Go to hell.'

'Shhh. Just listen.'

Both fell silent again.

A half-minute passed, then there it was. Very low, almost blending into the background. Even as hard as it was to hear, Quinn could tell it was not something that belonged in the hushed hills.

By silent agreement, they moved toward the sound side-by-side. It seemed to be coming from just beyond the pile of rocks directly in front of them.

'Around, or over the top?' Nate whispered.

'To the top, but not over. Let's see what we

can see from there.'

The closer they got to the top, the easier it was to hear it. When he first heard it, Quinn had thought it was like the sound of a distant freeway. But now he realized it was more like a hum than a drone.

The valley was almost in complete shadow when they reached the top. And here, the sound was much louder, the hill no longer shielding the noise.

When Quinn brought night vision binoculars back to his eyes, he saw the fence right away. Rather, fences. There were two running parallel to each other, and disappearing off to the left and the right. The only break was at the point where they met the road. There a gate closed the gap. Next to it was a concrete building no more than fifteen feet square — enough room for some bunks, a table, a hot plate, and some storage. *Guardhouse*, Quinn thought. Light spilled out of the solitary window on the east side.

Nate tapped Quinn once on the arm, then pointed a dozen feet right of the outpost. Quinn stared at the spot for several seconds before he made out what had caught Nate's attention. There were three men standing in a loose group. Quinn assumed they were talking, but they were too far away to hear anything.

Nate tapped him again. But instead of pointing at anything, he made a waving motion with his fingers like he wanted to pull back, then he retraced their path down the hill. Quinn followed.

'Did you see it?' Nate asked, once they were off the hill.

'The men?' Quinn said. 'Yeah, I saw them.'

'Not the men,' Nate said. 'The fence.'

'I saw it. What about it?'

'It didn't seem odd to you?'

'Tell me what you saw,' Quinn said.

Nate seemed to be lost in thought.

'What?' Quinn asked.

Instead of answering, Nate started walking along the edge of the hill, toward the fence.

'Wait,' Quinn said. 'What did you see?'

'I might be wrong,' Nate said. 'I want to get a closer look first. We should be able to approach it right up there.' He was pointing along a gully to the right.

As they neared the fence, the hum grew louder again. It was . . . *electronic*, Quinn thought.

They came around the edge of a rock that looked like a gigantic T-bone steak, and found themselves only twenty feet away from the double fence.

The hum was loud enough now that Nate had to raise his voice above a whisper to be heard. 'I was right,' he said.

Each fence was a series of thick wires strung horizontally from one post to the next with no more than six inches between them. The posts were made of some type of composite material and were placed every ten feet. The planners had taken the extra step of staggering the two fences so that their posts didn't line up. And as for the sound, it was coming from the wires. Each crackled and hummed with electricity.

345

Quinn looked first left, then right. It was the same setup for as far as he could see.

'How the hell do we get through that?' Nate asked.

But Quinn said nothing. It was better than saying he had no idea.

# 26

'We've got an alert on the old road.' The guard's voice was clear, though a bit overamplified.

Tucker moved his handheld radio closer to his mouth. 'Any visual?'

'No,' the guard replied. 'Just the motion sensor.'

'Still going off?'

'It was a single notification. Just happened.'

The system didn't use simple motion sensors like some people had in their homes or offices. These devices were more refined, weeding out most extraneous movement and only reporting on objects that were large enough to be human. Over the two months they had been deployed, there had only been one false alarm. Perhaps this was a second; Tucker wasn't going to take any chances. The Dupuis woman had friends out there somewhere. Maybe they had decided to come for a visit.

'Send someone to check,' Tucker said. 'But do not intercept yet. I want to know how many people are out there first.'

'Copy,' the guard said.

Tucker heard the guard relay his instructions, followed by a distant grunt of agreement.

'I'm sending a team out to you just in case you need some backup,' Tucker said. 'Should be there in five minutes.'

'All right.'

'Report back the moment you know anything.'

Tucker didn't wait for an acknowledgment before clipping the radio to his belt. He used Yellowhammer's built-in PA system to order one of the other security teams to the main gate.

He reached for his desk phone, but stopped before picking it up. With the helicopters due to leave in just over eight hours, he knew Mr. Rose would still be in the lab overseeing the final preparations. The old man would not be happy to be disturbed. Better to find out if the alarm was real or not, and implement an appropriate response before filling his boss in, Tucker thought.

He still picked up the phone, but instead of Mr. Rose, he called his contact in Toronto — a guy named Donald Chang.

'You get anything from Montreal yet?' Tucker asked.

'Hold on,' Chang said. 'Let me bring it up.'

Tucker could hear the clacking of a computer keyboard. Once it stopped, Chang came back on the line.

'There wasn't really anything at the house,' Chang said. 'Plenty of prints, but they mainly belonged to the family.'

'Mainly?' Tucker asked.

'The other ones check out as members of the Montreal Police Department. Which makes sense, of course. Unless you think the people you're looking for might be cops.'

'I don't,' Tucker said.

So the Dupuis house was clean. Tucker was

only mildly disappointed. It had been a long shot at best.

'I did get a hit from the license plate on the car you were following, though,' Chang said.

'What kind of hit?' Tucker asked.

'Police found it in Brossard, on the other side of the St. Lawrence River.'

'You got prints from inside?' Tucker asked, hopeful.

'No. It was clean. But we did go ahead and check motels in the area. The car matched a description given by a man staying at a Comfort Inn that night. There were three people, actually. Two men and a woman. One of the men and the woman stayed together. The other had his own room. They left the next morning. No one knows exactly what time, they just left their keys in the rooms.'

'Did you get any names?' Tucker asked.

'The couple registered as Mitch and Sissy Booth. The other guy as Vince Salas. But they were phony. Home addresses didn't check out.'

'How did they pay?'

'Same credit card for both rooms,' Chang said. 'The name on it was Mitch Booth. It was good, but I back-checked. It's the only time it's ever been used.'

Prepared false IDs. No prints. A disposable car.

Professionals.

'What about security cameras? The motel had to have one.'

'You're going to love this,' Chang said.

'What?'

'They had a jammer.'

Tucker said nothing.

'The camera in the motel office takes stills every ten seconds, low res. At the beginning of each day, they burn the previous twenty-four hours to disk. My guy got a look at the night the people you're looking for checked in. But at the time they would have been in the office, the pictures were just digital crap.'

'So other than knowing where they stayed, you've got nothing?' Tucker said.

'Not exactly nothing,' Chang said. 'There is another camera. Parking lot security. Whatever type of jammer they were using, it looks like it had to be within thirty feet or so of a camera for it to work.'

'So you got them on the parking lot camera?'

'Yes. It's from a distance, and not very clear, but it's something.'

'Send it to me.'

'Should be in your email now.'

'Thanks,' Tucker said, then hung up.

His laptop was in a shoulder bag next to his desk. He pulled it out and booted it up. Mr. Rose's technicians had installed a wireless system that worked throughout the facility, so as soon as his desktop appeared, he activated his email. The message from Chang was there, complete with two attachments. He highlighted both and opened them.

The first showed a grainy night-time shot of a parking lot. There were dozens of cars parked in neat rows. Though the photo was black-and-white, he thought one of the cars parked next to

350

the motel building looked very much like the car he had followed in Montreal. Beside it were three people. The two closest had their backs to the camera and were opening the doors on the passenger side of the vehicle. One was the woman. She was short and thin, but other than that she was unidentifiable. On the other side, facing the camera, was the second man. But his head was lowered in preparation to climb into the car, leaving only the top visible. He could have been anywhere from eighteen to sixty.

Tucker brought the second image forward. Same angle only a few seconds later, he guessed. The woman who had been climbing into the back seat was just a shape through the rear window now. The driver had also disappeared.

But the man who'd been getting into the front passenger seat was still there. It looked like he was just about to slide in, but in doing so he had turned and given the camera his profile.

Tucker leaned in toward the computer screen. There was something about the man. Something familiar.

He knew if he just concentrated for a minute, it would come to him. He switched back to the first shot, looking at the man's back. Nothing special there. Lean, but not thin. A little under six feet tall. He looked strong — not rippling-muscle strong, but useful strong. Like he was the kind of guy who could do a lot of things.

Tucker clicked on the second picture. It confirmed what he'd seen in the first. A man of action. He flipped between the photos, letting the images dance on the screen in front of him.

Back.

Profile.

Back.

Profile.

Back.

Profile.

Stop.

All of a sudden he was remembering snow. Not the snow that capped the peaks just outside the entrance to Yellowhammer. German snow. Berlin snow.

*Jonathan Quinn.*

That's who he was looking at. Jonathan-fucking-Quinn. Tucker had last seen him on a sidewalk in Tiergarten in the middle of Berlin almost a year and a half earlier. They'd made a deal. Tucker had given up his boss's where-abouts, and Quinn had let him walk away alive.

Jonathan Quinn. *Goddammit.*

He looked back at the first picture, this time concentrating on the woman getting into the back seat. Like before, he could only see her back, but now that he knew what to look for, her hair and her height gave her away.

Dark, probably black, and a little longer than it had been in Berlin. As for her height, she didn't even look like she cleared the top of the Jetta.

Orlando. She'd been on that sidewalk with Quinn and Tucker. There had been murder in her eyes. His murder if she had had her way. Couldn't really blame her. He'd been involved in the abduction of her son, after all. But a deal was a deal, and Quinn had made her keep it.

If Tucker's and Quinn's roles had been reversed, he wasn't so sure he would have been as honorable as the cleaner had been. Honor, he knew, was mostly bullshit anyway.

The other man had to be Quinn's assistant. *What the fuck was his name?* Tucker realized he wasn't sure he had ever heard it. Didn't matter anyway. Quinn was the important one.

But in reality, their presence didn't change anything. Tucker seriously doubted Quinn and his team even knew about Yellowhammer. How could they? Even if they had been able to get to Marion and talk to her, they would have learned nothing, because she knew nothing. Tucker was sure of that now. He believed her story about the African girl. Playing the part of the good Samaritan, she had unintentionally gotten in the way. That had been all there was to it.

They'd been hunting her not so much to get the child back, but because they were worried she'd known more than she did. She'd been a potential leak that needed to be stopped. Tucker's fault, really. He knew that. The army colonel he'd hired in Côte d'Ivoire had been too heavy-handed. Tucker had told him a less direct approach was best. Fewer questions that way. And much more cooperation. But the man had gone in with a whole squad, acting all tough and demanding. Stupid.

Tucker closed his laptop and leaned back in the chair. The only thing that stopped him from giving the order to get rid of the Dupuis bitch at that moment was the *what if* floating in the back of his mind. *What if* Quinn had actually made it this far? *What if* it was one of the cleaner's team poking around outside the fence? Or better yet, *what if* it was Quinn himself who had tripped the motion sensor?

Tucker liked to believe he was always thinking ahead and preparing for all the different possibilities. Covering his own ass just in case. If Quinn somehow got the upper hand — which Tucker thought very unlikely — Marion Dupuis could then become a bargaining chip. Tucker could play to Quinn's honor again, giving him the woman and walking away clean. Or better yet, he could use Dupuis to trap the cleaner, then threaten to kill the woman if Quinn didn't tell him everything he knew. It would be an interesting experiment to see how far Quinn's honor went.

Tucker couldn't help but smile at the possibility.

* * *

Marion was getting worried. She'd been locked in her dark cell for hours without another visit from the Australian or the old man with the creepy eyes. From the little experience she'd had, that was unusual. Until now, they hadn't let her go for more than two hours without another round of questioning.

She kept time by pacing the cell and brushing the fingers of her hand along the wall, letting them guide her so that she wouldn't run into anything. She slowed her pace so that it took a

354

full thirty seconds to make one circuit, then began counting laps, one minute for every two, an hour for every 120.

A couple of times she lost count and had to estimate, but she didn't stop until she reached 800. By her estimate over six and a half hours. But it wasn't her legs that stopped her. It was her fear.

*Six and a half hours and no visitors?*

No one had even come to see if she needed to use a toilet. She didn't. She hadn't drunk enough liquids in the last twenty-four hours to warrant that.

*Something must be wrong,* she thought. Could they have decided they didn't need her anymore, and were just going to let her die?

Maybe everyone was gone. Maybe there was no one left here but her.

She started breathing faster as her fear took a sharp turn toward panic.

Without even realizing it, she began circling the room again, hoping to reassure herself that she'd get out of here. Somehow. But it didn't work. She knew her life, the life she wasn't ready to give up yet, was almost over.

*No.* Not just her life, she reminded herself.

'God, please,' she said out loud. 'Please watch over Iris. Don't let them hurt her. Please. Don't let them.'

# 27

'Dammit,' Nate said.

Quinn looked up. They had been trying to move into a position with a better view of the guardhouse. Nate had been on point, fifteen feet in front of him. He was still there, but instead of standing, he was on the ground. Quinn raced forward, his eyes darting around as he knelt down next to his apprentice.

'Are you hurt?' Quinn asked.

There was a pause. 'I tripped on something,' Nate said. 'A bush, I think.'

Quinn tried to give Nate a hand up, but Nate said, 'I'm fine.' Then pushed himself to his feet unaided.

Nate was about to start up again, but Quinn stopped him. 'Wait. Did you hear that?'

In the distance he had heard a scrape. Like a shoe slipping on rock. But the sound didn't come again.

'What was it?' Nate asked.

'I think someone's out there.'

'A guard?'

'Must be.' Quinn thought for a moment. 'Go around the right side of that hill.' He pointed at a mound of rock rising ahead of them another fifty feet. 'I'll go left. Let's meet back here in ten minutes.'

Nate nodded.

'And Nate,' Quinn added as Nate was about to leave.

'What?'

Quinn smiled. 'Don't trip.'

★ ★ ★

Tucker had grown impatient waiting for word about the possible intruder, so he had the guard at the gate patch all communications with the search team to his radio. Now he sat staring at the small black unit on his desk, listening to bouts of dead air between bursts of digitally encrypted transmissions.

'Base to four,' a voice said.

The two-man team had been joined by the four men Tucker had sent. The man in the guardhouse was Base, while the searchers were numbered two through six.

'Four,' another voice replied, his tone hushed.

'Status.'

'Grid H-3 clear.'

'Move to H-4.'

'Roger.'

'Base to five.'

'Five here,' the new voice said. Before Base could ask for a status, he went on. 'I have a visual. Repeat, I have a visual.'

'Grid?'

'A-2. Near the fence. Looks like a male.'

Tucker couldn't help himself. He picked up his radio and pushed transmit. 'What's he doing?'

There was a pause, then five said, 'He's prone. No movement.'

357

'Is he injured?' Tucker asked.

'Doesn't appear to be. His eyes are open and active.'

There was dead air for a moment.

'Base requests instructions,' the man at the guardhouse said, his question directed at Tucker.

'Is he alone?' Tucker asked.

'I haven't seen anyone else,' five said.

Tucker thought for a moment. 'Have your man stay there and keep an eye on him. Report any movement. Have the others move in and check surrounding area to make sure he's alone.'

'Roger,' Base said. 'Five hold position. Two, four, and six sweep grid points B-2, B-3, and A-3. If clear, proceed to A-4. Three, move to A-1 to cover any potential forward movement by intruder.'

Guards two, three, four, and six all replied with 'Roger.'

Then the radio went dead again.

* * *

'I've got movement.'

Nate's voice was so low, Quinn almost thought he was imagining it. As if he could see where Nate was, he turned to the west, but the only thing there was the hill that separated them.

'What is it?'

'Looks like one of the guards. He's at my two o'clock, a hundred and twenty feet away, but coming in this direction.'

'Standard patrol?' Quinn asked.

'Definitely not. He's sweeping, and keeping

low. He's looking for something.'

'Is he alone?'

'I . . . don't see anyone else.' Nate's voice lacked confidence.

'Where are you?'

'I found a crevice between two boulders. Southwest corner of the hill.' He paused. 'I can also see a motion sensor. It's about forty feet in front of me.'

'Did you trip it?'

'I . . . I don't think so.'

'If you think you can, back out of there,' Quinn said. 'Otherwise hold tight until they're gone. I'll go up the hill and see if I can get an overview.'

'Copy that.'

Quinn turned to his right and began ascending the hill.

⋆    ⋆    ⋆

'B-4 clear,' two said.

Several seconds later, six added, 'A-4 also clear.'

*Good*, Tucker thought. *He's alone.*

He pushed the transmit button on his radio. 'Close in and apprehend. I want to talk to him, so don't kill him.'

'Roger,' Base said. 'All units close in on A-2, but hold at least fifty feet out from intruder, then report when in position. Five, you have ground command.'

'Roger,' five said.

The first 'in position' came forty-five seconds

after the order was given. The last, a minute and a half later.

'Close to twenty-five feet,' five said.

Silence.

'Hands in the air!' five called out, his voice booming from the receiver.

It was followed in quick succession by similar calls from the other guards.

Tucker waited for the sound of gunfire, but there was none. *Good*, he thought.

'On your feet,' one of the guards called out. Tucker had lost track of who was who. 'On your fucking feet!'

'Get up! Get up!'

'Drop your backpack to the ground, and put your hands on your head!'

'On your head, goddammit!'

'Four, six, search him.'

'I've got a gun,' a guard said. Six? 'Spare mag in his pants pocket.'

'Backpack?' Tucker recognized the voice this time. Five.

'A couple more mags. Surveillance equipment. Some rope.'

'Use it to tie his hands.'

'Left hand down.' Several seconds passed, then, 'Now your right.'

'Intruder secured.' Five again, his calmer tone denoting that this message was meant for Base and Tucker.

'Who is he?' Tucker asked.

'Name!' five shouted.

There was silence.

'I said give me your goddamn name!'

More silence.

There was a loud thwack. Tucker knew the sound well, rifle stock against flesh.

'Get the fuck back on your feet and tell me your name.'

Silence, then another smack.

'Doesn't seem to want to cooperate, sir,' five said.

'Take him to the guardhouse and put him on the camera,' Tucker said. 'I want to see his face.'

'Roger,' five said, then to the others, 'Let's move.'

\* \* \*

Ten feet from the top of the hill, Quinn heard yelling coming from the other side.

'Nate?' he said.

No response.

He scrambled to the crest on all fours, crawling over the rocks and stopping only when he had a shielded position from which he could see what was happening.

At the base of the hill was a fifty-foot-wide gap of scattered boulders and sand. And standing in the middle of it were five men. Five armed men, Quinn noted. They stood in a loose circle around a sixth man who lay on the ground.

'Nate?'

Still nothing.

Quinn pulled out his binoculars and aimed them at the group. It was apparent the guards were not happy with the guy they were surrounding. Several aimed their weapons at him.

'Get the fuck back on your feet and tell me your name,' the guard closest to the man's head yelled.

As the man stood up Quinn trained the binoculars on him, knowing what he'd see.

Only he was wrong. The captive wasn't Nate.

'Nate,' Quinn said. 'Where are you?'

The response came in two short, low bursts. 'Can't. Talk.'

Quinn swept the binoculars back toward the hill he was on, but didn't see anything. He tried again, this time turning on the thermal-imaging overlay first. Unlike before, this time two small ovals stood out. They were poking out of the back of a crevice created by a couple of the large rocks that were leaning together.

'Tap your toe,' Quinn said.

'What?'

'Tap your toe.'

Quinn watched as one of the ovals moved upward, then tapped back down against the rock it had been lying on.

'I can see your feet.'

'You can see my feet?' Nate whispered.

'Just me,' Quinn said. 'They don't have an angle on you.'

Quinn returned his gaze to the group in the clearing. Who the hell was the guy they had caught? Was he out here alone? Quinn sensed he must be, because they had seen no sign of anyone else. One man, okay. Maybe Quinn could account for having missed a single person, *if* the

362

guy was ahead of them. But two or more, no way.

What were the guards thinking, though? They had to be wondering if there were more people out here. If they started looking, Quinn and Nate were going to have to make a serious effort not to be found.

Down below, two of the security men had hold of their captive, while a third was saying something, this time his voice too low to be heard. A few seconds later, they started walking as a group in the direction of the guardhouse.

'We're moving,' Quinn said.

'Back to the car?' Nate asked.

'No. We follow.'

'What about the sensors? We'll trip them.'

'I know,' Quinn said. 'Wait where you are. I'm coming to you.'

* * *

Quinn took two chances. First, he decided that any motion sensor alarms they might set off would be attributed to the group with the prisoner. Since no one had come looking for them, that part seemed to have worked fine. Second, he decided to see if they could get to the guardhouse before the others. He figured that by keeping close to the fence, the guards wouldn't notice them as they passed in the darkness. That, too, had paid off.

A ridge of stones standing upright like a collection of monoliths less than a hundred feet from the concrete structure acted as perfect cover. Quinn found a gap between the rocks that gave him a good view of both the guardhouse and the short valley that led up to it.

'Don't know if this is the right time to mention this or not, but we're kind of trapped here, aren't we?' Nate said. 'I mean, when we head back, we're going to trip the sensors again. And this time I don't think they'll ignore it.'

'We're not going back,' Quinn said. 'At least not yet.'

'Wait, we're going to try to get *inside* the fence?'

'Maybe.'

'Didn't you promise Orlando this was just a simple recon, and we wouldn't be doing anything that could get us into trouble?'

'I guess I was wrong.'

The truth was Quinn hadn't planned on making an incursion at all, but the opportunity presented itself, and instinctively he realized it might be their best chance at getting in. In his job, listening to those instincts wasn't a luxury. He trusted them, and this time they had said, 'Move!'

From the left, toward the other end of the valley, there was the sound of several footsteps. The others had arrived.

Quinn peeked between the rocks at the guardhouse. The door had opened halfway, and there was the shadowy form of a man standing just inside. As Quinn angled to the right so he could get a look at the guards, he pulled out his camera phone. They had closed into a tight group around their prisoner. Quinn snapped several photos as they approached the guard-house. Once everyone was inside, he chose the best pics and attached them to a hastily prepared email.

Need ID on man tied up.

He started to address it to both Orlando and Peter, then changed his mind and sent it to Peter only. Best to let Orlando relax and not worry.

'You've been checking for sensors?' Quinn asked Nate.

His apprentice nodded. 'They were placed about every fifty feet through the hills, but the last one's more than a hundred feet back there.'

'So there's none up here?'

'I didn't say that. I just meant I hadn't seen any more.'

The lack of sensors this close to the guardhouse made sense. If there had been any, every time a guard went for a walk or to relieve himself the alarm would sound. That was an annoyance no one would want to deal with.

'Okay,' Quinn said. 'As close as we can get.'

He stepped out from behind the rock and hoped to God that he was right.

# 28

'I see them,' Base said.

Tucker picked up his radio. 'About fucking time.'

It was unfair, he knew. The rocks out there were a bitch. But dammit, he hating waiting this long. He wanted to know who was sneaking around their operation, and what he wanted.

Two minutes later, Base said, 'Ready for video hookup.'

Tucker already had the video window open on his computer. The light level was a little low, but he could still make out several of his men moving around in the background. Then a face appeared on the screen. Tucker recognized him as a guy named Carter.

'You have a picture?' Carter asked.

'Yes. Could use a little light.'

'Hold on.'

A few seconds later, the picture lightened up by twenty percent.

'Better,' Tucker said. 'Let me see him.'

'Over here,' someone barked on the other end.

A body moved into the shot. Male, dark clothes.

'Can't see his face. I need to see his face,' Tucker said.

Someone adjusted the light on the other end, illuminating the intruder's face. Tucker couldn't help feeling a moment of disappointment. He'd been hoping the man was Jonathan Quinn. He would have liked to have seen the look on the cleaner's face once he realized who was in charge here. A fucking laugher that would have been. But apparently Mr. Quinn had lost the Dupuis woman's trail.

'Who the hell are you?' Tucker asked.

The man kept his face neutral and his mouth shut.

A rifle butt swung into the frame and slammed into the captive's stomach. The man doubled over and fell out of the frame.

'Get the fuck up,' a voice off camera yelled. 'You hear me? Get the fuck up.'

Tucker could hear retching off camera, then something scraping against the concrete floor. For several seconds nothing happened, then the captive's head moved back into the frame, rising unsteadily from the bottom.

'Let me ask you again,' Tucker said. 'Who the hell are you?'

'No,' the man said.

This time the rifle hit him in the kidney. The man flew forward, screaming, almost running into the camera.

Tucker smiled. Not because of the man's pain, he was ambivalent about that. He smiled because the man spoke, and in Tucker's experience once someone opened his mouth, he would eventually tell whatever he knew.

'Bring him in,' Tucker said.

He could hear Carter starting to say 'Yes, sir,' but the guard was cut off as Tucker quit the program.

He pushed himself away from his desk and stood up. There were two empty cells along the hall where they were keeping the woman. One of those would be fine for their new guest.

He took a deep breath, then picked up the phone and punched in the number for the lab.

'Yes?' The voice was young. One of the technicians.

'I need to talk to Mr. Rose,' Tucker said.

'He left a couple of minutes ago. Headed up to the main level.'

Tucker hung up without saying anything, then rushed out of his office hoping to catch his boss before the old man disappeared into his quarters. Mr. Rose's rule number one: If the door to his private room was closed, he was not to be disturbed. There wasn't even the phrase 'except in cases of emergency' tacked on. If he was inside, all could wait until he reappeared.

Tucker passed only one other person in the corridors on his way to the elevators, one of his security men on patrol. When the facility had been built, it was designed so that a hundred people could work inside at the same time. Mr. Rose's operation was manned by less than half that amount — twenty security personnel, seventeen technical staff, Mr. Rose, and Tucker. Thirty-nine total. Of course, that wasn't counting the Dupuis woman. Or Mr. Rose's special packages.

When he reached the elevator, the car was already there and empty.

Frowning, he headed to Mr. Rose's suite, hoping he wasn't too late. As he turned onto Mr.

Rose's hallway, he nearly ran into the old man. He was standing just five feet around the corner, talking to a technician Tucker had seen a couple times before.

Whatever conversation they'd been having had stopped the minute Tucker appeared.

'Glad I caught you,' Tucker said.

Mr. Rose just stared at him.

'We've caught an intruder.'

That woke the old man up. 'What? Where? Here in the base?'

'No,' Tucker said. 'He was outside the fence, near the gate. He tripped the sensors, then hid when my men went to find him.'

'But they caught him.'

'Yes,' Tucker said.

'Who is he?'

'I don't know yet. He wouldn't give us his name. My men are bringing him here right now.'

'Into the facility?' Mr. Rose did not sound happy.

'I can question him here, and we can run his prints through the system.'

'Do a complete scan of him before you bring him down,' Mr. Rose said. 'Understand me? We can't chance anything jeopardizing the operation.'

'Okay. Sure.'

'Not 'okay, sure'! It should not even be an option. You should have already thought of that.'

'Of course,' Tucker said. He'd known his mistake even as he'd spoken the words. He tried to do a little damage control. 'It's standard operating procedure is all I mean. We'll definitely do it.'

'That's not what it sounded like.'

'I apologize if I was unclear.'

'You were,' Mr. Rose said.

No one spoke for several seconds.

'Was there more, Mr. Tucker?'

'No,' Tucker said. 'That was it.'

'Give me a full report when you are done talking to him.'

'Of course.'

* * *

'Come on, come on, come on.' The words were more in Quinn's head than spoken.

He and Nate had crawled to within a foot of the gate. It was built like the fences, horizontal wires about half a foot apart. And while it looked like it could also be electrified, it wasn't humming like the double fence that converged to meet it.

'Come on,' he whispered again.

Getting to the other side should have been simple. They should have been able to slip through the deactivated fence while the others were inside with their prisoner. The problem was that one of the guards had decided it was a good time to take a leak. And even though he had finished, he was taking his sweet time zipping up and rejoining his friends inside.

Each second longer meant it was a second closer to more of the guards coming back outside. Perhaps they would take the prisoner

370

through the gate and to the Yellowhammer facility. Maybe even after they were gone, someone would flip a switch turning on the power to the gate. Quinn's best chance was to move now, before any of that could occur, but the son of a bitch seemed to be enjoying a little alone time.

Finally, the guard finished up and went back inside.

*About goddamn time*, Quinn thought.

He glanced at the window. No one seemed to be keeping tabs on the outside. What was inside was more interesting to them at the moment.

He gave Nate a quick nod, then crawled forward into the pale light that illuminated the gate. Once he was moving he didn't stop. He pushed his backpack to the other side first, then squeezed between the wires. They were pretty taut, but they gave enough to let him through. Nate followed right behind him.

Once they'd both made it, they ran in a crouch down the road until they found a good spot from which to keep an eye on the gate. Turned out their precautions were unnecessary. It was another ten minutes before the door to the guardhouse opened again. This time, though, it wasn't another pee break. It looked like the whole squad had come out, and with them the prisoner.

The gate opened and the group passed through. They continued down the road, passing less than a dozen feet away from Quinn and Nate's position.

Once they'd gone by, Nate looked at Quinn,

his eyebrows raised in a question.

Quinn nodded.

Without a word, they began to follow.

★  ★  ★

The elevator let Tucker out in a secure room at ground level. The walls, the floor, the ceiling, they were all concrete, and at least two feet thick, built to withstand a direct, pre-nuclear era attack. Of course, these days you wouldn't need an atomic bomb to do the job. A single bunker buster would destroy the whole facility.

Tucker pressed his palm against the security-release pad next to the door, and was greeted with the gentle whoosh of the lock releasing.

Tucker entered the main part of the structure. From the outside it looked like a small one-room cinderblock hut built in a small clearing between piles of boulders. Most people would mistake it for something left over from one of the handful of failed mines that were spread through the Alabama Hills.

Inside, there was another palm reader near the exterior door, and on the wall above it, a ten-inch television monitor. Tucker touched the power button on the monitor, and the feed from a camera mounted on the cabin's roof appeared. It provided a wide shot of the entire visible area in front of the cabin, and since it was in night vision mode, everything was in tones of green.

Tucker's men had just come out of the dry wash to the left and were seventy-five feet away, on the other side of the road. Tucker scanned the

372

hills behind them. He didn't expect to see anyone, but he had a hard time believing their new guest had come alone. What he saw was rocks, and nothing else.

Tucker placed his palm on the reader. This time the sound was more a heavy click than a whoosh. He pulled the door open, but stayed in the shadows as his men closed the distance.

The prisoner was walking in the middle of the group, his head down. Not defeated, more like he was conserving his energy.

*Thinks he'll be busting out of here*, Tucker thought. But that wasn't going to happen.

Once everyone was inside, Tucker then led the way to the waiting elevator car. It was large enough to hold all of them with plenty of room to spare.

It wasn't until the doors shut that he turned to the prisoner.

'Look at me,' Tucker said.

The prisoner didn't move.

One of the guards reached out and pushed the man's chin up so that Tucker could see his face.

'Who the fuck are you? And what are you doing on my land?' Tucker said.

The prisoner smiled like he was the smartest man in the room and had no interest in talking to any of them.

Tucker shook his head. 'You don't want to mess with me.'

The man let out a laugh.

Tucker counted to five, then punched the guy in the face, knocking him backward into the wall. He slumped down, blood pouring from his nose.

They left him there until the doors opened again.

'Put him in the room two doors down from the woman,' Tucker said.

He stepped through the opening, then headed for his office. He'd let the bastard stew in his own blood for a while before he started the serious questioning. But he wouldn't wait too long.

He didn't want to let his own anger fade.

# 29

Quinn and Nate watched from a distance as the guards walked into what had to be the main entrance to Yellowhammer. Someone had been waiting for them just inside the door, but who-ever it was remained in the shadows, unidentifiable.

Quinn knew if they were going to try to get inside, this wouldn't be the way. He examined the map Peter had sent them, then glanced up to get his bearings.

'We'll head for that hill over there,' he whispered, pointing at a mound to the northwest.

'Should we check in?' Nate said.

Quinn shook his head. 'It's fine. We'll let her sleep.'

'We've been gone a long time. I'll bet she's not sleeping.'

Nate was right. Knowing Orlando, she was still waiting up for them.

'I'll text her, okay?' Quinn said, annoyed.

'Fine. Okay. Whatever you want.'

Quinn pulled out his phone and tapped in a quick message, then pressed Send.

Still on recon. All good. Get some sleep.

'Happy?' Quinn said to Nate.

'I'm always happy. I was just watching out for you.'

Quinn stared at him for a moment, then broke away. 'I'll lead.'

★ ★ ★

There was no cinderblock hut covering the back door to Yellowhammer. There was no need. It had been built utilizing the existing entrance to a mine hidden by several boulders. Quinn only knew this because of a notation on the map. Finding the actual entrance was another story.

They fanned out, each taking a section of the hill that looked like the best bet. At first Quinn thought he'd come up dry. It was just more rock on rock. A glance over at Nate told him his apprentice was doing no better.

Quinn walked twenty feet up the slope and took another look around, not expecting much. But then his eyes stopped on a flat-top rock sticking out from the side of the hill.

He made his way over to it, half walking, half slipping across the gravelly surface. There was something about the surface of the rock. Some of the color along the top seemed odd, lighter.

*Scrapes*, he realized as he got close.

There were dozens of them, each leading toward the edge of the rock that hung out into the air. Something had been moved. Something big. He peered over the side. There, leaning against the scraped rock, was another slab.

'Over here,' he called out.

Nate jogged over.

'That rock doesn't belong there,' Quinn said. 'I'd say it was up here not long ago.'

'That thing must weigh over a ton,' Nate said. 'How the hell would they have moved it? Couldn't have just manhandled it.'

'Helicopter,' Quinn said. 'The same way they get in here.'

It was the only piece of machinery that would have been able to do the job, given the physical restrictions of the location. And once the job was done, the entrance would be sealed off.

'I hate to point this out,' Nate said, 'but we don't have one of those.'

'We don't need it. We just need to move it enough to get in.' Quinn pointed toward the right edge. 'It's already leaning a little. We just need to help it along.'

He pulled off his backpack and removed the twenty-foot piece of climbing rope he had coiled at the bottom.

'Slip this over the top. Then get up there and push the rock with your feet. I'll pull the rope. Careful you don't fall once it starts moving, though.'

'Ha-ha,' Nate said.

Once everything was in place, Quinn said, 'On three. One. Two. Three.'

He pulled as Nate pushed. At first nothing happened. He wondered if perhaps the rock was lodged in tighter than he had assumed.

'Again,' he said.

Nate groaned. 'Come on, you son of a — '

Then it moved. An inch at first, then two, then six. When it finally stopped, there was a gap three feet wide by almost five tall.

It wasn't until Nate came down and was

helping him coil up the rope that Quinn realized he had made his apprentice push with his legs. Or leg rather. Nate's missing limb hadn't even occurred to him. And, he had to admit, it seemed not to have made a difference.

'You want me to lead, or you?' Nate asked as they pulled their packs back on.

'Have at it,' Quinn said.

Nate smiled, then slipped into the newly created opening.

★ ★ ★

It looked at though it had been decades since anyone had used this route into the underground facility. Twenty feet in, there was a door all but rusted shut. But time had weakened the metal so much they were able to wrestle it open without breaking out any of their gear.

Using flashlights, they made their way down a set of stairs that had been cut into the earth, then covered with a layer of concrete that had long ago started to crack. The walls and ceiling of the tunnel had also been reinforced, but weren't doing any better. There were patches where concrete had fallen and broken into pieces on the steps.

As they descended, the tunnel made a constant, gradual turn to the left, providing them no more than fifteen feet of forward visibility. So it was almost without warning that they reached the end of the tunnel.

'Where's the door?' Nate asked. The dead end was covered with more of the ancient concrete.

'We must have missed it,' Quinn said.

'I didn't see one.'

Quinn pushed by him and headed back up the tunnel. He swung his flashlight back and forth so he could get a good look at the walls on either side.

Nothing.

He continued on for fifty feet before turning back and making a second pass.

'Is it possible they never finished it?' Nate asked.

'It's finished,' Quinn said. 'Why else cover this end with the concrete? If they'd still been working on it and stopped, we'd be looking at raw earth.'

'Maybe they covered it up when they decided not to finish it. Some sort of safety precaution.'

The possibility rang truer than Quinn wanted to admit. But there was one other fact that negated it.

'Then why did someone block the entrance with the rock?' Quinn asked. 'These guys are serious. They would have checked this tunnel first. If it was unfinished, they wouldn't have wasted the effort moving that slab in place.'

He ran his flashlight over the end of the tunnel, then flipped it around and tapped the metal handle against the surface. There was a dull echo from the other side of the concrete.

'It's hollow,' Nate said, surprised.

'Apparently.'

'What do we have to do? Bust through? That won't be too subtle.'

Quinn said nothing as he examined the

379

surface. It was something near the edge where the end of the tunnel met the wall on the left that caused him to pause. He moved the beam of his flashlight closer, the circle of light condensing to a bright spot on the concrete. He then moved the beam up the wall a couple of feet, then tilted it down until it almost reached the floor before returning it to its original spot.

'What's this look like to you?' he asked.

Nate stepped over and looked at the illuminated surface.

'The crack?' he asked. 'We've seen tons of them on the way down. Wait . . . are you thinking we might be able to push this in?'

Quinn moved the light upward again. 'What about here?'

'Another crack.'

Quinn shook his head. 'Not another.' He moved the light down the wall back to where he'd started. The crack was continuous, curving gradually toward the center as it traveled up.

'Let me see that,' Nate said.

Quinn handed him the flashlight. Nate performed the same examination Quinn had a few moments before, looking both up and down the wall. The crack started near the floor and continued all the way up to an apex at the center of the tunnel's dead end before traveling back down to the floor near the other wall.

'What the hell?' Nate said. 'A door?'

'That's what it looks like to me.'

'But how do we open it?'

'Excellent question.'

380

First they tried pushing on it, but it didn't budge.

'Maybe it can only be opened from the inside,' Nate said.

*A very distinct possibility*, Quinn thought.

'Look for a release,' Quinn said. 'Something that you'd press or maybe step on.'

They searched for five minutes but found nothing. Quinn stood staring at the wall, trying to think of another possibility. Twist the door like a dial? Doubtful. What if they needed to push the door at an exact spot? Perhaps, but . . . it didn't seem like the right answer, either.

Maybe Nate was right and the only way to open the door was from the other side. If that was the case, they were done here, and might as well figure out a way to get off the facility grounds without drawing attention.

Quinn's phone vibrated against his leg. He reached in and pulled it out. As he pressed his thumb against the screen to release the lock, he paused. His phone had *rung* in his pocket. They were a good fifty feet underground, and he shouldn't have been able to get a signal. There was only one reason he could think of that would explain it. The facility must have been wired with an antenna so cell phones could be used. Large businesses did it all the time, wiring their buildings so you could still get a signal in the elevator or while you were sitting on the toilet. Progress.

He looked at the name on the screen. Peter.

'You got my email?' Quinn asked.

'Yes. Where the hell are you?'

'Exactly where I told you we were going.'

'Yellowhammer?' Peter asked.

'Yes.'

'And that's where you took the picture?'

'Do you know him?'

'He . . . works with my client. His name is Kevin Furuta. He's CIA.'

'CIA? What the hell is he doing here?'

Peter didn't answer.

'What's he doing here, Peter?' Quinn asked again.

'I'm not sure.'

'How the hell did he even know about this place?'

'After you told me about your meeting with Primus, I informed my client. He must have thought it necessary to send Furuta in for a look. Probably figured he could get in and out before you even arrived.'

'Pretty goddamn stupid, if you ask me,' Quinn said.

'I don't disagree.' There was a pause. 'Do you think you can get him out?'

'Get him out? I don't even know if I can get in yet. And if I remember correctly, that's not my priority.' But even as he said it, Quinn knew he'd do what he could.

Peter must have known it, too. 'Keep me posted,' he said, then hung up.

Before Quinn put the phone back in his pocket, he realized he had a text waiting. It was from Orlando and had been sent while Quinn and Nate had been searching for the back door entrance.

Where are you?

*She knows*, Quinn thought.

He typed in a quick response that implied they were in a safe position doing a basic recon. Her response was almost immediate, and confirmed his thoughts.

Bullshit

He put his phone back in his pocket. They could argue about his decision later; doing it now and by text would be counterproductive.

'Did I hear you say that guy was CIA?' Nate asked.

Quinn nodded.

'Well, that's awesome. Did he bring any friends with him?'

'I don't think so.'

Quinn started walking back up the tunnel toward the surface.

'Where you going?' Nate asked.

But Quinn didn't answer. Since the door was a bust, he figured their next best chance was one of the ventilation shafts. Though if Tucker's group had gone to the trouble of blocking the entrance to the emergency exit, they surely would have done something that would keep anyone from using the vents. Still, Quinn had to try.

When they reached the rusty door, Quinn stepped through first, then turned to make sure Nate shut it behind them, only Nate wasn't there.

Quinn stepped back inside. Nate was ten feet down the tunnel, looking toward Quinn but not at him.

'I think I might know how it works,' Nate said.

Quinn was quiet for a moment, then glanced over his shoulder at the rusted metal door. 'Are you thinking that — '

'Yes,' Nate said. 'Stay here.'

Without further explanation, Nate ran back down the tunnel.

Thirty seconds later his voice crackled in Quinn's ear.

'Can . . . ou hear . . . Quinn, can . . . ear me?'

'You're breaking up.'

' . . . ose the do . . . '

'What?'

' . . . e door . . . ose . . . oor.'

'You're not coming through.'

'Close . . . e door.'

That was enough. Quinn reached out, grabbed the handle of the rusty door, then pulled it closed. As he did, he noticed a lever built into the frame. It was in the down position.

' . . . id yo . . . lose it?'

Quinn thought about it for another second, then reached out and flipped the lever up.

For a moment there was nothing. Then, ' . . . aaa. That d . . . ome . . . down. Come . . . '

Quinn raced back down the tunnel. At the bottom he found Nate standing near where the tunnel had ended. Only now the artificial wall had moved out of the way.

'Closed circuit,' Nate said. 'All you had to do was close the door.'

Quinn thought about telling him it had nothing to do with whether the door was open or closed at all, but decided to save it for later. It was good for Nate to feel like he'd accomplished something. It had been a good guess anyway. And if Nate hadn't suggested it, Quinn would have never seen the lever.

'And you're going to love this,' Nate said.

He shone his light through the opening. The tunnel went on for another ten feet, but straight and level now.

And at the end, a door. A real door.

'I think we've found the way in.'

# 30

Tucker looked at his watch. It had been thirty minutes since the prisoner had been taken to his cell. He would have liked to leave the guy sitting in the dark a little longer, but there was no time for that.

It wouldn't be long before he and his team would have to pitch in on the final preparations of the shipment. And by this time tomorrow he would be on his way to Bali, the job complete, and his final payment sitting safely in his offshore account.

He wasn't even worried about what would be next after that. At some point he would have to find more work. But his pay on this one had been pretty damn good, so it would be a while before he'd have to make any calls.

He radioed one of his men to meet him near the detention cell, then pushed himself away from his desk.

It was time to find out what the asshole knew.

★ ★ ★

The door from the tunnel let out into a wider corridor. Quinn went through first, his SIG with suppressor attached in his right hand. Nate, also armed, stepped out of the tunnel as soon as Quinn was clear.

Quinn signaled to his apprentice to leave the

tunnel door cracked open in case they had to make a quick exit, then leaned forward just enough to peek around the corner.

Empty, both ways. He stuck his head out a little farther for a better look.

His first impression was that they'd suddenly found themselves inside a naval ship, or more accurately, perhaps, a submarine. All the walls were metal, and thick with layers of gray paint. Along the ceiling and hugging the top of one wall were pipes of various diameters running lengthwise down the corridor. Lights hung down between the pipes every ten feet or so, and gave the hallway plenty of illumination.

To the left, the corridor went another fifty feet, then turned to the right, out of view. To the right, it continued half again as far before dead-ending at a closed door. Somewhere in the distance was the sound of a door closing. He paused, listening, but there was nothing else.

He pulled out the Yellowhammer blueprints from his backpack and located their position. This particular section was at the north end of the facility. The corridor to the left that made the ninety-degree turn ended in what appeared to be a storage room. The rest of the base lay to the right, through the closed door.

The map showed that just beyond the door was the main east-west corridor. Compared to the passageway they were in, there was a much greater chance it would be occupied.

He folded the printout and put it into his pocket.

'Stay here,' he mouthed to Nate.

He could see the reluctance in his apprentice's eyes, but Nate nodded anyway.

Quinn approached the door at the end of the hallway. The handle was a lever, not a knob. Down to unlock, up to lock. Quinn pressed his ear against the door, his free hand resting on the handle. Quiet.

Slowly he pressed down on the lever. There was a muffled groan as the bars holding the door in place moved out of their sockets. Once they were free, Quinn paused. If anyone had heard the noise, they'd show up any second.

When no one did, he pulled the door back a few inches, testing the hinges. They were smooth and silent.

The corridor beyond was much like the one he was in, only larger. Again he listened for sounds of life, and again he was greeted with silence.

He pulled the door open farther, then stepped over the threshold.

He knew from his examination of the blueprint that there was another corridor about twenty yards to the east that led to the elevator. It was the only way to the facility's main exit. Beyond that, the hallway he was in disappeared around a bend to the left. To the west, there was another intersecting corridor running to the south. No elevator down this one; it led to living quarters from when the base was fully staffed.

The majority of the facility was to the west, so if there was any activity, that's where he would find it. Quinn ducked back into the hallway where he'd left Nate, then motioned for his apprentice to join him near the door.

'I'm going to see if I can find Peter's friend,' Quinn said.

'You want me to come with you?'

'No. Stay here and watch my back. Let me know if anyone comes down the hallway.'

Nate didn't look happy with the answer.

'Problem?' Quinn asked.

'No. It's fine.'

'Good,' Quinn said. 'I'm not sure how well our radios are going to work down here. If we lose contact for more than twenty minutes, get back into the tunnel. Give me another fifteen, then get the hell out of here.'

As Quinn started to open the door again, he heard a metal groan somewhere in the distance. Immediately he pulled the door closed, leaving the barest of cracks so he could hear what was going on.

A door farther down the hallway shut, then there were steps moving toward Quinn's position from the east. The person's pace was steady, not rushed. Quinn soon became aware of a voice, too.

' . . . him now. Have two men meet me there, then the rest of you should go downstairs and help get things ready to go.' Male, with an accent. Australian, and unforgettable. *Leo Tucker.* Just like Hardwick had promised.

'Okay,' a second voice said. It was tinny, coming over a radio.

Tucker was close now, within twenty feet.

*Just keep walking,* Quinn willed him. *Just keep walking.*

'Once I finish with him, I'll join you in the lab,' Tucker said.

'Petersen and Linden are on their way to you.'

'Good.'

Quinn wanted to peer through the crack to see if he could get a look at what was going on, but he resisted the urge, and instead held the door steady so that Tucker would have no reason to notice it wasn't closed.

Tucker continued past without breaking stride. Quinn waited until the footsteps began to recede, then pulled open the door and looked out.

Tucker had almost reached the west end of the hallway where it turned to the south.

Quinn looked back at Nate. 'Twenty minutes,' he whispered, then began following the Australian.

\* \* \*

Tucker couldn't help feeling a bit of respect for his captive. The man was good. He'd clammed up tight and was refusing to speak again.

'Torture, is that what you're waiting for?' Tucker asked the man. 'Maybe some bamboo shoots under the fingernails? A few good kicks to the kidneys?'

The man did what he'd been doing for the last fifteen minutes. He smiled, a grotesque fake smile that made Tucker want to pistol-whip him.

'Well, hate to disappoint,' Tucker said. 'But torture's not something I'm into.'

This time he was the one who smiled, then he

390

moved his gun away from his side and shot the man in the knee.

'Oh, wait,' Tucker said as the man howled in pain. 'I forgot, I am into torture. I just don't like to work at it.'

He shot the man in the other knee.

The prisoner screamed, then fell off the chair onto the floor.

'Who the fuck are you?' Tucker said.

The man writhed in pain, unable to respond.

'Perhaps I'll do your elbow next. Is that what you want?'

'No,' the man gasped. 'Please.'

'You answer my questions, and we'll bind those up for you. Give you a little something for the pain, too. How's that sound?'

'Please,' the man repeated.

'Who are you?'

'Furuta,' the man said, his voice labored. 'Kevin Furuta.'

'All right, Mr. Furuta. This is progress. Who do you work for?'

'Please. My legs. Help me.'

'You answer my questions first, remember? Questions with an s. That makes it plural. You know what plural means, right?'

'The Agency,' Furuta said. 'I work for them.'

'Now, that's interesting. Why would the CI-fucking-A have an interest in us?'

Furuta said nothing.

Tucker raised his gun and pointed it at the man's arm.

'Come alone, did you?' Tucker asked.

'No,' Furuta said.

But the answer came too fast, and Tucker knew it was a lie.

'There's a strike team waiting close by. If they don't hear from me soon, their orders are to attack.'

'Oh, Jesus Christ. Where did you get that line? Out of some fucking Bruce Willis film? You're alone, Mr. Furuta. And you're royally screwed.'

'No. Really, they're there.'

'Enough,' Tucker said.

He shot the man in the left elbow. Furuta screamed again, then fell silent. Tucker kicked him to see if he was still conscious, but the man had passed out.

'Patch him up?' Petersen asked.

'Fuck no,' Tucker said. 'Let him bleed out. He's no use to us anyway. Even if the CIA is interested in us, we'll be gone before they can do anything about it. You've got to love bureaucracy.'

Linden opened the door and let Tucker pass through first. Once they were all in the hallway, Tucker glanced back at the room Marion Dupuis was in.

'Are we bringing her along?' Petersen asked.

'No,' Tucker said. 'Leave her to rot. She's caused us enough problems.'

'You're in a generous mood tonight,' Linden said.

'Thanks for noticing.'

They exited the short hallway and shut the door behind them.

# 31

Marion had heard them bring the other one in. At first she thought they were coming for her again. Either they had decided it was time for more questions, or had realized she had nothing to offer so were coming to get rid of her. Oddly, it was the former she feared most. At least if they had decided to kill her, she'd have nothing to lose. She could fight with all she had left, and if by some miracle she freed herself, she could try to find Iris. She knew there was zero chance of that happening, but she clung to the idea, thinking maybe, just maybe . . .

She had pressed her ear against her door, hoping to hear what their intentions were. But the men had not come to her cell. Instead, she heard another door open down toward the main exit. Feet scuffled across the floor, then someone barked, 'Get the fuck in there.'

This went on for over a minute. A struggle of some sort. That much was obvious. It ended with a smack and a grunt. Then the door slammed closed.

'Asshole!' someone yelled. The voice had come from inside the hallway.

'Chill,' a second voice said.

'You see this? I'm bleeding.'

'Just a scratch.'

'Fucking asshole!' the first voice yelled again.

393

'When we get the word, I want to be the one who offs him.'

'Come on,' the second voice said.

The door at the end of the hallway opened, then shut. A second later, all was quiet again.

Another prisoner, she thought. Somebody else with a child? Someone who had been able to put up more of a fight than Marion had?

When they had taken her out earlier, she had counted two other doors, both on the same side of the hallway as the one to her cell, and behind them rooms she imagined were very much like her own. The door that had slammed shut hadn't sounded close enough to be from the room next door. So whoever their new captive was, he or she had to be in the room nearest the exit.

If there was just some way she could communicate with him. She thought for a moment, her eyes searching the blackness for an answer. The idea that came to her wasn't perfect, but it was something.

She removed her tennis shoes, then began tapping one against the metal door. Maybe the other person would be able to hear it.

*Tap-tap-tap.*

Silence.

*Tap-tap-tap.*

Still nothing.

*Tap-tap-tap . . . tap-tap-tap . . . tap-tap-tap . . . tap-tap —*

She stopped. Had she heard something?

She waited, but the only thing she heard was her own breathing.

*Tap-tap-tap . . . tap-tap-tap . . . tap —*

*Clank.*

*Clank.*

*Clank.*

Marion almost cried. The other person had heard her.

For the next five minutes they tried to communicate with each other, tapping back and forth but with no more meaning than an acknowledgment that they knew the other was there, confirming that they were not alone, but little more.

The other prisoner's responses began to lag, then finally stopped altogether. Marion continued tapping for several minutes, trying to get him to return her signal, but he had either lost interest, or worse, lost consciousness.

As a last resort, she found the crack between the door and the frame with her finger, then moved her mouth over.

'Can you hear me?' she yelled.

But she knew it was useless. Where the door had transmitted and amplified the tapping of her shoe, it also acted as an effective buffer, bouncing her voice back into the room and letting very little of it pass through.

She slumped to the floor, knowing that nothing had changed for her. In thirty minutes, in an hour, in a day — at some point they *would* come for her. She stared at the floor, almost numb to the possibility now.

When the hallway door opened again sometime later, she thought this time was it. Her turn to die. Only once again it was the door at the other end of the hallway that opened, not hers.

She could hear raised voices, but could not make out the words. She figured they were giving the new prisoner the same treatment they had given her.

Then a loud crack reverberated down the hall, and a few seconds later, another.

Gunshots. She had heard them in Africa, only more at a distance. Here the source of the sound was only a couple dozen feet away at most, and the metal hallway didn't help, enhancing the noise instead of dampening it.

Marion scrambled into the corner, pulling her knees to her chest and pressing her hands against her ears. She didn't want to hear the screams of pain, but they seeped through her fingers anyway.

When she thought it was over, a third gunshot rang out.

This time she was the one who screamed.

★ ★ ★

Quinn almost blew it at the last turn. Tucker had stopped just ten feet away, in front of a door. Two others were standing there with him. Quinn pulled back before any of them could see him.

If they exchanged any words, Quinn couldn't hear them. What he did hear, though, was the door opening, and the men passing through. Once the door closed, he peeked around again.

The corridor was empty. He waited a moment to see if they were coming right back out, then stepped around the corner and approached the door. Like the others he had passed, it appeared solid. There was a small, faded metal sign attached to the wall next to the door. Etched in it were the words: HOLDING CELLS.

Looked like he'd found where they'd taken Furuta.

Quinn glanced around. There were several other doors along this stretch of corridor. He approached the one that was directly opposite and placed his ear against it. He could hear nothing. As he started to open the door, he heard a muffled gunshot behind him. Then another.

*Son of a bitch*, Quinn thought. Had they just shot Furuta? If so, the agent was either dead, or close to it. And there was nothing Quinn could have done about it.

He yanked the door in front of him open, hoping he'd find an empty room. It was a small space. Big enough only for the built-in desk and metal bunk missing a mattress at the other end. A guard's room that didn't look like it had been used since the base had been decommissioned.

Quinn ducked inside and closed the door, sealing himself in darkness. He was there less than a minute when he heard another shot.

'Nate, can you read me?' he said.

Dead air.

'Nate?'

'I can hear you,' Nate said. The signal was weak.

'Okay. Stand by. I might need your help.'

'Copy that.'

The sound of a door opening into the corridor

kept Quinn from saying anything else. He leaned forward, listening.

'You two go help Mr. Rose.' It was Tucker again. 'Tell him I'll be there in a few minutes. Want to check in with the gate first.'

There was a grunt of assent, then the clacking of feet on the metal floor walking away. By the sound of it, they were heading back in the direction Quinn and the man had come.

'Unfriendlies heading your way,' Quinn said. 'Keep your head down.'

'Copy that,' Nate said.

Quinn knew every second counted. If Furuta was injured, he would need immediate attention. Still, Quinn waited a full minute before he opened the door and stepped back into the hallway.

He hesitated at the door to the holding cells, knowing there was a possibility someone was stationed inside. He tightened his grip on his gun, then pressed down on the lever and opened the door.

Inside was a short hallway with three doors down the left side, but no sentry. Quinn stepped through and closed the door behind him.

There were numbers painted on each of the doors: 1, 2, and 3. Cells, Quinn knew. There were no locks, because none were needed. The way the doors latched would keep anyone inside from being able to get out.

He unlatched door number one and pulled it open.

Right on the first try.

Furuta lay in the middle of the floor, a bloody mess. His knees had both been blown out. He had another injury, too, but Quinn couldn't see where it was at first. Somewhere on his torso or arms. His shirt was soaked with blood.

His elbow, Quinn realized. He kneeled down next to the man and felt for a pulse. It was there, but faint, and disappearing fast. The man was bleeding out.

Quinn yanked the laces from Furuta's shoes. He used one for each leg, tying them tightly around the thighs just above the damaged knees. He knew it was futile, but he had to try. As he searched for something he could use on the man's arm, Furuta's eyes opened.

'Hold on, buddy,' Quinn said.

He pulled off one of Furuta's socks, but before he could wrap it around Furuta's bicep, the man stopped him.

'Who are . . . you?' Furuta whispered.

'Peter sent me. I'm here to get you out.'

'No . . . your name.'

'Quinn.'

Furuta actually smiled.

'Just be quiet and let me get you patched up.'

'Too tired,' Furuta said. 'Won't . . . work.'

The man's eyes drifted shut as Quinn tightened the sock around Furuta's arm. He then stood up and moved back into the small hallway.

'Nate, I'm going to need your help.'

'Where are you?'

Quinn gave him directions. 'Have the others passed your position?'

399

'Two minutes ago. No noise in the hallway now.'

'Okay. Be careful. I don't think there's very many of them, but there's enough.'

'Copy that.'

Quinn pulled out his phone. Full signal strength. There was definitely some sort of antenna set up throughout the facility.

He didn't want to make this call, but he had no choice now.

The call rang only once before it was picked up.

'Where are you?' Orlando said.

Quinn hesitated. 'Inside Yellowhammer.'

'*Inside?*'

He could tell she wanted to say more, but was holding back.

'I need your help.'

'Tell me.'

The shift was amazing. From pissed to all business in a split second. She was a pro, after all, though Quinn knew at some point in the near future pissed would make a harsh return.

He told her where he'd left the car, then gave her a quick overview of the outside area surrounding Yellowhammer.

'I'll be there in thirty,' she said, then hung up.

Quinn stepped back into the room and checked Furuta's pulse again. Still weak.

'Hey,' he said as he moved Furuta's chin back and forth. 'I think maybe you should try to stay awake.'

The man's eyes remained closed.

Quinn slapped him, not too hard, but enough to sting. 'Wake up.'

This time Furuta's eyelids peeled open.

'Stay awake, okay?' Quinn said.

'Losing . . . it,' Furuta said. His eyes closed, but then opened again. 'Other one.'

'What?'

'Other one . . . tapped.' His hand twitched on the floor. 'Tapped . . . other one.'

He tried to move his head, his eyes turning upward like he was looking at something beyond him.

'Other one,' he repeated.

This time when his eyes closed, they didn't reopen. Quinn felt for a pulse, but there was none. Too much blood on the floor, and not enough still in the veins. Kevin Furuta was dead.

'Goddammit,' Quinn said.

He'd known this was going to happen. He'd known the moment he'd seen Furuta's shattered body. But that didn't make it any easier.

He closed his eyes and thought for a moment. Maybe it would be best to get the hell out of there. The main reason they'd entered the facility was lying dead at Quinn's feet. They'd learned enough already for Peter to mobilize a full-on assault. There was little more Quinn could do without increasing the chance of discovery. Maybe it was time to —

The latch to the main corridor door groaned. Quinn ducked into the corner of cell number one. He could hear someone step into the hallway, then close the door behind them.

'Quinn?' The voice was a whisper.

Quinn stepped around the opening to the cell and found Nate standing a few feet away.

Nate gave him a nod, but showed no other reaction.

'Any problems?' Quinn asked.

'No one. Very quiet.'

Quinn was beginning to think all of Tucker's people were helping this Mr. Rose he'd heard the Australian talk about and were somewhere else in the facility.

Nate looked past Quinn into the cell. 'That him?'

Quinn nodded.

'They really messed him up, didn't they?'

'He's dead.'

'He's . . . son of bitch. Do we still take him with us?'

Quinn looked back through the door at the body. 'No. We can't ri — '

He stopped himself.

*The other.*

Glancing to his right, he could see the two other cell doors. Numbers two and three.

*The other.*

He approached the door to cell number two.

'What are you doing?' Nate asked.

Quinn held up a hand to silence him, then pulled out his gun again. Carefully he released the door's latch and pushed it open. The only light inside was that which spilled in from the hallway, but it was enough for him to see the room was empty.

He moved over to cell three.

'Pull out your flashlight,' he said to Nate.

He waited until his apprentice had the light on, then he repeated what he had done with the previous door.

Only, unlike cell number two, there was someone there.

# 32

Marion barely registered the hallway door opening for the third time. She'd moved into the corner farthest from the door, and had curled against herself. If anyone was talking, she didn't hear. She just rocked back and forth, her mind searching for someplace happy, something to help her forget.

Ice skating with her family as a girl. The school trip she'd taken to New York when she was in high school. Kissing Reynard Moreau in an empty math classroom. He had been more nervous than she. She could remember feeling him shake even as his lips touched hers.

But she couldn't hold on to any of the memories for long before they slipped into an image of Iris, eyes filling with water, lower lip quavering, her whole body emanating fear and confusion.

Marion rocked harder, trying to force her mind away from any thoughts of the child. But when they did, what replaced them were the faces of her mother and father and her sister, all staring at her with lifeless eyes.

She was jerked into the present by the sound of the latch to her door moving.

They'd come for her. Finally, they'd come.

It was her turn now.

*Let the first bullet kill me*, she prayed. *Dear God, please.*

She stared at the door as it swung open. She saw the shadow of a man, a gun at his side.

When the beam of a flashlight moved across her face, she started to scream.

'Hey, hey,' a male voice said. 'It's all right. Don't yell. It's okay.'

But she knew it wasn't okay. She'd seen the gun in his hand. And though her eyes were now shut tight, she could feel him approach her.

Her scream turned into a sob, and tears began pouring down her cheeks.

'It's all right,' he repeated, much closer now.

Why did he keep saying that?

'Nate, move the light out of her eyes.'

The glow on her lids lessened, but didn't go completely away.

'It's okay,' the man said. 'We're here to help you. Take a breath. Relax.'

Despite herself, she did what he said. After a moment, she allowed her eyelids to part.

The man was in front of her, a warm smile on his face. She almost smiled, too, then she realized who he was.

It was the man who chased her in Montreal.

The man who had tried to stop her in front of her parents' house.

He wasn't here to help her.

He *was* here to kill her.

She started screaming again.

'It's okay. It's okay,' he said.

'You tried to catch me,' she said. 'At my parents'. You killed my parents!'

'I never even met your parents,' the man said. 'I'm sorry they're dead, but I had nothing to do with it. I was there to help you. Like I'm here now.'

Easy words. 'You killed them. You killed my sister. Now you're going to kill me, too!'

'Listen to me. I am *not* here to hurt you. I'm here to get you out.'

She stared at him, unable to believe it.

'Your name is Marion Dupuis. You smuggled a child into the States. A little girl from Africa. You were trying to save her.'

'You killed that man in New York,' she said. 'I saw your picture on TV.'

The man almost laughed. 'The same people who brought you here set things up to look like I murdered someone. We're the same, in a way. These people aren't friends to either of us.'

'I don't believe you.'

'I get that. And that's fine. But think of it this way: If you think you're going to be killed anyway, what's it going to hurt coming with us?'

'I think I hear something.' The voice came from the man holding the flashlight. Nate, he'd been called.

'Check,' the other man said.

Nate disappeared into the hall, plunging the room back into semi-darkness.

'Keep quiet,' the man with the gun whispered.

She did as she was told, a part of her wanting to believe the man's words.

Several seconds passed before Nate returned.

'Two people,' he said. 'Passed right by, though.'

'Good,' his partner said. 'Now what's it going to be? You come with us and see if we can get you out of here? Or stay and die for sure?'

'Who are you?' she asked.

The man hesitated, then said, 'I'm Quinn. My friend's Nate. So, what's it going to be?'

She wanted to go, but . . .

'Iris,' she said.

'What?'

'The child,' she said.

'Iris,' Quinn repeated.

'I won't leave without her.'

Quinn went silent as he turned to the side and stared at the empty corner of the room for several seconds before looking back at her. 'What if we get you someplace safe, and then I go look for her?'

'I'm not leaving her.'

'The place I mean is still within the facility. But we'll have a better chance to find her if I go alone.'

She could see Nate glance at his partner, concern on his face. 'I told you I don't trust you,' she said.

'Without us you won't even have the chance to find her.'

He was right, and she knew it. *Oh, God,* she thought. *What choice do I have?*

The simple answer was none.

She nodded. 'Okay.'

'Can you walk?' he asked.

'I'm fine.'

Quinn held out his free hand to help her up, but she avoided it and rose on her own.

'From now until we get you hidden, you have to do exactly as I say, and no talking.'

'Okay.'

He looked at her feet, and she followed his gaze.

'What?' she asked.

'Do you have any shoes?'

'Right . . . yes.'

She spotted her tennis shoes and started to sit down so she could put them on, but he said, 'Not yet. You'll be quieter in bare feet. But once we get outside, you'll need them.'

'All right.' She was starting to believe him.

'Just don't drop them.'

She nodded, then followed him out the door of her cell.

It was weird to be there without the guards pushing her around. It felt almost like she was doing something wrong. As they approached the entrance to the main corridor, she glanced into the open door of the first cell, and jerked to a stop.

There was a man covered in blood lying in the middle of the floor.

'He's dead?' she asked, surprised she could manage the words.

'Yes,' Quinn said.

'I heard gunshots,' she said.

'I heard them, too.'

'I tried to let him know I was here. That he wasn't alone.'

'I know,' the man said. 'That's how we found you. He told us.'

'He . . . told you?'

But he didn't answer. Instead he ushered her toward where Nate stood near the exit.

'Later,' he whispered to her as she passed.

'Back to the tunnel?' Nate said.

'Yes,' Quinn said. He looked at Marion. 'Ready?'

She hesitated. 'I don't know.'

He gave her one of his warm smiles again. 'That'll have to do.'

★  ★  ★

Quinn let Nate take point, and had Marion Dupuis walk between them.

It had been touch and go with her back in the cell. She'd understandably associated him with her kidnappers. Given the circumstances, Quinn would have done the same. But at least they'd gotten her to come along, and even better, she seemed to be starting to trust him.

They had made it almost halfway back when Nate stopped abruptly. His hand flew up, palm toward Quinn and Marion, telling them to freeze. They were about ten feet from where the hallway took a ninety-degree right turn.

Footsteps. Heading their way.

Quinn did a quick scan of the immediate area. No doors, no alcoves, no place to hide. They would never make it back to the previous section without being either heard or seen.

He listened again. It sounded like it was just a single person. Tucker perhaps?

He put his hands on Marion's shoulders and pushed her against the wall.

'Stay here,' he mouthed.

She nodded, her eyes were wide with fear.

To Nate he mouthed, 'Quietly.' Then motioned for him to get as close to the corner as possible.

Once his apprentice was in position, Quinn took two steps out into the center of the corridor, then waited.

The steps were steady but hurried, as if whoever it was had somewhere to be.

Two steps away.

One.

A man — not the Australian — rushed around the corner, his forward momentum taking him within three feet of Quinn before he realized he wasn't alone. He was wearing fatigue pants and a black T-shirt. The barrel of an M16 peeked above his shoulder.

'Who the hell are — ' the man started to say.

Nate smashed the butt of his pistol against the back of the man's head, forcing him to stumble into Quinn.

Nate hit him again, and the man sagged against Quinn, unconscious.

Blood from a cut caused by the blows trickled down his neck and onto the floor.

Without missing a beat, Quinn tossed the M16 to Nate, then hoisted the man over his shoulder. Nate was already kneeling on the floor, wiping away the blood with a piece of cloth he'd gotten from his backpack.

'Come on,' Quinn whispered, motioning to the woman.

'You're taking him with us?' she said.

'We can't leave him here.'

She didn't seem to like the idea, but she didn't protest further.

Soon they were back in the unused northern hallway that led to the facility's neglected emergency exit, no one else interfering with their escape.

'All the way into the tunnel,' Quinn said.

Once they were surrounded by the old concrete again, he set the man on the ground. He patted the prisoner down. In the guy's pants Quinn found a roll of cash and a cell phone.

'Tie him up. Gag him,' Quinn said to Nate. 'Shoot him if you have to.'

'He's one of the guards,' the woman said. 'You weren't lying to me, were you?'

'No. I wasn't.'

'You'll find Iris?'

Quinn hesitated. 'I'll try.'

'Please. She's only a little girl. I can't imagine what they'll do to her, what they've already done. Please. Please find her.'

Quinn nodded, wanting to promise but knowing that he couldn't.

To Nate he said, 'Keep all the doors closed in case they come looking for him or for her.'

'Right.'

'I might be gone awhile,' Quinn said. 'You'll be safe here. But if it's within an hour or so of dawn, get her out of here before it's too light.'

Nate didn't appear to be happy about the idea, but he nodded.

'Orlando's on her way,' Quinn said. 'See if you can reach her by phone. She can help you, especially if you need to get out without me.'

'But they're leaving tonight,' Marion said.

'What?' Quinn asked, surprised.

411

'I overheard them talking outside my cell. They said they would be out of here before sunup.'

'Son of a bitch,' Quinn said. 'You're sure?'

'I don't know, but it's what I heard.'

'Okay,' he said, trying to sound reassuring. He looked at Nate. 'Stay with the plan. But chances are I'll be back before you have to leave.'

'I'm counting on it,' Nate said.

'So am I.'

# 33

Quinn was pretty sure most of the activity was taking place on the lower level, the one the map had indicated contained the laboratory. He didn't even want to think about what that might mean, what the bastards might be doing there.

The problem he faced was how to get down there without being detected. As far as he could tell, there was only one direct route. The elevator. Unfortunately, he couldn't just get on and ride down without taking a huge risk of getting caught. And while his job was full of risks, the smaller they were, the better.

Before leaving the northern hallway, he looked at the map again. There had to be stairs somewhere, didn't there? OSHA would have had a field day with this place. Of course, it had been built thirty years before the Occupational Safety and Health Administration was even formed. But there still had to be some other way down. It wouldn't make sense not to have a backup.

But if there was, it wasn't on the map.

Short of tunneling through the rock by himself, it looked like the elevators were his only choice. Or, more specifically, the elevator shaft.

According to the map, there were two elevator cars running side by side in a shaft that went from the lowest level up to the surface. If he could somehow get into the shaft, he could make his way down without being seen. Except the only way in would be through the elevator doors. That meant taking the hallway on the other side of the main east-west corridor.

He swore under his breath, counted to three in his head, then reentered the Yellowhammer labyrinth.

\* \* \*

The sentry at the guardhouse reported that there had been no further activity outside the gate. Good news for sure, Tucker thought. It was just further confirmation that Furuta had come alone.

Tucker guessed that the man had been an advance scout, probably had received a tip and had been checking it out first before calling in a whole team. Intelligence gathering, the stiffs at the Agency would have called it. Even if Furuta had somehow gotten word back to his people — which Tucker was confident he hadn't — they wouldn't be able to mount any kind of response before Tucker's team evacuated in a few hours.

The radio on his desk beeped, then the voice of one of his men came on. 'Tucker?'

'Go for Tucker,' Tucker said.

'Mr. Rose is asking for you.'

'Tell Mr. Rose I'll be there in just a bit.'

'Said you should be here supervising us.'

Tucker tensed. 'Tell him I'll be there in just a bit.'

'Sure. Got it.'

Tucker felt like throwing the radio across the room. What did Mr. Rose want him to do? Take care of security? Or babysit a bunch of grown men who could handle a packing job just fine on their own?

*Whatever*, he thought. Mr. Rose was the one paying the bills. If he wanted Tucker to come down to the lab to help, fine.

He radioed the guardhouse one last time just to make sure nothing had changed. All was still quiet. He switched to channel four.

'This is Tucker,' he said into the mic. 'Everybody up.'

He waited for a moment, then repeated the message.

A sleepy voice came over the speaker. 'What time is it?'

'We'll be loading the helicopters in a couple hours.'

'A couple hours? Hell, I'm going back to sleep.'

'Get up,' Tucker said. 'And wake the others. I don't need any of you still groggy when you fly us out of here.'

There was a pause. 'We'll be fine.'

'Get up or you won't be paid.'

'Goddammit,' the pilot said.

'Check in with me after you eat.'

Tucker slipped the radio into the holder on his belt, knowing the pilot would get his flight teams moving. Maybe he'd stop in the kitchen and get a bite himself before heading down to the lab.

Anything to delay being near the cargo.

★ ★ ★

Quinn wished he had a wrecking bar. He would have only needed the small, foot-long version. It would have made things a hell of a lot easier. What he did have was a nine-inch flat blade screwdriver.

He worked it between the sliding doors of the elevator on the left. There was a rubber lining inside, so he had to be careful not to rip it. Once the screwdriver shaft was all the way in, he pushed sideways, trying to create an opening between the doors.

There was resistance at first, the doors holding their position as he applied pressure. Then the right half gave an inch. He jammed the fingers of his right hand in, holding the door in place, then dropped the screwdriver on the floor at his feet and used his left hand to grab the other half.

As he pushed his hands away from each other, the doors began to part. A few inches, then six, then a foot. But at twenty-four inches they stopped, some now-ancient security device kicking in.

He leaned through the opening. It was dark and he could see neither the bottom nor the top of the shaft. At least the elevator car wasn't there.

He scanned the walls just inside, looking for something to anchor his rope. There were several pipes to the right, but he wasn't quite sure how he would reach them. The most promising thing he found was above the opening — a steel bolt sticking out of the wall several inches. It was nowhere near a perfect solution, but Quinn thought he could use it to maneuver over to the pipes.

He positioned his leg in the gap so that his knee pushed against one side of the door, and his foot against the other. He then worked his backpack off and removed the rope from inside. As he was trying to zip the bag back up, it slipped out of his hands and fell to the ground, hitting the handle of the screwdriver. The tool rolled away from the bag, under Quinn's foot, and into the gap.

He whipped his head back inside, but could see nothing. Then, a few seconds later, there was the crash of the screwdriver hitting bottom.

Quinn froze.

Had anyone on the lower level heard? He waited, expecting to see a flood of light as someone below opened the elevator doors to investigate. But the shaft remained dark.

He was just beginning to relax when he heard the footsteps.

They were coming down the hallway toward the elevator.

Quinn grabbed his bag off the floor and moved it into the shaft, hanging it off the bolt he was going to tie the rope to.

He only had seconds now. He squeezed through the opening and grabbed the rail that ran across the top of the door. The sliding sections closed again the moment he was out of the way.

He could hear the steps come into the elevator alcove, then stop. There was a moment of nothing, then the sound of an electric motor starting somewhere below Quinn.

Quinn looked behind him to see if he could tell which car was on its way up. But it was too dark.

The sound got louder and louder. Quinn kept his eyes on the darkness below him, looking for any change, prepared to jump if the car appeared directly beneath him.

The whir grew louder and louder. Then he saw the outline of a car moving up. Not below him, but next to him.

The car stopped seven feet to his left. There was a slight delay, then he heard the door open and the waiting passenger get on. As soon as the doors closed again, the motor restarted, and the elevator plunged back down into the darkness.

Quinn donned his backpack, then inched over to the pipes he'd spotted earlier, and attached the end of his rope to one of them. Once it was tied off, he cinched the loose end around his waist and began a controlled descent into the inky well below.

★   ★   ★

'Quinn?'

Marion looked up. Nate seemed to be talking to himself. When he noticed her, he said, 'Radio.' He turned his collar out so she could see the black dot attached on the inside. 'Quinn?'

'Maybe he's hiding and can't talk,' she offered.

Nate frowned. 'Maybe. But he should have done a radio check by now.'

Before he could call out his friend's name

418

again, there was a buzzing sound. He shot a hand into one of his pants pockets. When he pulled it back out, he was holding a vibrating cell phone.

'Maybe his radio's not working and he's using his phone,' she said.

'It's not him,' Nate said, looking at the display. He flipped it open. 'Hi.' He listened for a moment. 'I'm in the emergency exit tunnel ... No. He went back in ... about fifteen minutes ago ... I can't get through. I think he can't get a signal on the second level ... There's a reason, a good one ... Wait, wait. Orlando, let me talk for a moment ... I didn't go with him because I'm not alone. We found Marion Dupuis. She's with me ... No, no kid. That's who he went back for ... are you there? ... Yes. Said if he didn't get back in a few hours, I was to try and get Marion out ... Where *are* you? ... Jesus, you're as crazy as he is ... You need to watch out for the motion sensors. They go all along the road, then fan out in a wide arc as you near the gate. Maybe you should wait at the ... Okay, okay. But you're not going to be able to get through the gate without them knowing ... What's that mean? ... Orlando? ... Orlando?' He pulled the phone away from his ear. 'Shit.'

Orlando had been the name the other man, Quinn, had mentioned before he left. Marion assumed it was another member of their team.

'What did your friend say?' Marion asked.

Nate continued to stare at the ground for a few seconds longer before looking at her. 'She's

419

on her way to help us.'

'That's good, right?'

He forced a smile, then turned and walked back down the tunnel toward the facility corridor. 'Maybe I can get a signal if I go back into the hallway.'

'Don't. Please,' she said. 'I mean Quinn wanted us to wait here.'

Nate nodded. 'All right. I'll give him another fifteen. If we don't hear from him by then, I'll go back in. That fair?'

'Sure . . . yes. Very fair.'

It wasn't the fear of being discovered that had made Marion stop Nate. It was the fear that he might actually get ahold of Quinn. And when he did, Quinn would tell them that Iris was dead.

At least this way, she could hold on to hope a little longer.

# 34

For an hour and a half Tucker had played the good boy, standing beside Mr. Rose as they both watched the others get the cargo ready. The technicians had started the job by prepping the solution that would put each package — as Mr. Rose had dubbed them early in the project — under for as long as would be needed, then administering it one by one. Tucker's men then moved the gurneys each package was on into one of the two storage rooms nearest the elevator.

Tucker purposely didn't look at any of their faces. It wasn't because he was afraid of feeling a sudden rush of sympathy. In fact, quite the opposite would have been true. Their faces, their bodies, turned his stomach. They were just . . . *wrong*. He'd felt that way since he'd picked up the first one in Bangladesh two months earlier. Still, they were the key, the method in.

But not the delivery device itself. That was also a stroke of genius. No one would suspect a thing. And when it was over, not only would the targets be eliminated, but the unwanted brats, too. The fact that Mr. Rose was using them in this way made perfect sense to Tucker. It was economical. No waste at all.

After the cargo was in the storeroom, they packed up the remaining materials and wheeled everything on carts to the small trash incinerator

421

at the far end of the second level. There could be no evidence left.

'What time is it?' Mr. Rose asked as the last cart was wheeled down the hall.

Tucker looked at his watch. 'Eleven fifty-three.'

'They're running slow. This should have been done twenty-three minutes ago.'

'We're still ahead of schedule.'

Mr. Rose turned his laser eyes on Tucker. 'That is *not* the point. Done by eleven-thirty was what we agreed to.'

Knowing it was useless to argue, Tucker said, 'You're right. My apologies.'

'I don't want your apologies, Mr. Tucker. I want your efficiency. Tomorrow is a *very* important day. Everything must run smoothly.'

'It will. We've gone over it dozens of times. My men know what to do.'

'They'd better, because if something goes wrong and you somehow get away, I will find you. And I promise, I will not kill you.'

Despite himself, Tucker felt a shiver go down his back. He knew Mr. Rose had vast resources. Hell, he'd been able to assemble and pay for this operation in a matter of months. And it hadn't been cheap, not even close. Forget what he was paying everyone. The travel, the special equipment, Yellowhammer, it had all cost big-time.

'I understand,' Tucker said. 'Everything will be fine.'

Mr. Rose stared at him for another several seconds, then said, 'I want the helicopters in the air by one-thirty.'

'I thought the plan was to go at two.'

'One-thirty,' Mr. Rose said.

There was no need for Tucker to respond. Mr. Rose had already turned and walked away.

* * *

Quinn had waited in the elevator shaft for forty-five minutes before he felt it was safe to sneak into the lower level. Even then, he'd been forced to duck into an unused office before he'd been able to get very far.

Several people had gone by. There had also been the unmistakable sound of wheels rolling over the metal floor. Less than a minute later a second set of wheels passed his door. This went on for a quarter hour, with another cart each minute.

The only time he heard any conversation was when the last cart passed by.

'. . . of there. I don't want to leave anything for . . .'

The voice trailed off, and was replaced by just under sixty seconds of silence before Quinn could hear the footsteps returning. It was the same pattern that had occurred every time. The cart would go by, and, soon after, footsteps would return on their own.

But this time after the steps receded, no new cart wheeled past. Quinn waited several more moments, then opened the door just enough so that he could listen unimpeded.

There were voices off to the left. Distant and indecipherable. He also thought he heard another cart. He waited to see if it might be headed in his direction, but it never grew closer. He opened the door wide enough to slip through, then stepped out into the corridor and looked to the left toward the noise. The majority of the facility was in that direction. Whatever Tucker's people were up to was going on in that area. Quinn was sure of it.

It took him less than a second to make his decision. Right first. See what they were doing with the carts. Maybe it would help explain what was going on. If not, he would have only lost a few minutes tops.

He headed down the corridor. There were three doors between where he'd been hiding and the elevators. The first was another empty room like the one he'd been in. The second was the same again.

But the third was different. Even though it was dark, Quinn could tell it was larger than the other two. He sensed depth. He stepped inside and closed the door behind him. He then pulled out his flashlight and turned it on.

He started to move the light across the room, but he didn't get far before he froze.

In the beam were two of the carts and part of a third. Not carts. Gurneys, like in a hospital, complete with an attached IV stand, plastic bag full of liquid, and a tube leading down to the distinctive form of a human being under a sheet.

*Holy shit*, he thought.

He started to move the light again, scanning the room. More gurneys, each with its own lump on top. He could see now there were straps holding each of the bodies in place. He counted seventeen total.

He took a deep breath, then approached the nearest one.

A head stuck out from under the sheet, lying on a pillow. A mop of brown hair hung down over the face. By its length Quinn guessed the person was female. He glanced at the sheet and watched it move up and down several times.

*Alive.*

But there was something about the person that seemed off. He moved the light from one to another of the nearby gurneys. They all looked similar. The bodies under the sheets were small, taking up little more than half a bed's length.

Children.

He played the light through the rest of the room.

The same.

The same.

The same.

On each gurney, the sleeping form of a child.

'Oh, God,' he said under his breath.

He knew it shouldn't have been that much of a surprise. He was looking for the girl who had been with Marion Dupuis, after all. But this was not what he'd expected. Not a room full of kids strapped to hospital beds.

He closed his eyes for a moment and brought up the picture of Iris he'd seen on the passports Marion had left in Montreal. Then he began moving from bed to bed looking for the girl. But he didn't get too far before he noticed an even more disturbing pattern.

None were the regular kids he'd see playing in the park, or clinging to their mothers at the sight of a stranger. These children were different. 'Special,' Quinn's mother would have called them. 'Gifts from God.'

Three of the first five children he looked at had the unmistakable facial features of Down syndrome. He knew the look, had seen it himself as a kid in the face of his cousin. She was the 'gift from God' his aunt had been given. Sarah. So sweet, so trusting. A bad heart had taken her life when she was just eleven. Quinn hadn't thought about her in years, and was surprised by the level of sadness he felt at the memory.

Though the other two children did not look like they had Down's, it was obvious they had some other genetic affliction. Quinn continued through the room, going bed to bed. More disabled children. They all must be, he realized.

What the hell was going on?

A mix of anger and horror and compassion welled in his chest. It was all he could do to keep his feelings from taking over. He needed to remain objective and alert. He needed to figure —

A noise to his right stopped him.

It was only a few feet away. A moan, soft but pleading.

Quinn turned toward it, his light sweeping over the nearby beds.

The moan again.

He zeroed in on it. A young boy, his half-open eyes squinting at the light, but still looking in Quinn's direction. Like just over half of the others he'd seen, he appeared to have Down's.

As the boy moaned again, there was a movement under his sheet. A hand, Quinn guessed, trying to reach out but held in place by the strap.

Quinn hesitated a moment, trying to keep his emotions in check. He was already halfway to the boy's bed before he realized he'd even moved.

'Aaaa,' the boy said.

Quinn knelt down beside him.

'Hey, buddy. It's okay,' he said, then stroked the boy's hair. He wasn't sure if the kid understood him or not. Iris was from Côte d'Ivoire, so God knew where he was from. His pale skin meant he could have most likely come from Russia, any part of Europe, North America.

'Mowno.'

The sheet moved again.

Quinn reached over and slipped his hand under it, taking the boy's hand in his. 'It's okay,' Quinn said. 'Go back to sleep.'

The boy smiled, his eyes continuing to look into Quinn's.

'Sleep,' Quinn said.

'Aaaa mowno.'

Quinn gently rubbed the boy's hand. 'Sleep,' he whispered.

The boy's eyes fluttered, then shut, before popping open again, his hand squeezing Quinn's as if he were afraid it wasn't there anymore.

'Shhh. Sleep,' Quinn repeated.

Even though he knew the others could return at any moment and find him there, he stayed

427

where he was for another five minutes, long after the boy had fallen asleep.

★ ★ ★

There were four children with skin dark enough to indicate they might have come from Africa. But they were all boys. There was no sign of Iris.

Quinn checked again, but the result was the same. No Iris. Not in this room anyway. There must have been another room with more children. The thought was at once comforting and disturbing. At least it would mean Iris might still be alive, but more sleeping children?

He'd have to find out. But first he knew he was long overdue checking in with Nate. He toggled a switch in his pocket that changed his microphone from off to active.

'Nate, can you read me?' he said. 'Nate?'

Nothing at all. He'd feared as much when he realized just how far this level was below the other.

'Nate?' he said.

Only silence.

He pulled out his phone and was happy to see that the signal strength was as strong as it had been above. Whatever boost they had used on the first level must have also been implemented here.

He was not surprised to see that he had several text messages. His phone was on silent, so he hadn't known they'd come in.

Four of the messages were from Nate. One,

428

though, was from Orlando. He read them in the order received.

From Nate:

10:23
Checking in. Don't think we have radio sig.

From Nate:

10:47
Everything all right? LMK

From Nate:

11:13
Pls respond. Do U need help?

From Orlando:

11:33
What the hell do you think UR doing going in alone?

From Nate:

11:49
Assuming no signal, but just in case. Orlando's outside the fence, and she's pissed.

Instead of typing a response, Quinn called.
'Are you all right?' Nate said.
'I'm fine,' Quinn told him, keeping his voice low. 'But it might be a while before I'm done.

Get Marion out of there. See if Orlando can create some kind of distraction so you can get out the gate.'

'She's on the other line,' Nate said. 'Let me conference her in.'

'No. Don't do — ' But Quinn's words came too late. He was already on hold.

A second later the line clicked live again.

'Quinn?' Nate said.

'I'm here.'

'Orlando?'

'Are you crazy?' she said. 'What the hell do you think you're doing in there? You're going to get yourself killed.'

'Listen,' he said.

'No. I'm not going to listen. You pull out now. We've got more than enough for Peter to act on. Let's leave it to him.'

'He'd never be able to get here in time. They're moving out soon. Within the next hour or two would be my guess.'

'Doesn't matter. You should *not* be down there by yourself.'

'Listen, goddammit,' he said. 'I've found something.'

'I don't care what you've — '

'Children,' he said.

That stopped her. 'What?'

'I've found children. At least seventeen and probably more.' He told her about the room full of gurneys.

She didn't say anything for several seconds, then when she did speak, her voice was low and controlled. 'You're sure they're all alive?'

430

'As far as I can tell.'

'Iris?' Nate asked.

'Who's Iris?' Orlando asked.

'The child who was with Marion,' Nate said. 'That's what she calls her.'

'Can Marion hear you?' Quinn asked Nate.

'No, I've moved up the tunnel.'

'She's not here.'

Nate and Orlando fell silent.

'That means one of two things to me,' Quinn said. 'Either they've . . . gotten rid of her . . . '

'Jesus,' Nate said.

'Or,' Quinn went on, 'there's another group of children somewhere.' He explained about hearing the gurneys being wheeled into the room, then his discovery of them. 'But I also heard something else being pushed in the other direction. Sounded similar to the gurneys that had rolled past me. So I think it's likely there's another room with more kids in it.'

'What the hell are they doing?' Nate asked.

'I don't know, and at the moment it doesn't matter,' Quinn said. 'That's why I can't leave yet. I have to find them. I have to see if there's something I can do . . . we can do.'

Orlando, who had been silent through the entire explanation, said, 'I think I can get onto the base without anyone knowing. I found a weak spot, a dry riverbed that's been eroding the dirt from under the wires. I think I can dig myself under.'

'No,' Quinn said. 'Just stay out there. See if you can cause a distraction for the guards at the gate. Everyone's tied up here, so I don't think

431

they'll get any immediate help. It just needs to be enough to allow Nate and Marion to get out without being caught.'

'That's a stupid idea,' she said. 'I'm coming under. I'll meet up with them at the tunnel, then bring Marion out myself the way I came. That way Nate can stay in case you need him.'

'It's too much of a risk,' Quinn said.

'Don't talk to me about too much risk,' she shot back. 'This is *not* open for discussion.'

There was a click on the line.

'Nice going,' Nate said. 'She hung up.'

Quinn took several breaths, allowing himself to calm down. 'Text me when she gets there,' he said, then disconnected the call.

He gave one last look at the gurneys spread out behind him. Then, without realizing what he was doing at first, he found the bed with the boy who'd woken up.

'I'll take care of this,' Quinn said to him.

He then doused his flashlight and stepped back into the corridor.

# 35

Tucker entered the level one cafeteria at precisely 12:45 a.m. and found all four of the helicopter pilots sitting at a table finishing their meals. Their crew members sat at a nearby table silently scarfing down the remains of their sandwiches.

'It's time,' Tucker said. 'We'll have everything on board in forty minutes, then lift off right after that.'

'All right,' the head pilot, a guy named Seizer, replied. 'We'll meet you topside.' He stood and looked over at his crew's table. 'Let's go.'

Almost as one, the crew members and the remaining pilots all stood.

'We'll be ready,' Seizer said.

They filed out of the room.

Tucker glanced over at the table in the back where several of his men sat drinking coffee. 'We've got forty minutes to get the cargo up to the surface and into the helicopters,' Tucker said. 'You should be able to fit four packages per elevator car. I want both cars in constant operation. Should be able to have everything all topside by,' he paused, looking at his watch, 'fifteen after. Petersen's bringing the truck around.'

One by one they stood.

'This is what we're getting paid for, so let's not fuck it up,' Tucker told them.

433

As soon as his men were gone, he pulled out his cell phone.

'It's Tucker,' he said. 'We're in final prep and should be off the ground by one-thirty. Flight time a little less than two hours, so figure three-thirty worst case.'

'We're ready and waiting,' the man on the other end said.

'No problems?'

'None at all.'

'And the targets' schedule?'

'Unchanged. They'll be at the center at nine-thirty a.m.'

'Good. And the distractions?'

'Both cars already in place. I'll give you the detonators when you arrive.'

'Perfect,' Tucker said.

The distractions were a little extra something he'd added into the mix that Mr. Rose didn't know about. It was going to be his ass on the line, after all, so anything that could help with a successful escape was welcome.

He disconnected the call and headed for the exit, wanting to get down to the second level so he could supervise the first load himself. As he did, he checked his watch again, then smiled.

With any luck they'd actually be off the ground ahead of schedule.

★  ★  ★

Quinn had just begun his search for the second room when he heard someone talking. The voice was distant, but that could have been a trick of

434

the corridors. And, he soon realized, it wasn't just a single voice, it was several.

He knew he should find an empty room and hide out until he could move freely again, but he also knew he was running out of time. So he increased his pace, checking the rooms he passed, but finding nothing.

When he turned down an intersecting corridor, the voices grew louder. He crept forward, passing two hallways, then stopping before he reached the third. The voices were coming from around the corner. Though they were distant enough that he knew they were down the hall a bit, he could make out snippets of conversation.

' . . . time to take . . . fine.'

'We need . . . think?'

' . . . promise anything . . . best.'

He checked the lighting and realized he was in a deep shadow. He knew if he took a look around the corner, the risk of being noticed would be minimal. Keeping his motions slow, he leaned out just enough to see around the edge.

Forty feet away, the hallway widened out into a common area where over a dozen men were gathered. Most were big, ex-military types like the ones who had captured Furuta. A few were smaller, wearing white coats like doctors or lab workers. All were focused on the man standing in the middle. Tucker.

Quinn hesitated only a second, then crouched down and crossed the intersection. He moved as fast as he could, taking a back route to the room where he'd found the first group of children.

Maybe he could find a way to block the door, and at least slow Tucker's people down. He wasn't going to be able to stop them, not on his own, but if he could throw off their timetable, he might be able to get back to the surface and figure out some way to keep them from leaving.

Only he was too late.

Four other men were already at the room. Quinn could see them through the half-opened door. They were arranging the gurneys in some kind of order.

Quinn had no choice. He reentered the same room he'd hidden in earlier, this time leaving the door opened a crack.

The first thing he heard was one of the gurneys being wheeled out of the room and back into the hallway. Just before it passed the room he was in, someone called out, 'Hold on.'

The cart stopped.

'Let me get the drip going,' the voice said. 'We don't want them waking up mid-flight.'

*Flight?* Quinn thought. Maybe there was an airfield and a plane that could hold all the children.

'Hurry up,' a second voice said.

'Two seconds,' the first said. A pause, then, 'Okay. You're good to go.'

As the cart started up again, a second came down the hallway. Again the first voice — *one of the technicians?* — stopped it for a moment before letting it move on. After that, the carts began rolling out unhindered. The technician was no doubt getting each of the IVs going before they left the room.

Quinn pulled out his cell phone. He wanted Nate to get into a position where he could observe the main ground-level exit so that he could see where they were taking the children.

There was a voice message waiting for him. He pressed Play and put the phone to his ear.

'There are four Sikorsky Superhawks in a clearing about an eighth of a mile southwest of Yellowhammer's entrance.' It was Orlando. The Superhawk was a troop-transport helicopter. 'You said you thought they might be leaving soon. If so, this is how. I got Marion on the other side of the fence, so I'm going in for a closer look.'

That was it. There was no follow-up message. He couldn't call to get an update, either. The minute he'd open his mouth, those in the hallway would hear him. But at least he now knew how they planned to fly out. Not a plane. Helicopters.

He fired a text off to Orlando.

Status?

He didn't wait for a response before sending a second one, this time to Nate.

Have u heard from O?

He thought for a moment, then decided a third was in order.

Be ready. They're moving tonight. Be advised they have hostages. More soon.

He chose Peter's name from his addresses, then hit Send.

Another thirty seconds passed before he got any response. It was from Nate.

Last radio contact 30 min ago when she took M out. Have tried to reach her since, but no reply. U need me to come to u?

Quinn typed:

No. They're starting to clear out of here. O left message she spotted helicopters. Meet up with her. Disable them if u can.

It took Nate ten seconds to receive and reply.

OK.

Outside the room, another gurney rolled past. Once the noise of the wheels had faded, Quinn eased the door all the way shut. There was nothing he could do now but wait.

Wait, and hope he wouldn't be too late.

★ ★ ★

Peter had pulled all-nighters before. Hell, half the time he felt like he lived at the Office's headquarters, the rest of the world seldom conforming to Eastern Standard Time.

But tonight was different. He had a team in the middle of some serious crap, but his client, the only person who could provide the help they would need, had all of a sudden gone AWOL.

'I have visual confirmation from my agent on the ground that your man Furuta has been detained at Yellowhammer,' he had told Chercover the last time they'd talked.

'Visual?' Chercover asked, his tone unconcerned.

'I have a photo.'

'Send it to me.'

'What was he doing there?' Peter asked. 'I told you I was sending a team in.'

There was a pause. 'I wanted my own eyes on the ground.'

'That worked out well.'

'Is there anything else?' Chercover asked.

'I assume you'd like us to see if we can extract him.'

Again a pause. 'If the opportunity presents itself.'

Before Peter could say anything else, the line went dead.

That was the last time he'd been able to get through to Chercover. He'd started calling every ten minutes, but each time the line had gone directly to voicemail.

And now with this latest text from Quinn it looked like whatever was being prepped at Yellowhammer was going live, but Peter had no means with which to stop it. It was obvious now the threat had always been real. It would have been more than enough for Chercover to get actual government forces into action. But where the fuck was he?

Peter had other contacts he could go to, but it

would mean bringing them up to speed, which would delay any help. Still, he didn't see that he had any choice. The only question was who to bring in?

He pulled up his contacts list on the screen of his laptop and began scrolling through it.

There had to be one, someone who would trust him. Someone who could make things happen in a hurry.

*For God's sake*, he thought as he finished the L's. *Just one name.*

# 36

The sound of several large engines winding up startled Marion. She'd remained hidden behind the rock outcropping where the woman, Orlando, had left her. The buzzing electric fence they'd passed under was only a hundred feet away. She'd heard the familiar whirling roar before, back in Africa. Not a truck engine, not even a jet. Helicopters, and by the sounds of them, large ones.

To her it meant only one thing: those who had taken her and Iris were about to escape. But did they still have the girl? Or had Quinn, Nate, and Orlando been successful in rescuing her? Marion wanted to believe they had, but she feared the worst.

She'd been told to stay where she was no matter what. But how could she? How could she stay when Iris's life was still in danger?

The answer was she couldn't.

★  ★  ★

'Hey. What are you doing?' The voice had come from behind Quinn.

He'd been crouched in front of the elevator door, just starting to pry it open. Acting like nothing was up, he released the door, then dropped his right hand onto the grip of the SIG Sauer pistol resting on his lap. He stood, keeping his back to the new arrival.

'The doors got stuck,' he said.

'Turn around!'

The man was closer now. Quinn judged fifteen feet at most. And whatever weapon he was armed with — one of the M16s no doubt — it would be aimed at Quinn's back.

Quinn pivoted around, the barrel of his gun level with the man's gut.

'Who ar — '

*Thwack.*

The man dropped to the ground.

Quinn kept his gun on the man as he ran over, but there was no need to pull the trigger a second time. The guard was dead.

He dragged the body over to the elevator door, then removed the M16 from the man's shoulder and set it on the floor. He ripped the sleeve off the man's shirt, knowing he'd need it for cleanup. After prying the sliding doors of the elevator apart, he used the guard's shoulders to wedge them open. He then wiped up a small pool of blood where the man had fallen, and the trail of drops that led back to the elevator.

Once he was done, he dumped the man's body and the sleeve into the shaft, slung the M16 over his shoulder, then slipped through the doors himself, and over to his waiting rope.

★ ★ ★

Tucker was pissed.

He had four Superhawk helicopters sitting on the ground, but only three with rotors turning.

'I thought you said everything was working fine,' he shouted at the lead pilot.

'Everything checked out okay when we fired them up last,' the pilot said. 'I have our engineer looking at it now. Thinks he might be able to get it up and running in thirty minutes.'

'We don't have thirty minutes.' Tucker looked back at the helicopters. 'God*dammit*! We'll have to get everyone in three.'

'We all won't fit in three.'

'Then some people will just have to stay, won't they?' Tucker said. 'Get back to your aircraft. We go on schedule.'

'Yes, sir.' The pilot turned and walked away.

Tucker brought his radio up to his mouth. 'Petersen?'

'Yes?' Petersen's voice said on the receiver.

'Split the cargo between the three working helicopters. Just don't put the juice and the special package with the triggering mechanism in the same aircraft. Then divide up the men. Nonessentials stay behind.'

'So the fourth copter's out, then?'

'At least for now. Those who stay behind can take it out once it's fixed.'

'Copy,' Petersen said. 'Is Delgado with you?'

'I told him to do a final check of both floors before coming up. If he takes too long, assign him to helicopter four.'

'Copy.'

★ ★ ★

443

Quinn found Nate on a hill overlooking the makeshift heliport. Again the rocks played into their favor by creating several nooks from which they could observe what was going on without being seen.

'What happened to disabling the helicopters?' Quinn asked.

'Very funny. The crews were already there when I got here. Kind of think they might have seen me if I walked up and started messing with their engines.'

'What about Orlando?'

'I texted her what you wanted us to do, and said I'd meet up with her. She texted back 'OK,' but that was it. Haven't heard anything more from her.'

'Let me see those,' Quinn said, motioning for Nate's binoculars.

As soon as Nate gave them to him, he raised them to his eyes. Men were moving three-foot-long metal baskets from a truck to the helicopters. In each basket was one of the children.

'Only three of the helicopters are running,' Quinn said.

'Still?' Nate said. 'I was thinking they just hadn't fired the fourth one up yet.'

'Looks like someone's got an access panel open and is looking inside.'

Quinn continued his scan of the landing area, stopping only when he spotted a man standing on a boulder at the northwest corner. He touched the zoom. It was Leo Tucker.

He lowered the binoculars and handed them

to Nate. 'The man on the rock. At the far end.'

'What about him?'

'Just take a look.'

Nate lifted the glasses to his eyes.

'Son of a bitch,' he whispered. 'Is that . . . ?'

'Is that what?'

Quinn and Nate turned in unison toward the voice that had come from behind them. Orlando was a dozen feet away, crawling between two of the rocks.

Nate smiled, then glanced at Quinn.

'Where the hell have you been?' Quinn asked.

'I was trying to disable the helicopters,' she said. 'That's what you asked, wasn't it?'

'Doesn't look like you succeeded.'

'I could only get to one before they showed up,' she said. 'Sorry I didn't get myself shot taking care of the other three.'

'I didn't mean that,' Quinn said.

'Sure you did. That's exactly what you meant.'

It wasn't, but she seemed to be in an arguing mood, so he decided to change the subject. 'How's your shoulder?'

'It's fine,' she snapped. 'What were you two looking at when I walked up?'

'Nothing,' Nate said. 'Just looking at the helicopters.'

'Don't try to lie to me, Nate,' she said. 'I can always tell.'

Quinn hesitated a moment, then said, 'Give her the glasses.' She needed to know.

Nate looked at Quinn as if he wasn't sure he'd heard him correctly, then held the binoculars out to Orlando. She took the glasses as she knelt down between the two men.

'What am I looking at?' she asked.

Quinn pointed toward Tucker. 'There,' he said. 'That guy on the boulder.'

It only took her a couple seconds to zero in on him. Once she did, she froze in place, the binoculars seeming to meld with the skin around her eyes.

When she did move them away, her gaze remained riveted on the man on the rock.

'He's mine,' she said.

Neither Quinn nor Nate argued with her. How could they? She had business with Tucker — the kidnapping of her son, Garrett. The only reason the Australian was still alive was because of the deal he'd made with Quinn to reveal Garrett's location in exchange for being able to walk away. A deal Orlando had hated, but could think of no alternative solution.

But the deal expired the moment they found Garrett. Though they never talked about it, Quinn knew in Orlando's mind Tucker had been living under a death sentence to be administered at a time she deemed best — a time that looked like it might soon be approaching.

'Ah . . . unless we do something fast,' Nate said, 'we're going to lose him.'

'What?'

Nate pointed at the rock Tucker had been standing on. The man was gone.

'Correct me if I'm wrong,' he said. 'But it looks like they're all loaded up and ready to go. Our old friend just climbed on board the one farthest from us.'

Nate was right; all but a handful of the men had boarded one of the working helicopters. Within seconds, the helicopter nearest them lifted into the air. The other two soon joined it.

'Down!' Quinn yelled.

They pressed themselves against the rocks as the helicopters rose in the air high enough to spot them. But soon all three aircraft were flying west toward the mountains.

'I think we just lost control of the situation,' Nate said.

'Exactly when did we *have* control of the situation?' Quinn asked.

'I don't see a problem,' Orlando said.

'You did see them fly away, right?' Nate said. 'All that noise a few seconds ago? The sudden breeze?'

She peeked over the rocks at the remaining helicopter. 'I'm betting one of them knows where their friends are headed. We just get them to fly us there.' She smiled, then pulled out a palm-size circuit board from her pocket. 'Of course, they'll need to put this back in first.'

Quinn smiled, thinking that maybe they still had a chance.

Then from the clearing below, they heard a woman scream.

# 37

Marion had been too far away when the helicopters rose into the air. Still she ran, stumbling around the last pile of rocks and into the clearing as they'd disappeared into the night. That's when she saw that one of the helicopters was still on the ground.

Blinded by rage at what these people had done to her family, and by fear of what had happened to Iris, she sprinted toward the helicopter, a scream fleeing from her throat. Ahead, several of the men gathered around the downed helicopter stepped out to get a better look at her. One man raised his arm, pointing at her. In his hand was a gun.

She was dead, she knew it. But her rage would not allow her to slow her pace.

The man with the gun took a step toward her.

There was the crack of a shot.

She thought it should have knocked her to the ground, but she felt nothing. He must have missed. The next shot would get her for sure.

Only the man with the gun was crumpled on the ground.

*Crack. Crack. Crack-crack.*

Three more of the men fell to the ground. The remaining two were scrambling into the helicopter. One of them starting to pull the door closed when a voice yelled out, 'Stop!'

Both Marion and the man at the door stopped

moving at the same instant. From the rocks at the edge of the clearing, two people emerged. Nate and Orlando, Marion realized.

Orlando moved over to the helicopter, while Nate checked the bodies on the ground, then jogged over to Marion.

Before he reached her, he said, 'All clear.' Then to her, 'Are you all right?'

'Iris? Do you have her?'

Before he said anything, she could tell from the look in his eyes what the answer was.

'We're not through yet,' Nate said.

'But they're gone. She's gone.'

As if to contradict her, the remaining helicopter whirled to life. She glanced toward the noise, but was distracted by movement off to the left. It was Quinn emerging from a gap in the rocks, and carrying a rifle. He motioned to them, then pointed at the helicopter.

'Let's go,' Nate said.

'What? On that?'

'You want to stay here?'

She didn't need him to ask again.

★　★　★

'Pilot says he doesn't know where the exact landing site is,' Orlando said. 'All he knows is that they were supposed to fly toward the coast to a point forty miles southeast of a town called Santa Maria. They were to be given the final destination at that point. Do you know where he's talking about?' Orlando said.

Quinn nodded. 'I've driven by a couple times.

449

Highway 101 runs right through it. But are we sure he's telling the truth?'

'When I stuck my gun to the back of his head, and Nate convinced him he knew how to fly this thing if necessary, he was pretty eager to stay alive and help out.'

'Nate doesn't know how to fly helicopters,' Quinn said.

'Sure sounded like he knew what he was talking about,' Orlando said. 'Maybe he's been studying more than just the things you've told him to while he's been recovering.'

Nate had had a lot of time on his hands during his rehabilitation, and the work Quinn had given him probably wouldn't have filled it all up. Quinn guessed there was a chance he *did* know what he was talking about it. But hands-on knowledge? No way.

'Maybe the pilot's lying,' Quinn said. 'Just telling us enough to get us off his back.'

'I don't think so. But if you want, I can go push him some more.'

Quinn shook his head. He trusted her judgment.

'Have you talked to our other friend yet?' Orlando said, nodding toward the technician sitting against the opposite wall.

'Not yet.'

'Shall we?'

'Definitely.'

Orlando glanced at Marion. 'What about . . . ?'

Quinn would have preferred that Marion wasn't there, but the only other place he could send her was the cockpit, and Nate needed that

450

distraction even less than Quinn did.

'Not one word,' Quinn told the woman.

'I understand,' Marion said, her voice a whisper.

The seats in the passenger area had been arranged in single rows along each wall, creating an open space for the cargo they'd thought they'd be carrying.

An image of the baskets being loaded onto the other helicopters filled Quinn's mind as he moved over to where the technician sat waiting. Anger made Quinn grab the man harder than he'd planned, but what the hell? The son of a bitch deserved it.

'Come on,' he said. He pushed the man back across to where Orlando sat waiting. 'There.' Quinn pointed at the chair he'd been sitting in a few moments earlier.

Once the man was down, Orlando grabbed his right hand and placed his thumb on the screen of her cell phone.

'What the fuck?' the man said as the screen lit up.

A bright light glowed on the screen for a moment, then went out. Orlando let go of his hand, then tapped the phone twice bringing up the keyboard.

While Orlando was busy with the phone, Quinn crouched down so that he was eye level with the technician. He pointed his SIG at the man's chest.

'What's your name?' Quinn said.

The man shook his head, then said, 'I'm not talking.'

451

'Really?' Quinn looked at Orlando. 'Door.'

Instantly she was on the move. Quinn then grabbed the technician and pulled him back to his feet.

As Orlando threw the side door open, the cabin was filled with the mixed roar of the wind and the engine. Within seconds the temperature dipped to near freezing.

Quinn shoved the man in the back, moving him near the opening. The man got to within two feet, but would go no more. Quinn placed the barrel of his gun against the back of the man's head.

'Take a good look,' he yelled. 'There's a hell of a lot of wilderness out there. By the time someone finds your body, you won't be much more than bones. But I guess that wouldn't be something you'd need to worry about. It's the fall you're thinking about, isn't it?' He paused. 'You won't have to worry about the fall, either. I'm going to shoot you in the head as I push you out. So, really, it's the bullet you need to be worried about. Now, what's your name?'

The man said something, but his words were lost in the wind.

'Sorry, didn't catch that.'

The man twisted his head, mindful of the gun still pointed at him. 'Leary. William Leary.'

'You're not lying to me, are you, William?'

'No, sir. Not lying.'

'And you'll answer all my questions?'

'I'll tell you everything I know.'

Quinn let him stand there for a moment longer, then nodded at Orlando to shut the door.

'So, William,' Quinn said after he returned the man to his seat. 'What's going on with the children?'

Leary looked between the three of them. 'You have to understand, I didn't have a choice. I didn't know what I was getting into when they hired me, and by the time I got to the base it was too — '

'Orlando, get the door.'

'No! No!' Leary said.

'Then don't lie to me, William. You knew what was going on. You were a part of it.'

William licked his lips. 'I swear I didn't know what was going on. Mr. Rose threatened to kill me if I didn't help them.'

'Who is Mr. Rose?' Quinn asked.

'Mr. Rose?' Leary said, confused. 'He's the big boss.'

'The Australian?'

'That's Tucker. He was in charge of manpower outside of the lab. Security, things like that. And I think he's the one who brought the children here.'

'So, what? You answered an ad, and took the job without knowing what it was?'

'Yeah. Exactly.'

'You're lying,' Orlando said. She was looking at the display on her phone.

'What are you talking about?' Leary said.

'Tell us about Wright Memorial Hospital,' she said.

He stared at her, unable to speak at first.

'Don't remember that?' she asked. 'Then how about Helene General Hospital? Or even the

453

Rosen Medical Center.'

'How did you . . . ' Leary's voice dropped into silence.

Quinn looked at Orlando. The thumb scan she had done had apparently come up with gold.

'He's a doctor,' she said. 'Only he's a little screwed up. Likes to sell drugs he took from work to schoolkids. Must have half a dozen aliases. Or did I get the wrong William Leary?'

The look on the man's face told them she was right.

'What kind of doctor?' Quinn asked the man.

He hesitated, trying not to look at Orlando. 'General practice.'

'Huh,' Orlando said. 'Then they must have got it wrong on your record.'

'What's it say?' Quinn asked.

'Says that Dr. Leary here is an anesthesiologist.'

'I-I haven't done that for a while,' Leary stammered.

'How long is a while?' Quinn asked.

'I stopped a couple years ago, okay?'

'Stopped?' Orlando asked.

Leary let out a defeated breath. 'My license was revoked. Happy? But then Mr. Rose found me. And he offered me a hell of a lot of money.'

'What did Mr. Rose want you to do?' Quinn asked.

'Keep the children sedated until we need them.'

'Need them for what?'

'You don't know?' Leary said. 'But isn't that why you're here?'

No one said anything.

Finally, Leary said, 'As a diversion. To get the explosives in.'

No one said anything for nearly thirty seconds.

'What explosives?' Quinn asked.

'They're built into the juice boxes,' Leary said. 'Binary explosives. Clear liquid. Looks harmless.'

'How does it work?' Quinn asked.

'I didn't work on them directly.'

'But you know,' Quinn said.

Leary looked away, then nodded. 'I heard something.'

'What?'

'I was told the chemicals inside were kept in two different compartments inside the pouches. Apparently they're only dangerous once the divider between them is removed and they mix together. The boxes will go in with the kids.'

'Into where?'

'That I don't know.'

'You've got to be kidding,' Quinn said.

'I don't! Really!'

Quinn stared at him, watching to see if he was lying. But he wasn't. 'How are the boxes triggered?'

The technician glanced at the floor. 'One of the children,' he said. 'One of the children is the trigger.'

Quinn heard Marion gasp, but she said nothing.

'How does it work?' Quinn asked.

'It . . . em . . . eh . . . '

Quinn's hand shot out, shoving the man's head against the wall.

455

'How does it work?' he repeated.

The man's eyes were wild in fear; for a few seconds his gaze fell on Marion as if he were scared of her the most. 'One of the children has the triggering device implanted in her thigh, just below the skin. It has to be activated first. A handheld device. I only saw it once, but it looked like a cell phone.'

'Who has it?'

'I don't know. Mr. Rose or Tucker, I would guess.'

'So they activate it,' Orlando said. 'Then what?'

Again he glanced momentarily at Marion. 'When the trigger, the child, enters the room where the boxes are, a signal from her prompts the membrane inside to dissolve. Then thirty seconds later . . .'

'Jesus,' Orlando said.

'So one of the children is the trigger,' Quinn said.

Again the glance.

'Yes,' Leary said.

'Which one?'

No answer.

'Which one?'

'The new one,' Leary whispered, this time doing everything he could not to look at Marion. 'The African girl.'

'Oh, God,' Marion said. 'Oh, God, no.'

Quinn shot her a glance, and she grew quiet again.

'One of you was a surgeon?' Orlando asked.

'N-No,' Leary said.

A stillness filled the cabin before Orlando asked her next question. 'Then who implanted the device in the girl?'

Leary dropped his chin to his chest. 'Don't make me answer that.' It was answer enough.

Quinn pushed the man's head back up. 'We need to know the target, William.'

'I told you, I have no idea,' Leary said. 'I just know they needed the children to make it happen. They had to be special needs. Really, that's all I know.'

'So you don't know where the kids came from?'

The look on the former doctor's face said differently. 'I overheard something, maybe.'

'What?'

'Just that it was easier to obtain what they needed outside the U.S. In some other countries children like them aren't as well cared for. They're easier to . . . obtain. Tucker would bring them back in twos or threes. One time it was half a dozen. We fed them and kept them quiet.'

'By sedating them,' Orlando said.

Leary stared straight ahead, not looking at anyone.

'Door,' Quinn said.

'No!' Leary yelled as Quinn hauled him back to his feet. 'I don't know who the target is. Please, believe me.'

'I believe you,' Quinn said.

Orlando was at the door.

'Open it,' Quinn said.

457

'But you just said you believed me,' Leary said.

'You're right. I did.'

The door flew open, and the noise level in the cabin once again became deafening. Leary tried to turn, but Quinn had a tight grip on his neck.

Once again, Quinn maneuvered him so Leary faced outward with Quinn's gun against the back of the man's head. For a second he thought he could hear Leary say, 'Please, don't.' But then an image of the gurneys parked in the storage room flashed in his mind.

Pulling the trigger of his SIG was one of the easiest things he'd done in a long time.

# 38

'Furuta's dead,' Quinn said into the phone.

'Nothing I could do. They let him bleed out.'

'Oh, Christ,' Peter said.

'We've got a bigger problem than that.'

'What is it?'

Quinn paused for a moment. 'We're in a helicopter. Heading toward Santa Maria, California. Check the map, you'll see what I mean.'

Nothing for a moment, then, 'Okay, got it. That's about seventy miles north of Santa Barbara. I'm not sure what you . . . oh, shit.'

'Yeah, I know.'

Peter had seen what Quinn already knew. A little more than another hour north of Santa Maria was the small coastal town of San Simeon. And just beyond San Simeon, Hearst Castle. Not a castle, really, but about as close to it as you got in the States. It was a colossal home built by the late newspaper magnate William Randolph Hearst, and was the inspiration for Xanadu in the old Orson Welles film *Citizen Kane*. For decades now it had been run as a tourist destination by the State of California.

Usually it wouldn't even be a blip on the radar. Nothing to draw the attention of someone like Quinn or Peter. But as Hardwick had pointed out to Quinn, Hearst Castle was playing host to a group other than tourists this week. In fact, no tourist had been allowed near the place for the last ten days. Its remote location yet luxurious setting made it the perfect place for this year's G8 summit meeting — a meeting of the heads of state from all the 'Group of Eight' nations.

The meetings had begun in the mid-seventies with only six participating nations. They grew from the need for a more global stance to the oil shortages and recession of the time, then continued to grow and expand in the following decades until it had become arguably the most important international meeting of the year.

Every year the meeting would rotate to another of the member nations: Canada, France, Germany, Italy, Japan, Russia, the United Kingdom, and the United States. It was designed to provide an opportunity for the leaders of some of the world's most powerful nations to discuss whatever issues were deemed important at the time. And this year, it was the U.S.'s turn to host.

'Impossible,' Peter said. 'The government's got the whole area sealed off. Highway 1 is closed just north of Cambria and south of Gorda. No way anyone can get close even by air. And bringing a bunch of kids with them? Not a chance.'

'Check the schedule.'

'Hold on.' The line went silent for several seconds. 'Nothing. There are meetings all day for the next two days. There *is* a dinner each night.'

'Entertainment?' Quinn asked.

Peter paused again. 'Yes. But nothing matching your group of children. Yo-Yo Ma tonight

460

and Harry Connick, Jr., tomorrow.'

Quinn frowned. 'It doesn't matter. We know basically where they're going. You should be able to pick them up on radar, and if not, you get a large enough force out there, you'll find them before dawn.'

Peter said nothing.

'What is it?' Quinn asked.

'I can't get ahold of my client at the Agency.'

'What?'

'He's dropped out of sight. Not answering his phone.'

'Then call somebody else.'

'I've been *trying*, but no one is taking my calls.'

'What the hell are you talking about, Peter? You've got a ton of people you can reach.'

'The Office has been shut out,' Peter said. 'The word has gone out not to deal with us.'

'What? How do you know that?'

'Because the goddamn Assistant Director of the NSA told me right before he hung up.'

'You've got to keep trying,' Quinn said. 'My team and I can't do this alone.'

'I realize that.'

'Then stop talking to me and do something about it.' Quinn ended the call.

He looked out the window. Where the black mass of the mountains didn't block out the sky, he saw stars. He stared at them, his mind going blank.

'You should try to get a little sleep,' Orlando said. 'You've been going almost twenty-four hours. Even thirty minutes will help.'

461

'You've been going as long as I have.'

'Took a nap at the hotel when I thought you were just on a little scouting mission.'

It was hard to miss the sarcasm in her voice, and it wasn't the funny kind, either.

'I'm sorry,' he said. 'The opportunity to get in came up, so I had to take it.'

The left side of her mouth turned up in a smirk.

'All in all,' he said, 'it looks like it was a good decision.'

He knew she couldn't argue that. Still, she looked like she wanted to put up a fight.

'I'm sorry,' he said again.

She closed her eyes and rubbed her forehead. 'Sleep. Don't sleep. I don't care.'

She got up and walked to the other end of the passenger hold.

Quinn wanted to go after her, but he thought maybe it was best not to. Despite her nap, she had to be as tired as he was. She just needed a little space, he thought.

He slumped in his chair and stared at the floor. At what point his own eyes closed and he fell asleep, he had no idea.

★  ★  ★

'We're here.' It was Nate's voice, very close to Quinn's ear.

Quinn opened his eyes. The cabin was dim, but he could see Marion Dupuis stretched out on the other side of the cabin.

The roar of the engine was unchanged, and

462

from the way everything was still moving up and down, side to side, Quinn knew they were still in the air.

He sat up. 'The pilot,' he said.

'Orlando's watching him.'

'How long was I out?'

'A little over an hour.'

Quinn blinked several times, then looked out the window. Night still, but the massive Sierra Nevada mountains were gone. In the distance he could see the glow of a city on the horizon. He checked his watch. It was a few minutes before 4 a.m.

'Where exactly are we?' he asked as he stood up.

'Those lights out there are from Santa Maria. We're about forty miles south, right where the pilot said he was to receive his next instructions. But there's no sign of the others.'

'North,' Quinn said. 'They'll be on the other side of Santa Maria somewhere. As close as they can get to Hearst Castle without drawing any attention.'

'It's a pretty tight perimeter up there. There's a message on the radio warning of a no-fly zone starting south of Arroyo Grande. That's only about fifteen miles beyond Santa Maria.'

'I need to see a map,' Quinn said.

'There's one up front.'

★ ★ ★

There were only two seats in the cockpit. Orlando sat in the one on the left, the gun in her hand pointed at the pilot. He was sitting in the one on the right.

They both glanced over as Quinn leaned between them.

The look on the pilot's face was tense. Quinn noticed sweat streaks running past his eyes and down his cheeks.

'Where's the map?' Quinn asked.

'Behind my chair,' Orlando said.

Quinn grabbed it. It was a book kind of like the *Thomas Guide* he had in his car, only not quite as thick. He found the page showing the central coast of California, then traced a line along Highway 101 between Santa Maria and Arroyo Grande. There were a couple of smaller towns in between. There was also plenty of wilderness and hilly areas where a helicopter — or even three — could land unnoticed.

'We'll go here,' Quinn said, pointing at a spot on the map and showing it to both Orlando and the pilot.

The place he'd chosen was just a few miles southeast of Arroyo Grande, on the edge of a town called Los Berros. He knew they were pushing it to try and get in that close to the no-fly zone, but he didn't know what other choice he had. The other helicopters most likely hadn't gone that far, so there was a chance Quinn might be able to get in front of them. A small chance, granted, but it was something.

The pilot banked the helicopter to the right, then flew north, bypassing Santa Maria and keeping several miles to the east of the highway.

Less than a minute later a voice came over the

radio. 'Aircraft traveling north-northwest nearing Nipomo, be advised we have you on radar. Please identify yourself.'

'That's us,' the pilot said.

'Take us lower,' Quinn said.

'There are hills down there,' the pilot protested.

'Then try not to hit them.'

'Unidentified aircraft, please respond.'

The helicopter dove down several thousand feet until it was only a hundred feet above-ground.

'Hug the terrain,' Quinn said, knowing it would cut down on their radar signature.

'Unidentified aircraft, you're instructed to head south-southeast to the Santa Maria Public Airport. You are to land and await further instructions. Please confirm.'

On the ground below, Quinn could see scattered homes. Most were dark at this hour, but a few had lights on.

'Two miles,' Orlando said.

'Unidentified aircraft. Please be advised you are nearing a no-fly zone. If you enter the zone, you *will* be shot down. Unidentified aircraft, please respond.'

'One mile,' Orlando said.

'Company,' Nate said.

He was standing behind Quinn and pointing over Quinn's shoulder and out the front window to the left.

A black spot on the deep blue sky was rapidly approaching. Within seconds it buzzed by them.

'I'm turning around,' the pilot said.

Orlando raised her gun. 'Nate,' she said, 'you ready to take over?'

'Absolutely,' Nate said.

'Jesus,' the pilot said. 'They're going to shoot us down.'

'Shut up, and keep on course,' Quinn said.

'He's back,' Orlando said. She motioned with her chin at the window beyond the pilot.

Pacing them a hundred feet to the east was an Apache attack helicopter.

'Unidentified aircraft, this is Captain Muñoz of the U.S. Army. I'm here to escort you back to Santa Maria. I'd advise not trying anything stupid. Do you understand?'

'*Now* what do you want me to do?' the pilot asked.

'Tell him you understand,' Quinn said.

The pilot hesitated a moment, then keyed his mic. 'I understand, Captain.'

'You will make a one-eighty-degree turn to the left, then fly south to Santa Maria.'

The pilot looked at Quinn, who nodded back.

'Roger,' the pilot said.

'First let's get you some altitude. Take her up to a thousand feet on my mark. Okay?'

'There,' Quinn said. He pointed at a clearing just ahead. It looked like someone's field. Perhaps a place for horses. There were several houses in the area, and a thick grove of trees lining two of the sides.

'Did you understand my instructions?'

'Tell him yes,' Quinn said. 'But when he tells you to go up, I want you to take us down fast into that clearing as close to the trees as possible.'

'I'll need at least a hundred feet of clear space.'

'Make it fifty,' Quinn said. 'Any more and I will kill you the moment we're on the ground.'

'Did you understand my instructions?' the voice on the radio repeated, now without any trace of friendliness.

'I understand,' the pilot said.

'Nate,' Quinn said. 'Go back with Marion. Secure for a rough landing.'

Without a word, Nate was gone.

'All right,' the captain in the Apache said.

The clearing was close now.

'Let's take her up,' the captain said.

Quinn could feel the helicopter rise. Just a few seconds more.

'Now!' Quinn yelled.

The Superhawk immediately switched direction, heading straight down for the ground.

'Unidentified aircraft, cease your descent!'

'As close to the trees as possible,' Quinn reminded the pilot.

The ground was rushing up at them.

'Pull up,' the captain said. 'Pull up now!'

With a loud *whap*, they hit the ground. Quinn, who'd been holding on to both seats, tumbled forward, landing halfway in the pilot's lap. He pushed himself up, then yelled, 'Everybody out!'

The pilot started to unbuckle himself.

'No,' Quinn said. 'Not you.'

He punched the man hard in the face, stunning him.

467

In the main cabin, Nate already had the door open and was helping Marion to the ground. Orlando was right behind them. Quinn was pleased to see the pilot had put them even closer to the grove than he'd hoped.

'Go,' he said as he jumped out. 'Into the trees.'

Above and behind him, he could hear the Apache coming in for a landing, but he didn't look back. With a crew of only two, no one from the Army helicopter would be following them. At least not on foot. If the helicopter went airborne again, it might be able to spot them. But that's where leaving the pilot of the Superhawk behind came in. He would occupy them, at least long enough for Quinn and his team to get away.

'Head west,' Quinn said as soon as they were all under cover. 'Better chance we'll find a ride in that direction.'

But the noise of the helicopters had woken everyone in the area, and several people were outside trying to see if they could figure out what was going on. It forced Quinn and the others to keep to the trees, slowing their progress.

After a couple of minutes they reached a blacktop road heading east to the hills and west toward Highway 101. The highway was where they wanted to be, so they moved westward parallel to the road, staying under the cover of the trees. They passed a couple of hills, then a short bridge above a dry creek bed.

That's when Quinn heard the Apache power up again.

'Back, back,' he said. 'To the bridge. Get under.'

Nate and Orlando understood why at once. But Marion looked confused. Quinn grabbed her by the shoulders and pulled her with him down into the dry creek.

There was only about four feet of clearance under the bridge. After Nate and Orlando scrambled underneath, Quinn pushed Marion's head down and all but shoved her in after them. He could hear the helicopter rising into the air as he ducked down and joined his team.

'What are we doing here?' Marion said.

'Thermal imaging,' Nate said. 'They'd be able to spot us even in the trees.'

'Oh,' she said.

'Marion,' Quinn said, 'I need you to stay focused. If you want us to save Iris, we need you to do this. Okay?'

'I'm fine,' she said. 'I just didn't know, okay?'

Quinn stared at her for a second, then nodded.

Outside they could hear the Apache flying in a circle, looking for them.

'Nate,' Quinn said, 'I noticed a house not far down the road on the left. You see it?'

Nate nodded.

'After the next circuit, when the Apache is heading away from us, I want you to sprint over there, but keep low. You think you can get there before they look back in this direction?'

'I think so.'

'Will your leg hold up for that?'

Nate paused. Quinn had asked the question honestly, with no hidden agenda. Nate seemed to have sensed it. 'It'll hold up,' he said. Not a boast, just information.

'Good. When you get there, act normal. You can even look up at the helicopter as it flies over. Then find us a ride, but don't come back until the Apache is gone.'

'Got it,' Nate said.

Quinn gave him a pat on the back. 'Now get ready. As soon as it turns away, go.'

Nate moved to edge of the bridge. Above them, the helicopter circled past.

Nate smiled. 'Why don't you guys get some rest,' he said. 'I'll be back in a bit.'

Then as the helicopter turned away, Nate slipped into the darkness.

# 39

'Here's the authorization, officer,' Tucker said in his best mid-American accent as he handed several pieces of paper to the Highway Patrol officer standing outside the bus.

'Don't really need to show those unless you're going past Cambria,' the officer said. But he glanced at the sheets anyway, then handed them back.

'We'll have to take a look inside, though,' the officer said.

'Sure,' Tucker told him. 'I'll open the door. But do me a favor and try to keep quiet. Most of the kids fell asleep on the ride, and I'd like them to stay that way for a while longer if possible.'

The officer smiled. 'No problem.'

Tucker pushed a button and the door to the school bus he was driving folded open. Two officers climbed aboard. The second one — the same guy who'd checked Tucker's papers — whispered as he passed, 'We'll only be a minute.'

Tucker watched in the mirror as the two men walked down the aisle, looking from left to right at the sleeping children. The only two other adults on the bus were Tucker's men, Petersen and Linden. They were all he needed now. The rest had been sent south on a detention mission that at last word had gone off without any problems. The officers nodded at Tucker's men,

471

but otherwise seemed not to have any interest in them.

As they made their way back out, the main officer said, 'All good. Thank you. You have a big day ahead of you. Enjoy.'

'Thanks,' Tucker said. 'I'll just be glad when it's over, and I can get these kids home.'

The officer chuckled. 'Yeah, I bet.'

As soon as the door was closed, Tucker put the bus in gear and headed west on Highway 1 toward Morro Bay.

\* \* \*

The sun had come up and the world had come back to life. Quinn had finally given up any hope of spotting Tucker and the children on the highway, so they'd stopped at a café in Shell Beach to figure out what their next move should be.

When Quinn returned from the bathroom, he found Orlando sitting at their table alone with her laptop open in front of her. Marion was still in the bathroom, and Nate was out finding a new car, something that hopefully wouldn't be reported stolen for several hours.

'There's a report about the helicopter going down,' she said. 'They think we were some kind of protestors trying to embarrass the government by attempting to enter restricted airspace. But they think they thwarted us.'

' 'Thwarted?' ' Quinn asked.

'That's what it says, 'thwarted.' '

'I've just never heard the word spoken before.'

472

She shook her head, but she was smiling. After a moment, she said, 'I got to thinking.'

'About?'

'Schedules,' she said. 'Peter told you there was nothing on the leaders' schedules that would seem to connect with whatever it is Tucker is up to, right?'

'Right.'

'What if it's not the leaders they're after?' she asked.

'What do you mean? Like, someone lower level? Secretary of State or something like that? Wouldn't their schedules be pretty much the same as their bosses'?'

'No. You're right. I was just thinking of something else.'

'What?' he asked.

But before she could respond, Marion reappeared.

'Shouldn't we go or something?' she said. 'Why are we waiting?'

'As soon as Nate gets back, we'll leave,' Quinn said.

'But Iris?' Her eyes pleaded with him to understand.

'We haven't given up, okay? We just need to try and figure out where she's — '

'I know,' Orlando said.

Quinn looked at her.

'I know what they're going to do,' Orlando said.

'What?'

'It's not the leaders they're after, not directly.' She turned her laptop around so Quinn could see it. 'It's their wives.'

'Wives?' He wasn't sure he'd heard her right.

But on the screen was the itinerary for the First Lady of the United States. And there listed in bold, and to begin at 9:30 a.m.: *Spouses' Tour of the R. J. Oliver School of Special Education, Morro Bay.*

Quinn stared at the screen. A school focused on the teaching of the mentally disabled. A wonderful photo op for the spouses of the G8 leaders — seven women and one man, the husband of the German Chancellor. A public face of caring while God knew what their other halves were discussing behind the closed doors of Hearst Castle.

'What is it?' Marion asked.

Quinn looked at his watch: 8:20. Seventy minutes. Less than that really, because once the VIPs were on-site, it would be too late.

'You're staying here,' he said to Marion, his tone dead serious.

'No way,' she said.

'Then we're all dead,' he said. 'You. Us.' He paused. 'Iris.'

Her stare was defiant, but he could see hesitation creeping in. After a moment, she started unconsciously chewing on her lower lip, then she nodded.

'Good,' he said. 'We passed a motel a couple blocks south of here, remember?'

Another nod.

He pulled some cash out of his pocket, peeling off two hundred dollars.

'Here,' he said, handing it to her. 'Use a false

name. Something easy to remember.'

Orlando snapped her laptop closed. 'Nate,' Orlando said, nodding toward the window.

Nate was standing in front of the café, next to a Nissan Maxima.

Quinn dropped a few bucks on the table to pay for the coffee, then stood up.

'Please bring her back,' Marion said.

'That's the plan,' he told her.

★ ★ ★

The closer they got to San Luis Obispo, the more police and Highway Patrol cars they saw. No checks yet, but Quinn knew there would be some ahead.

'Get off here,' Orlando said, glancing up from her computer screen.

The sign read *Los Osos Valley Road*.

'Not the PCH?' Nate asked. The Pacific Coast Highway was the direct route from San Luis Obispo to Morro Bay.

'This'll get us there, too,' she said. 'Just comes in from the back side.'

Nate nodded, then turned up the off-ramp, stopping at the top. 'Which way?' he asked.

'Left.'

They passed through the outskirts of San Luis Obispo and entered a more open farm country framed to the right by a series of dramatic hills.

Quinn's phone began to vibrate. Though Peter's name was on the display, it wasn't Peter's voice that spoke. It was Sean Cooper, the guy who had gotten them the car in New York.

'Where's Peter?' Quinn asked.

'There's a team of federal investigators sitting in his office right now.'

'What the hell?'

'He gave me his phone once we realized what was going on. Told me to leave and call you.' It sounded like Sean was walking fast, his breath audibly punctuating each word.

'Where are you?' Quinn asked.

'Out. Near the National Archives.' D.C., of course. Where the Office was located.

'So what you're telling me is that I shouldn't expect any help,' Quinn said.

'That's what I'm telling you.' A pause. 'One more thing.'

'What?'

'Don't call us. It'll be . . . safer for you that way. If things calm down, we'll be in touch.' Another hesitation. 'I'm sorry.'

Quinn hung up. There was nothing more to say.

★ ★ ★

When they reached Los Osos, they turned onto South Bay Boulevard. According to Orlando, that would take them to State Park Road, which wound around the local golf course before becoming Main Street in Morro Bay.

'What's the plan?' Nate said.

'We get as close to the school as we can,' Quinn said.

'And then?'

*And then* . . . That was the real issue. Quinn

476

had been trying to figure the best answer to that question since they'd left Marion in Shell Beach. One solution had come to mind, but he was hoping to come up with a better one before he had to act.

'Just drive,' he said.

A minute later Nate eased off on the gas. Ahead, five cars were stopped in the road. Parked on the shoulder at the front of the line were two Highway Patrol cars.

*Checkpoint*, Quinn thought.

Quinn pulled his SIG out of his backpack and slipped it under his seat. Though the last thing he wanted to do was use it, it needed to be accessible. He heard the zipper on Orlando's backpack open a second after his. Their thoughts once again parallel.

'Orlando and I are here on vacation,' Quinn said, creating a quick legend. 'Nate, you live up here. We're visiting you, so you wanted to show us Morro Bay.'

'Got it,' Nate said.

'The car?' Orlando asked.

'Don't worry,' Nate said. 'No one will notice it's gone for another couple hours.'

Quinn looked at him, a question on his face.

'Grocery store cashier. She was rushing to get to work on time. Never saw me.'

Nate pulled to a stop behind the last car in line. There were only two officers manning the checkpoint. One stood near the center of the road, leaning down to talk to the drivers as each car approached. The other stood just off the blacktop. His job was to observe, and react if needed. Low-level security, trying to weed out the obvious crazies.

Slowly the line inched forward. The officer seemed to be spending no more than a couple minutes or so with each vehicle. Just enough time to get a vibe from those inside, and check the trunks. So far, no one had been turned back.

As the car in front of them finished its check, Quinn said, 'Nice and relaxed.'

Nate eased the car forward, then rolled his window down.

'Morning,' the officer said.

'Morning,' Nate said.

'How you doing today?' The officer's gaze moved through the cabin, stopping for a second on Quinn and Orlando.

'Doing well,' Nate said. 'Can't beat the weather.'

The officer smiled. 'Are you locals?'

'I am,' Nate said. 'Arroyo Grande. My friends are visiting. Thought I'd take them out and show them the bay.'

The officer glanced at Orlando again. 'So where are you visiting from?' he asked, his voice deceptively light.

'Los Angeles,' she said.

'I hear it's been hot down there lately.'

Before she could respond, Quinn jumped in, 'Not too bad. It'll be worse in September.'

'Now that's true,' the officer said. His eyes stayed on Quinn. 'You look a little familiar. Have we met before?'

Quinn could feel a chill run up his arms. *The police sketch*, he thought. It was a question he wasn't used to, so it caught him off guard.

'He's an actor,' Orlando said. 'Does a lot of commercials.'

'I've done a couple movies, too,' Quinn added, trying to sound appropriately defensive.

'But no one's seen those,' she said. Then, to the officer, she added, 'Straight to DVD.'

'No wonder you're not my publicist,' Quinn said.

'That must be it,' the officer said. He took a step back. 'I'm going to need to take a look in your trunk. Do you mind popping it for me?'

'No problem,' Nate said.

There was a dull thunk as Nate released the trunk. The officer walked around back and pushed it all the way open.

'Anything in there we need to worry about?' Quinn whispered through unmoving lips.

'Just the body of the owner,' Nate said.

'Funny,' Quinn shot back.

'I checked before I picked you guys up,' Nate said. 'Standard stuff.'

A few seconds later, the officer closed the trunk and returned to the driver's side window. 'All right. You all have a good day,' he said.

★ ★ ★

'We're so glad you made it, Mr. Lee,' Sylvia Stanton, principal of the R. J. Oliver School, said. 'Doris in Santa Maria had a child who had a meltdown this morning, so they had to cancel. Since you were coming from so far, I was afraid you'd have the same problem.'

'We're glad we're here, too,' Tucker said.

Ms. Stanton was under the impression that Tucker was Harold Lee, director of a school several hours south in Ventura. The real Mr. Lee was indeed supposed to be transporting a group of children to the event, but his bus had been stopped not long after leaving Ventura by the squad of Tucker's men that had split off and gone south in the dark hours of the morning. Mr. Lee would be thankful later, Tucker knew. At least he and his children would still be alive, as long as no one did anything stupid.

Tucker's biggest concern had been the security check at the school. Mr. Rose's tests at the Yellowhammer lab had shown the explosives' delivery systems would pass through the government's detectors without a problem, appearing to be exactly what they looked like: dozens of individual juice boxes. But passing tests in a lab wasn't the same as carrying the containers through the actual screening machines. And all Tucker could think about as they went through the Secret Service check was the fact that for the first month those same tests Mr. Rose performed had all failed.

But they had passed through without a problem, and soon Tucker and his remaining men had their cargo — the *children* and the explosives — settled in the school's cafeteria. That was when Ms. Stanton had offered to give him a tour of the facility.

'If it's not too much trouble, I'd be honored,' he'd said.

There were classrooms, an indoor gym, the

administration office, an outside play area, and even a swimming pool.

'Only three and a half feet at the deepest,' she'd told him.

But it wasn't the pool or any of the rest of the school that interested him. It was the Secret Service members stationed throughout. Since he'd already passed through the security check and was on the inside, their focus was on other things besides him.

'My God, do you have to feed them all?' Tucker said as they walked out of the auditorium where the assembly would be taking place. Just under a dozen agents had been stationed around the room.

'I know what you mean,' Ms. Stanton half-whispered. 'I'm told there are twenty others in the building alone, and more outside that I can't see.'

*Securing a perimeter that's already been breached*, Tucker thought. He had to force himself not to smile. 'How long have they been here?'

'The advance team arrived on Monday. But they moved in en masse around six a.m. this morning. And let me tell you, they searched *everywhere*.'

'Hey, did they have any of those dogs?' he asked. 'You know what I mean? The ones that sniff out drugs and explosives and those kinds of things? The kids would love to see that.'

'No dogs that I saw,' she said. 'They did have electronic devices with them when they were

481

searching the building. Perhaps those might do the same thing.'

*Not only might*, Tucker thought, *but did*. He said, 'I don't know. I guess.'

While they were standing in the lobby outside the auditorium, Petersen entered from the hallway back to the cafeteria on cue. In his arms was the trigger.

Tucker smiled as if pleasantly surprised. 'Eric, could you come here for a moment?'

Petersen walked over.

'Ms. Stanton, I'd like you to meet one of my teachers. This is Eric Jones,' he said, using Petersen's temporary alias. 'Eric, this is Principal Stanton. She's in charge here.'

'Pleasure to meet you,' Petersen said.

'Good to meet you, too,' Ms. Stanton said.

'Sorry, I'd shake your hand, but I'm a little tied up.'

'I can see that,' Ms. Stanton said, smiling at Iris. 'She's beautiful.'

Tucker could tell she meant it. He reached out and took the girl — the trigger — from Petersen. 'This is Iris.'

Iris's lower lip quivered. She leaned away from Tucker as he took hold of her, like she was weighing the merits of falling to the floor versus staying in his arms.

'Would you like to hold her?' Tucker said.

Ms. Stanton smiled. 'Of course.'

Iris must have sensed the woman's kindness, for she hugged Ms. Stanton tightly, laying her head on the woman's shoulder.

'Hello, Iris,' Ms. Stanton said. 'You are just so

pretty.' She looked at Tucker. 'Is she verbal?'

'Unfortunately, no,' he said. 'She'll make several sounds, but no words yet.'

'That'll come, that'll come,' Ms. Stanton said.

He let the two bond for a few moments longer, then said, 'If I understand correctly, when the First Lady and her guests arrive out front, we're each allowed to have a child with us.' He had only learned this after he arrived. He had planned on keeping the girl in the auditorium with the others, just safely out of the detonation range. This, though, would be so much better. He could always revert to the original plan if his idea was shot.

'Yes, that's correct,' Ms. Stanton said.

Tucker smiled again. 'Iris is the one who will be out front with us.'

'Excellent.' Ms. Stanton kissed Iris on the cheek. 'We'll just have to be careful none of the ladies try to take her home with them.'

Tucker grinned. The last piece of the plan was in place.

# 40

They left the car on main street, then walked into the residential neighborhood northeast of the business district. It was already ten minutes after nine, the checkpoint having eaten up more time than they could afford.

'You going to tell us that plan yet?' Nate asked.

'Not yet,' Quinn said.

'You don't have a plan, do you?'

Before he could reply, Orlando said, 'Not a good one.'

Quinn frowned at her, knowing she had a pretty good idea of what he had in mind. 'I'm open to other suggestions,' he said.

'Yeah. I know.'

'You guys are giving me a lot of confidence right now,' Nate said.

'It'll be fine,' Quinn said.

The closer they got to the school, the more cars they found parked on the street. There were a lot of people, too. Most walking up the hill in the same direction they were. The curious out to see political royalty, something that had never occurred in this part of the country.

Quinn, Orlando, and Nate blended in, becoming just three more members of the crowd.

The school was located just off Ridgeway Street on Owens Avenue. It backed against a

484

small wilderness area that separated it from the Morro Bay Golf Course. Quinn wished they had time to sneak in from the rear, but he knew they didn't. In less than fifteen minutes, the limos would begin to arrive. And once that happened, there'd be carnage.

As far as two blocks away, people were taking up positions along the street, trying to get the best view they could. Sheriff's deputies and policemen were spread out along the road, keeping people on the sidewalk as much as possible.

Quinn took the lead, weaving through the crowd to get them as close as possible to the school. They made it to within thirty yards before the growing crowd forced them to stop.

They could see the school building now. It was older, low-slung, and very 1960s. It had a parking lot in front that was empty with the exception of two black Suburbans. Secret Service, no doubt. The crowd had been allowed to within ten feet of the lot's entrance, but had been stopped from going any farther by several police officers.

'I count at least half a dozen Feds in the lot,' Orlando whispered in Quinn's ear.

He nodded, then looked at his watch. 'Goddammit,' he said. Eight minutes until the scheduled arrival.

Reluctantly he pulled his backpack off his shoulders and handed it to Nate.

'What are you doing?' Nate asked.

'Not now,' Quinn said.

485

'You'll need me,' Orlando said. 'At least to get started.'

Quinn nodded.

'Is there something I should know about?' Nate asked.

Quinn pulled him close so he could whisper in his ear. 'Stay here. If we're not successful, do what you can to help with the aftermath. Otherwise we'll contact you.'

'Where are you going?'

'Where do you think we're going?' Quinn asked. 'To stop this.'

'And you don't need me?'

'At the moment, no. There's just no sense in all three of us going down.'

Nate's brow furrowed, but he only said, 'Okay. We'll meet up after.' Quinn hoped Nate was right.

★ ★ ★

'We're all set,' Tucker said into his phone. He was standing in the lobby with a few of the other attendants and the handful of children who had been selected to greet the targets out front when they arrived. The rest of the children, and, most important, the delivery devices, had been moved into the auditorium to await the arrival of the guests.

'The trigger?' Mr. Rose asked.

Tucker glanced at Petersen. He was a few feet away with Iris in his arms. 'In place, ready to go.'

'Good.'

Tucker wasn't sure where Mr. Rose was. After

486

the helicopters landed, the old man had taken one of the waiting vehicles for himself and disappeared, leaving the execution of the plan in Tucker's hands.

'What about the schedule?' Mr. Rose said.

'We've been told everything is running on time.'

At that moment, Ms. Stanton entered the lobby from the auditorium, looking both nervous and excited. Tucker smiled at her and gave her a nod. She smiled back and started walking toward him.

Into the phone he said, 'The transfers?'

'Once the job is complete, you will get the rest of your money. Just like we discussed.'

'Fine,' Tucker said. 'Gotta go. We're getting close.'

'Don't disappoint me,' Mr. Rose said.

Tucker disconnected the call just as Ms. Stanton reached him.

'I'm told there might be a few minutes' delay at most,' she said.

'I would have expected more,' Tucker said, his tone light. 'These things never come off on time.'

She put her hand near her mouth like she was about to tell him a secret. 'I think it helps that we're one of the first things on their agenda for today.'

'I think you're probably right.'

They both laughed at the non-joke.

'So is Iris ready?' Ms. Stanton asked as she looked over at the girl.

'She'll be plenty ready when they arrive.'

'Of course she will be.' Another smile, then, 'I

need to check on the others. So just hold your position until you're given the word to go outside.'

'It's the moment we've been waiting for,' Tucker assured her.

★ ★ ★

The crowd parted with reluctance as Quinn and Orlando elbowed their way to the front. When there was only one row between them and the loose line of cops holding everyone back, Quinn leaned down and whispered in Orlando's ear, 'Five seconds. That's all I'll need.'

She turned and kissed him on the cheek. 'I love you,' she said.

Quinn moved into position, going to the right against the stone half-wall that lined the parking lot. Once he was there, he looked back and gave Orlando a quick nod.

She waited a moment, then turned sideways and began trying to squeeze around the woman who was in front of her.

'Hey, watch it,' the lady said. 'I've been waiting here for hours, so back off.'

Orlando ignored her, and continued to push until she'd worked her way to the front.

'I said I was here first,' the woman said. 'Move back.'

'You move back,' Orlando said.

'Officer,' the woman said, her voice rising. 'She pushed me out of my place.'

The officer nearest them looked over. 'There's plenty of room for everyone, ma'am,' he said.

'Yeah,' Orlando said. 'So just shut up and chill.'

'She's been there all morning,' a man who was probably the woman's husband or boyfriend said. 'Now move back.'

'I'm here now, so I think I'll stay. Thanks.'

'I don't know who the hell you think you are,' the woman said. She was almost yelling now. 'But that's my spot and you're going to move.'

'Everyone calm down, all right?' the officer said.

'I'm not going anywhere, bitch,' Orlando said.

The woman gaped at her.

'You do *not* call my wife 'bitch.' ' Husband, then. Not boyfriend. He moved in close, doing the male intimidation thing.

'What are you going to do? Hit me?' Orlando said, then laughed.

'Hey,' the officer said. 'Everyone, *calm down*.'

But the crowd in the immediate area was already craning their necks to see what was going on, then repeating what they'd heard to the others around them.

'I'm calm,' Orlando said. 'Tell her to calm the hell down.'

'Officer, I haven't done anything wrong. This . . . woman tried to — '

'I didn't *try* to do anything.'

Quinn saw what he'd been waiting for. The officers on either side of the one who was trying unsuccessfully to control the situation had started to look over to see what was going on.

'Lady, you'd better leave before something bad happens,' the husband said.

'Did you hear that?' Orlando said. 'He threatened me. Hey, did you hear that? I can press charges for that, you know.'

That did it. All three of them began yelling over the top of one another.

Quinn watched the cop nearest him, the last before the wall. He was looking toward Orlando and the others, leaning ever so slightly in their direction. Then, as the yelling became even more intense, he turned to the people in front of him and said, 'Stay here.'

The moment he stepped away to help calm the crowd, Quinn moved to the front.

'He told us to stay here,' someone said.

'I'm with the press,' Quinn said, knowing that would stop them for a few moments.

He made it all the way to the end of the half-wall, and was just turning into the parking lot entrance when a voice shouted behind him, 'Hey! Stop!'

He raised his hands in the air, but he kept going.

'Stop or I'll shoot!'

But Quinn knew that wasn't true. Just beyond him several kids had been moved out of one of the buildings onto the sidewalk at the other side of the parking lot. Any shot would have had a very good chance of hitting them.

Not only the kids, though. There were a dozen Secret Service agents also in the line of fire. Most of them were now drawing their own weapons and heading in Quinn's direction.

'Sir, you need to stop right where you are.' This time it was one of the agents who spoke.

'It's time,' Ms. Stanton said.

Tucker took a deep breath, then removed the electronic activator from his pocket. It had been built into the handset of his cell phone so it would pass unnoticed.

'You're sure we're far enough away?' Petersen asked, glancing back toward the auditorium where the explosive devices were waiting.

'Plenty,' Tucker said.

Petersen turned Iris so that her leg was accessible.

'Naaaa,' Iris said, actually scowling at Tucker.

'Just hold still,' he told her.

'Naaaa.'

He touched the series of buttons that engaged the activator. On the display screen a simple bar graph appeared. It was yellow and hovered near the bottom of the screen, but the closer it got to the triggering device embedded in Iris's leg, the higher the bar rose.

Iris tried to push his hand away.

'Naaaa!' she yelled.

Tucker glanced up and saw that Ms. Stanton was looking in his direction.

'Just a little tired,' he said. 'After the drive and everything.'

'Maybe she should wait inside with the others,' Ms. Stanton said.

'She'll be fine,' Tucker assured her. 'I have a juice here for her. That should calm her down.'

Ms. Stanton didn't look convinced, but she didn't push any further.

'Hold this,' Tucker said to Petersen. He handed him the device. 'Just don't touch any of the buttons.'

Petersen shifted Iris so that he was holding her with only one arm, then took the activator from Tucker. Tucker reached into his pocket and pulled out a juice packet that looked exactly like its more deadly cousins inside, only it was the real thing. He'd grabbed it for just such an emergency. He freed the straw, stuck it in the hole, then held the whole thing out to Iris.

She looked at it, at first acting like she didn't want it.

'It's good,' Tucker said. 'Come on, take it.'

She finally grabbed ahold of it, and started sucking on the straw.

'Good girl,' he said.

He retrieved the device from Petersen, then moved it over the implant. As the bar on the display filled the screen, he pressed the # and the 7 keys at the same time. The bar graph was replaced by a circle that began turning white in a slow wave, following an invisible second hand as it moved around the dial.

'Hold her still,' he said.

When the advancing white filled three-quarters of the circle, the words *Configuration Confirmed* flashed twice before disappearing, and the edge of white accelerated. In less than two seconds the circle was complete, and the words *Activation Confirmed* flashed above it.

'Mr. Lee. Mr. Jones. Are you coming?' It was Ms. Stanton again.

She was near the door, holding it open so the

last of the greeters could head outside.

'Coming now,' Tucker said.

He slipped the phone into his pocket. As soon as he could, he'd dump it. He didn't need it anymore. The triggering implant inside Iris was now active. Less than a minute after the girl got within twenty-five feet of the binary explosives, they would detonate.

'Sorry about that,' he said to Ms. Stanton as he stepped outside. 'She's fine now. Just needed a little juice.'

He smiled at her, but the look she gave back was less than approving.

God, he couldn't wait to get away from all these kids.

The parking lot where they'd arrived in the bus was now devoid of all but a couple of government vehicles. But they wouldn't be a concern. During the upcoming confusion, Tucker would simply be able to run out the gates like he was afraid for his life, then walk the few blocks to the car that had been staged for his escape. Less than thirty minutes after the spouses of the G8 leaders had been killed, Tucker and his men would be on the 101 Freeway headed south toward Los Angeles. And once in L.A., no one would ever find them.

'All those holding children please move to the center,' Ms. Stanton said.

Petersen glanced at Tucker.

'You know what to do,' Tucker whispered.

Petersen walked over to where the other child minders were gathering. His job would be to get one of the VIPs to carry Iris into the auditorium.

'The rest of you, split up so you're in equal groups on either side.'

Tucker moved to the left and took position at the far end of the group, graciously declining offers to be closer to where the action would be.

'I'm just along for the ride,' he said. 'You all did the real work.'

One of the agents walked over to the group.

'My name is Agent Dettling,' he said. 'I'm in charge of the arrival. I just wanted to let you all know we've just received the five-minute warning. So please, no wandering around at this point. And when the cars arrive, Ms. Stanton will step out to greet the First Lady and her guests, but the rest of you should remain where you are like we discussed earlier. Now, are there any questions?'

There weren't; most of those present were either too excited or too nervous to say anything.

'Great,' Dettling said. 'Then everything should go smoothly.'

As he stepped away, the woman standing next to Tucker said something in a low voice.

'Excuse me?' Tucker said.

'What?' She sounded startled. 'Oh, my God. I'm so sorry. I was . . . well, I was practicing what I was going to say.'

Tucker laughed. 'No problem. Completely under — '

'Stop or I'll shoot!'

Tucker whipped his head around, looking toward the voice. It had come from somewhere beyond the street.

A man dressed in dark jeans, black T-shirt, and a jacket had entered the parking lot and was walking toward where Tucker and the others were waiting, his hands raised in the air. Several Secret Service agents already had their guns drawn, and aimed at the man as they walked quickly toward him.

'Sir, you need to stop right where you are.' The voice was that of Agent Dettling, but it hardly registered to Tucker.

What caused him to freeze was the man with his hands in the air.

Jonathan Quinn.

'Fuck me,' Tucker said under his breath.

* * *

Quinn stopped twenty feet into the parking lot, his arms still raised above his head.

A quartet of Secret Service agents walked toward him. Each had a gun trained on his chest. Behind Quinn, back toward the exit to the street, he could hear at least as many police officers closing in.

Quinn focused on one of the men in front of him. 'I need to talk to the agent in charge.'

'Sir, get down on your knees, then lay down on the ground,' the agent said.

'I need to talk to the agent in charge.'

'Get down on your knees, then lay on the ground. Now!'

Quinn knew they were going to rush him, but if they did, he'd lose what advantage he had.

'You need to call off the event,' he said. 'There's a bomb.'

Everyone stopped moving.

495

Tucker pulled out his phone and the piece of paper he'd been given when the helicopters had landed. Somewhere out in the streets surrounding the school there were two parked cars with enough explosives to get everyone's attention. The plan was to set them off thirty seconds after the bombs in the school were detonated, helping to create even more chaos so that Tucker and his men could get away. All he had to do was call the phone number on the paper, then the first would go off a moment later, the next twenty seconds after that.

He glanced at Petersen. 'Be ready,' he mouthed.

* * *

One of the agents lifted his wrist to his mouth and spoke too low for Quinn to hear.

'I'm not joking around,' Quinn said. 'Call it off. There's a bomb in the building.'

'On the ground,' the first agent said.

Quinn looked past him toward the crowd gathered on the sidewalk. It was a mix of adults and children, all staring at him, the children in curiosity and the adults in fear. All, that was, except the large man standing toward one end. The look he gave Quinn wasn't fear. It was anger.

*Hello, Leo*, he thought.

And several people away from Tucker, toward the middle of the group, was one of the men

Quinn had seen at Yellowhammer. He was holding Iris in his arms.

'It's him!' Quinn said, still keeping his arm raised, but pointing in Tucker's direction. 'The bomber. He's right there!'

The agents didn't turn around, their training keeping them focused on what they considered to be the primary threat. But Quinn had said it loud enough to reach the crowd at the sidewalk. Several of the adults and two of the agents who had held back looked where he was pointing.

'On the ground n — '

The agent's voice was cut off by the near-deafening boom of an explosion.

# 41

The crowd both inside and outside the school grounds started screaming. People began running in all directions. Before they could get even a few feet, a second bomb went off. Like the first, it was somewhere in the streets beyond the school grounds.

The chaos became total. Three of the agents watching Quinn took off in the direction of the explosions, leaving only the fourth to guard him.

'Over to the sidewalk,' the agent said.

He held his position, waiting for Quinn to pass by him. But when Quinn came abreast of the agent, he dropped low and rammed his head into the man's gut. The agent expelled a loud breath, then fell to the ground.

Quinn pinned the agent's arm down with a knee, preventing the man from using his gun. Then he punched the man twice in the face. It took a third hit, though, before the agent lost consciousness.

Quinn jumped up and sprinted toward the sidewalk near the school entrance. He all but expected another agent to come at him, but they were occupied elsewhere.

People were running everywhere. To the school, away from the school, in all directions. Some of the people who had been in the streets had moved onto the grounds, seeking shelter and adding to the frenzy.

*Where the hell is Tucker? Where is the other man?* Quinn thought. They were nowhere to be seen. Had they taken Iris? If so, were they inside or had they left?

Ahead at the door that led into the school, two women were trying to get the last of the children inside. The final child was a little girl who couldn't have been any more than five. African-American. And like the boy who had reached out to Quinn in the room at Yellowhammer, she also appeared to have Down syndrome.

'Come on, Iris. Let's go inside,' one of the women said.

'No!' Quinn yelled.

The women looked up in terror, then grabbed the girl and rushed her across the threshold.

Quinn raced down the sidewalk and threw the door open. He had to get to Iris before she triggered the explosives hidden somewhere inside.

That was if he wasn't already too late.

★　★　★

Tucker ran as fast as he could. Petersen, who had been built for strength more than speed, had fallen several paces behind.

Smoke, dust, and debris from the car bombs had begun to descend over the neighborhood, creating a milky haze. Some people were still screaming as they ran. Others had faces covered with tears, while a few tried to act the hero and urged everyone to remain calm.

'Get out of my fucking way,' Tucker said as he shoved a teenage boy into a parked car.

He just needed to get a few more blocks. A blue Honda Accord was parked waiting for him on Anchor Street. With so many Hondas on the road, it would provide a certain amount of anonymity. Tucker had memorized the license plate number, and been told the keys would be under the front seat.

The crowd thinned the farther he got from the school, some choosing one street thinking it would take them to safety, while others chose another. By the time Tucker was within a block of the car, there were only a handful of people still running with him.

He glanced over his shoulder to see how far back Petersen had fallen. He could only see four people. A man and a woman on the other side of the street, gripping each other's hands as they fled. And on his side, farther back, a teenage girl, and behind her several paces a woman.

Nowhere did he see Petersen.

*Jesus Christ*, he thought. Hell if he was going to wait more than a couple minutes tops. If Petersen didn't make it by then, he'd have to find his own way out.

Tucker began scanning the street for the Honda. It was only a few moments before he spotted it near the end of the block. As he started to open the driver's door, he heard steps running on the asphalt behind him. But before he could turn to see who it was, a voice yelled out at him.

'Don't even *think* about moving.'

★ ★ ★

The chaos outside the school was intensified inside by the restricted space of the lobby Quinn found himself in. There were adults and children everywhere, screaming and crying and consoling and whispering. They were all too preoccupied to notice Quinn joining them.

*My God,* he thought. *If the explosives are in here, we're all already dead.*

He knew he couldn't let that stop him. He whipped his head around, searching for Iris. There were kids everywhere, some even holding juice boxes, but he couldn't see the girl.

A set of double doors that led off the lobby flew open. From inside, several Secret Service agents rushed out.

'Get everyone into the auditorium with the others,' one of the agents yelled while his colleagues ran toward the doors to the outside.

*The auditorium,* the man had said. *With the others.* It was where the First Lady and the other spouses would have been taken. Where the best opportunity for total success would be. That's where the explosives would have been taken, Quinn realized. He had to keep Iris from entering the room.

The crowd surged forward, everyone but the agents wanting to get as far away from the outside as possible. Quinn tried to push through them to get to the front so he could see Iris before she went through the doors.

He was only ten feet away when someone said, 'Oh, my God. You're him. The guy from outside.'

501

Several people cried out in fear, while others tried to move away from him as fast as possible. Quinn glanced back at the doors to the outside, and was relieved to see all the agents were gone. Civilians he could deal with, Feds with guns were slightly more problematic.

'Out of my way!' he yelled as he rushed forward through the door to the auditorium.

The room was large. The stage at the other end of the room was at least a hundred feet away. Those inside were gathered near it. Some looked at him curiously, having no idea who he was. Against the wall near the stage was a low stack of boxes. Trays, really. He'd seen them before in markets. A couple dozen juice boxes plastic-wrapped to a cardboard base. *Oh, God.*

He scanned the room looking for Iris, but the girl wasn't there. He returned to the lobby.

Most of the people there had moved to one corner and were crowded together, staring at him as if they expected him to attack them all. As he started to raise his hands in front of him in an effort to make them relax, the door to the outside opened.

Quinn retrieved the gun he'd taken from the agent in the parking lot out of its temporary holding place under the waist of his pants behind his back, and pointed it at the widening gap.

'Hey. Chill out. I'm just here to see if you need any help.'

It was Nate.

Quinn allowed himself a relieved breath, then asked, 'Orlando?'

'Don't know. I've been alone since you left.'

Quinn nodded. With the chaos, it would have been surprising if they had found each other. He turned his attention back to the group cowering against the wall.

'Who's in charge here?' he called out.

There were a few murmurs, then several people looked toward a woman standing near the middle of the group. She appeared to be in her fifties, and had the look of a school administrator, caring but strong.

After a second, she said, 'Leave us alone. We won't bother you.'

'So you're in charge?' he said.

'Yes,' she said. 'I'm in charge of this school.'

'What's your name?'

She hesitated. 'Ms. Stanton. Now please, leave. You're scaring the children.'

'I'm sorry,' Quinn said. 'We're not here to hurt anyone.'

'Then what do you want?'

'I'm looking for a girl. She's about five, and African.'

'I'm not letting you take any of the children,' Ms. Stanton said.

Quinn ignored her. 'The girl's name is Iris.'

One of the women, a teacher perhaps, moved slightly.

'You have something to tell me?' Quinn said, looking at her.

'No,' she said.

He glanced at Nate, then pointed at the woman. 'Check.'

Nate walked over.

'Please step out,' he said to the woman.

The woman began to tremble, but she didn't move.

'What are you going to do to her?' Ms. Stanton asked.

'We're not going to *do* anything to her,' Quinn said.

'Please, I need you to step out,' Nate repeated.

For another couple of seconds she remained where she was, then her resolve crumbled and she moved forward.

Behind her was Iris.

Nate reached out to her. 'Hey, sweetie. Come here.'

The girl didn't move, so Nate leaned in and picked her up.

'Got her,' he said to Quinn.

'You can't take her,' Ms. Stanton said.

'I want you to listen to what I'm going to say very carefully. The man who brought this girl to your school today also brought several others. Correct?'

Ms. Stanton nodded. 'Mr. Lee came up from Ventura.'

'Mr. Lee?'

'That's who you're talking about, right?'

'Mr. Lee isn't who he said he is.' Quinn paused. 'He came here for one reason, to kill you and your special guests this morning.'

'What?'

'Those bombs that went off outside? There's more, only here in the school.'

'Impossible,' she said, though she looked terrified that it might be true.

'He brought juice boxes along with the

504

children, didn't he?'

'Sure. Everyone did.'

'Well, there isn't juice inside his. I'm guessing the ones he brought are in the auditorium right now, just waiting to go off. Get everyone away from them, then tell one of the agents.'

'My God,' Ms. Stanton said.

'Do you understand?' Quinn asked.

A pause, then, 'Yes.'

'Good.' Quinn looked at Nate. 'Let's go.'

'You can't . . . just kidnap her,' Ms. Stanton said, much of her defensive posturing gone.

'She and the others he brought were already kidnapped.' He turned and started heading for a doorway at the far end of the hallway.

'Then where are you taking her?' Ms. Stanton called out.

Quinn stopped a few feet from the exit and looked back over his shoulder. 'To her mother.'

* * *

Tucker knew he had few immediate options. Because of all the Secret Service and the inevitable security check, he'd gone to the school without a gun.

He thought about the last thing he'd seen when he'd looked over his shoulder. There had been only the two on his side of the street: the teenager and the woman. He had thought they'd been nobodies, but it looked like he'd been mistaken. The woman must have been Secret Service. She'd been dressed in street clothes,

505

working undercover in the crowd. That had to be it.

His brow furrowed. He'd been so caught up in trying to figure out how to get out of this, he hadn't even considered why the agent had been chasing him in the first place. Tucker had been just one of hundreds running through the streets. And as far as anyone should have been able to tell, he'd done nothing wrong.

Behind him, he could hear the woman stepping closer.

'Open the back door,' she said.

'Sure,' Tucker said. 'No problem.'

He took a step toward the rear of the car and opened the back passenger door.

'Now get behind the wheel,' she said. 'And shut the door once you're inside.'

Tucker hesitated. A Secret Service agent would have had him get on the ground, like they'd tried to get Quinn to do back at the school. If she wasn't Secret Service, then who the hell —

'Do it!' she said.

He moved back to the driver's door. As he slipped into the front seat, he could hear her get in behind him, then the thunk of her door closing just before he closed his own. He started to reach down for the seat release so he could fall back into her.

'Don't,' she said. It wouldn't have worked anyway. She'd already slid all the way across so that she was sitting diagonal from him.

He put both of his hands on his lap, wishing he'd requested a gun be left under his seat. But he hadn't thought he would need one at this point, and the last thing he had wanted was for the police to find it at one of the roadblock searches that were sure to go up soon.

'So are we going anywhere, or are we just staying here?' he asked.

'No, Mr. Tucker. We're not going anywhere.'

The back of his neck began to tingle. How did she know his name?

'Then . . . what are we going to do? You want some information? You need some names, is that it? We can make a deal. You promise to let me go, I'll tell you whatever you want.'

'No,' she said. 'No deal this time. This time I'm going to kill you.'

He turned so he could see who she was, unable to stop himself.

It wasn't the woman he'd seen running behind him. It was the smaller one, the one he'd thought was a teenager. Only she wasn't a teenager.

'Remember me?' she asked.

'You're Quinn's bitch.' He paused, thinking. 'Orlando.'

The small Asian woman smiled. 'Good. So I don't have to explain to you why you're never going to get out of this car.'

*No, she didn't,* he thought. He would have been out for blood, too, if he had run across the person who had once kidnapped his child. That was if he'd had any. He glanced past her, through the back window, hoping to see Petersen.

'No one's coming,' she said.

'Don't know what you're talking about,' he said.

'Your friend,' she told him. 'The big guy? He ran into a car back there. Don't think he's going to be up and around for a while.'

So he was on his own. *Fine*, he thought. His left hand drifted toward the door handle.

'We had a deal,' he said.

'That deal was done almost two years ago. And here you are messing with children again.'

'A bunch of defects. No one will miss them. Hell, we were doing a service.'

'We know about the explosives in the juice boxes and the trigger in the girl's leg,' she said.

His hand stopped for a moment.

'And as far as I can tell, we haven't heard any more booms,' she went on. 'Sounds to me like Quinn's neutralized the threat, so your mission's a bust.'

'I'll give you names,' he said. 'The people I was working for.'

'We already have the names. We don't need anything from you.'

'Look,' he said. His fingers were only inches from the handle. 'Your son's fine. Looks like these defe . . . ' He paused. ' . . . these kids are fine, too. So no reason I have to die. I didn't kill anyone.'

She smiled.

And just as the pad of his index finger touched the door release, she pulled her trigger.

# 42

Quinn and Nate worked their way through the buildings to the back of the school.

Iris clung to Nate, a short laugh escaping her mouth every few seconds. It had become a game to her, and that was fine with Quinn. Better that she was happy than crying.

When they reached the back of a rectangular building that butted up against the large grassy playground, Quinn stopped. There was a chain-link fence that ran along the back of the field, and just beyond it a wooded area that separated the school grounds from the golf course.

'We need to get over there,' Quinn said. He did a one-eighty, checking if they had been followed. So far so good. 'I'll go first. Once I'm over, I'll give you a signal, then you follow.'

'Got it.'

Quinn did one final look around, then sprinted across the grass. It took him just over ten seconds to reach the fence. He tossed the pistol onto the other side, then placed his hands on the top crossbar and pushed himself over.

Once rearmed and partially hidden by a nearby tree, he scanned the school. There was no one but Nate and Iris, so he gave his apprentice a single wave.

Quinn met them at the fence. Nate handed Iris over the top, and Quinn gently maneuvered her the rest of the way over. He then hugged the girl to his chest and turned to head for the cover of the trees. That's when he heard the shot.

Nate, already pulling himself over the fence, grunted, then fell to the ground on Quinn's side. Quinn darted behind the same tree as before, getting Iris out of any line of fire. He pulled his gun out, then peeked around the tree.

Nate was dragging himself along the ground toward the cover of the grove.

'Are you hit?' Quinn asked.

'I'm fine,' Nate said.

Quinn glanced through the fence back at the school. There were two men in police uniforms crouched near the corner of one of the buildings. Quinn aimed his pistol so that he would hit a spot in the grass off to their right, then pulled the trigger twice.

As he'd hoped, the sound of the shots sent the officers running for cover. It also caused Iris to yell out in surprise.

'Up. Quick, quick, quick,' Quinn said to Nate.

Nate got to his feet and lunged into the woods.

Quinn rubbed Iris on the back. 'You're going to be all right,' he said. 'No need to cry.'

'Here,' Nate said, holding out his arms.

Quinn handed the girl to him, and instantly she went quiet.

'You're just the one who made the big noise,' Nate said to Quinn. 'Don't take it personally.'

Quinn looked back at the school. The police officers were still out of sight, but he knew that wouldn't last for long.

'We need to keep moving,' he said.

If he headed south and a bit to the east, he knew they would get to the road that led to the golf course clubhouse, but that would be the first place anyone looked for them. So he turned left.

As they ran, Quinn pulled out his phone and called Orlando.

It rang five times, then clicked over to voicemail.

*Dammit*, he thought, then tried it again. Same response.

The trees were thinning to the right. Beyond was the green fairway of one of the holes. Not surprisingly, there was no one out on the course. The facility had no doubt been shut down due to security concerns for the now-canceled event at the school. Quinn moved to the left, keeping more trees between them and the open space.

After several minutes, he saw a wooden fence ahead of them that separated the course from the backyards of several houses. Once again he had Nate wait as he approached alone. What he was hoping to find was a gate behind one of the houses. No luck on that front, but what he did find was an empty house waiting for a new owner.

'Over here,' he called.

As Nate hopped the fence, Quinn saw that the shoe and pant leg near Nate's right ankle had been ripped apart.

'What the hell happened?' he asked.

Nate looked down at the damage. 'I got hit,' he said. 'But see? No blood. Bonus for missing a leg. I have to tell you, though, the vibration stung

511

like a son of a bitch.'

Nate was going to do fine, Quinn knew. Just fine.

As they headed across the backyard, Quinn's cell phone began to hum.

'Hold on,' he told Nate.

Orlando's name was on the screen.

'Are you all right?' he asked.

'Yes,' she said. 'I don't know where Nate is.'

'He's with me.'

'And the girl?'

'We've got her.'

He could hear her sigh. 'Thank God.'

'We could use a ride, though,' he said.

'That I can help with.'

He told her where they were. 'I'm going to leave Nate here with the girl. Pick them up and get out of town.'

'Where the hell do you think you're going?'

'I need to find Tucker.'

A pause on the other end. 'That won't be necessary,' she said. 'He's dead.'

And as soon as she said it, he knew where she'd been.

There was no statute of limitations on a mother's vengeance.

★ ★ ★

Hardwick had followed the car south on the 101 all the way to Santa Barbara to a motel called the Santa Barbara Beach Inn. He hadn't been seen because the person he was trailing had no reason to suspect he was being followed. Arrogance. An

512

arrogance that had served him well for years, but was ultimately going to bring him down.

He parked in the lot and got out of the car. The fat suit he'd worn when he'd met with Quinn was gone. He was leaner and in far better shape than he'd portrayed at the museum.

Once he found which room the man was in, he located a maid working alone on the second level. She hadn't put up much of a fight. It was too bad he had to kill her, but he couldn't leave anyone who would recognize him. He pulled her cart into the room where he'd left her, then shut the door. He would be long gone by the time anyone found her.

Her passkey in hand, Hardwick listened at the man's door. A TV was on inside, and somewhere water was running. A shower, he realized.

Perfect.

He used the key and let himself in.

The suite was nice enough. Not the Four Seasons, but livable. Of course, Hardwick would have never stayed there. He assumed it was chosen more for its low profile than for its décor. The living area consisted of a couple of couches, a small dining table, some odds and ends to give the space character, and a plasma TV hanging on the wall and tuned to CNN.

To his right was a door that led to a spacious bedroom, with attached master bath. That's where the sound of the shower came from.

Hardwick checked his watch: 9:15.

As if on cue, the shower turned off.

Hardwick made himself comfortable on one of the couches. From the bathroom he could hear first the flush of the toilet, then the sink turn on, then off.

When the man entered the living room, he wore only a towel around his waist. He crossed to the TV, and seemed annoyed by what he saw.

'Expecting something else?' Hardwick said.

The man whipped around, surprised. 'What are you doing here?' he said.

Hardwick smiled. 'It's such a big day for you, Anthony. I didn't think you'd want to spend it alone.'

'You will call me Mr. Rose,' he said, his tone as arrogant as his driving habits had been. Anthony was his given first name. No one ever called him that. 'And you're right. It is a big day. We should see the results in a few minutes.'

Hardwick stood up. 'I'm not talking about your little plan in Morro Bay. That, I'm fairly confident, isn't going to come off as you expect.'

'What are you talking about?'

'The LP has always had a plan, Anthony. And what we do in support of that plan is carefully worked out years ahead of time.'

'I'm well aware of the plan, *James*. That's exactly what I've been working toward. What I will have accomplished this morning will bring us just that much closer. This was all worked out months ago. The council approved my plan and has funded the operation. So whatever it is you're trying to tell me is just more of your bullshit.'

'The council. Right.' Hardwick smiled. 'Who do you think sent me?'

Mr. Rose's eyes narrowed as his lips pressed

together in obvious anger. 'Enough. You've overstepped your bounds. I'm sure the council has no idea that you're here.' He turned and started scanning the room, looking for something.

'Your phone's on the wet bar, if that's what you're searching for.'

This only seemed to make Mr. Rose angrier. He marched over to the bar, one hand holding up his towel, the other clenching and flexing as if it was the only thing keeping him from flying into a rage. After picking up the phone, he punched a couple of buttons, then raised it to his ear. Hardwick watched as Mr. Rose held it in place for several seconds, then moved it out so he could see the screen. His eyes grew wide as he read the message Hardwick knew would be there.

'Oh, I totally forgot,' Hardwick said, then looked at his watch. 'The council had your phone disconnected four minutes ago. Here. Use mine.' He pulled out his own phone and held it out to Mr. Rose.

Mr. Rose didn't move. 'I don't need to make a call to know that you're lying.'

'Then let me do it for you.'

Hardwick activated the speakerphone function, then dialed.

There were two rings, then, 'Hello?'

'Mr. Kidd, please,' Hardwick said.

Mr. Rose shot him a look.

'One moment,' the voice on the phone said.

'Didn't anyone tell you?' Hardwick said to Mr. Rose. 'Mr. Kidd's the chairman now.'

Movement on the other end of the line, then the hollow sound of another speakerphone being activated.

'James?' a voice said.

'Yes, Mr. Kidd,' Hardwick said. 'I'm here with Mr. Rose right now.'

'Ah. And you've delivered our message?'

'I'm in the process.'

'This is ridiculous,' Mr. Rose blurted out. He took several steps toward Hardwick and the phone. 'Where is Chairman Vine?'

'Is that you, Mr. Rose?' Mr. Kidd said.

'Where's the Chairman?'

'I'm the Chairman. If you're looking for Mr. Vine, he retired.'

'That's bullshit!' Mr. Rose yelled.

'It is not . . . bullshit,' a new voice said over the phone. It was older, and its staccato delivery was unmistakably that of the former chairman. 'I turned over power to Chairman Kidd ten weeks ago. So, Mr. Rose, you *are* talking to the Chairman.'

'Ten weeks?' Mr. Rose said to himself. He looked at the phone as if he could see Mr. Kidd on the other end. 'But my operation, you continued to fund it.'

'It was useful to us for a time,' Chairman Kidd said. 'We do owe you a thanks. Without your operation, we would have never been able to dispose of some of our more ardent enemies. The DDNI will no longer be hunting us, and as of this morning the Office has ceased operations. Those are both because of you.'

'But why try to stop what I was doing? I don't

understand. It served the plan.'

'Actually,' Hardwick said, 'it was decided that it would serve the plan better if your operation were to fail spectacularly. The result will be just as good as if you had succeeded in killing the targets. In fact, probably better.'

'It's all in service of the plan, Mr. Rose,' Chairman Kidd said. 'I think there is only one little matter left to take care of.'

'Wh . . . what?' Mr. Rose asked.

'Mr. Hardwick will fill you in.' Almost before the last word was spoken, the call was disconnected.

Hardwick glanced at the television. There was a handheld shot from a street where dozens of people were running. In the background, smoke was rising in the air. The graphic at the bottom of the screen identified the location as Morro Bay, California. In the text scroll beneath that, this information:

**SCHOOL VISIT BY G8 SPOUSES DISRUPTED PRIOR TO THEIR ARRIVAL ON THE CAMPUS • NO CASUALTIES YET REPORTED • CHAOS IN STREETS IN MORRO BAY • SCHOOL VISIT BY G8 SPOUSES . . .**

Hardwick looked over at Mr. Rose and saw that the old man was watching the television, too.

'I don't think we could have asked for a better result,' Hardwick said, smiling.

Mr. Rose looked at Hardwick, then at the useless phone he seemed to realize he was still holding. When he threw it, it wasn't a surprise. Hardwick was already moving toward him, the phone missing him by several inches and slamming harmlessly into the cushion on the couch.

Mr. Rose, though, displayed a surprising amount of speed. He was already moving toward the bedroom the moment the phone left his hand. Hardwick sprinted after him, getting to the door just before it closed all the way.

He shoved it open, knocking the older man back. Mr. Rose had one hand on the bed to keep from falling.

'The council knew you wouldn't take this well,' Hardwick said. 'And they just can't afford having you cause them any other problems. I'm sure you understand.'

Hardwick pulled his Beretta out from the holster under his jacket.

'You wouldn't fucking dare,' Mr. Rose said.

From a pocket in the jacket, Hardwick methodically removed his suppressor and attached it to the barrel of the gun. When he was done, he pointed it at Mr. Rose.

'Now everything is nice and clean. This operation of yours will be attributed to a small terrorist cell working out of Eastern Europe. G8 summit. Economic terrorists. Wouldn't be the first time. You, of course, will be branded the ringleader. The cool thing, though, is that in the process of carrying out your little terrorist plot, you were forced to kill several members of the

U.S. government who just happened to be enemies of the L.P. In fact, turns out they were the ones who wanted to take us down the most. Lucky us.'

Mr. Rose said nothing.

'And the best part?' Hardwick said. 'Those who aren't dead think we were trying to help them stop your threat. It puts us in a most . . . useful position. Again, thanks.'

'Fuck off,' Mr. Rose said, then dove toward the pile of clothes next to the bathroom.

Hardwick had been expecting the move. His first bullet caught Mr. Rose in the left shoulder, the second in the right hip. The man fell to the floor several feet short of the clothes pile that almost, but not quite, covered up the pistol that was beneath it.

Hardwick knelt down beside the old man. Mr. Rose drew in several rapid breaths, but he showed no fear, only anger.

'Don't worry,' Hardwick said. 'Your body won't be here for long. I planted enough evidence to lead investigators to this room before the end of the day. Which means I should probably be on my way.'

'Someday this will happen to you,' Mr. Rose said, teeth clenched. 'Someday they won't want you anymore.'

'I don't doubt it. But not today,' Hardwick said, then stood back up. 'Today, *you're* the one not wanted.'

He pulled the trigger one last time.

Once he was back in his car and on the road, he called the Chairman.

'It's done,' he said.

'Excellent.'

'Have you heard anything concrete about Morro Bay?' Hardwick asked.

'Two car bombs went off, but nothing else. It looks like your friend Quinn was able to minimize the damage. I still wonder if maybe we should have let the operation succeed.'

'No,' Hardwick said. 'This was perfect. If the targets had been eliminated, the focus would have been on finding the people behind the attack and exacting revenge. But now the focus will be more on prevention, more tightening of security. Paranoia, that's the key.'

'You're right, of course,' Chairman Kidd said. 'Excellent work, James. I believe it's now time for that vacation.'

'Yes,' Hardwick said. 'It is.'

He smiled to himself. Nothing was better than a job well done.

# 43

Marion came running out of the motel the minute she saw them pull into the parking lot. She'd been watching the news for over an hour, trying to see if she could spot Iris in the group of children being ferried away from the school. Reportedly they were taking them to a nearby medical facility as a precaution.

The reporter had said none of the children had been harmed. Marion had let out a prayer of thanks when she heard that. But where was Iris?

Quinn jumped out of the car before they were even parked.

'Back in the room,' he said to Marion.

'Why?' she asked.

He walked quickly up to her. 'Because we don't want to draw any attention.'

'Iris?' she asked.

'Inside, okay?'

As she turned to do as he said, she heard a familiar voice behind her call out.

'Goah.'

She whipped around. Nate had just emerged out of the back seat. In his arms was the one thing Marion wanted to see more than anything.

'Goah,' the girl said, smiling at Marion.

Marion rushed over and took Iris in her arms.

'Goah,' Iris repeated.

'Yes,' Marion said. 'Goah. Goah.'

In Marion's room, Quinn gave her an edited version of what had happened. There was no reason to let her know how close the girl had come to dying. If Marion sensed he was holding back, she didn't say anything. She seemed content just to hold Iris and kiss the girl's cheeks.

'We need to get her to a doctor,' Quinn told her.

'What? Why?' Marion said, scanning the child. 'Is she hurt?'

'The implant,' Quinn said. 'She needs to get it out.'

Marion touched the spot where the implant had been inserted. 'Right. Of course.'

'I know a place in L.A. Very discreet. And once they're done, we'll get you home.'

A dark look crossed Marion's face.

'Don't worry,' Orlando said. 'We'll make sure the papers you have for her will hold up. Iris will be yours now and always.'

'It's not that,' Marion said. 'I'm just not sure where home is now.'

* * *

In the wake of the Morro Bay attack, and the subsequent washing up on a beach in Virginia of another high-ranking CIA official — this one named Chercover — the Office was disbanded. But as much as the FBI wanted to pin the bombings and murders on the negligence of

Peter and his people, they couldn't.

Quinn didn't want to care. He was going to be through with the Office after this job anyway. Still, he couldn't help feeling a sense of loss. No matter how annoying Peter was, the Office had, for the most part, done some decent work.

Now there was a void waiting to be filled.

The last conversation he'd had with Peter had been short.

'I'll make sure your money is transferred before we close our accounts,' Peter had said.

Quinn frowned. It didn't feel right to be paid to stop the murders of dozens of children, let alone the others who would have died at the school. But he realized there was something he could do with his fee. Marion. He'd deposit it in her account. Of course, the amount would shock her, so he'd have to send her a note first so that she didn't do something stupid like tell the bank they'd made a mistake.

'I also thought you'd like to know about the children who'd been . . . ' Peter seemed to be unable to finish the sentence.

'What about them?' Quinn asked.

'All but one survived. The doctors say he had a heart condition that just couldn't handle the stress of being kept drugged for so long, followed by all the excitement at the school.'

'He?'

'A little boy. That's all I know.'

Quinn paused as an image of the boy on the gurney squeezing his hand pushed everything else aside. Though he didn't wish death on any of the children, he hoped for his own sanity that this boy was one of the living.

'One last thing,' Peter said. 'You remember the man you caught in the apartment building in New York before you discovered the DDNI's body?'

That seemed like years ago to Quinn. 'Al, right?'

'Al Barker,' Peter said. 'I was able to have one more conversation with him before the Feds showed up. I brought a picture of Hardwick with me that I'd taken from the NSA website. When he looked at it, he identified him as Mr. Monroe.'

'Monroe?'

'The landlord who owned the building. Remember?'

'What the hell?' Quinn said. Hardwick had *owned* the building where Quinn had found the DDNI?

'I think we've been played,' Peter said. 'I think we might have just done what the LP wanted us to do. But no one will believe me anymore. I'm out of the game. I just thought you should know so you can keep an eye on your back. Since you're still in good standing, they'll be concerned about you. You're one of the few out there who know they exist and can cause them a problem.'

Quinn let it sink in for a moment. Even if they had been set up, there had been no choice. Quinn had to do what he'd done. The alternative would have been a disaster. 'What are you going to do now?' he asked.

'Get drunk,' Peter said.

The line went silent for several seconds before it was replaced by the dead air of a disconnected call.

★ ★ ★

Nate sat behind the wheel of Quinn's BMW, his brand-new prosthesis pressing down on the gas pedal. They were heading south toward L.A., having retrieved the now-dusty car from where they'd left it in the Alabama Hills.

'You still want me to take you straight to the airport?' Nate asked.

Quinn glanced at the clock on the radio. By the time they reached the city, there would be less than two hours before his flight.

'Yeah. Straight there.' Tonight he'd be sleeping in a hotel in Minneapolis, and tomorrow, after a long drive north, he'd be having dinner in his parents' kitchen.

Quinn stared out the passenger window at the upsweep of the Sierra Nevadas. After a moment, he looked over at Nate.

'I've been thinking,' he said.

'Yeah? What?' Nate asked.

'I was thinking maybe you'd like to move into the guest room of my place.'

Nate stared at the road ahead, his expression impossible to read.

'I'm not going to be around that much,' Quinn said.

'Where are you going?'

Now it was Quinn's turn to stare out the window. 'San Francisco.'

A smile cracked on Nate's face.

'I guess I'm kind of asking you to watch my place for me,' Quinn said.

'What about my training?'

'Your training won't stop.'

Nate looked skeptical. 'Don't jerk me around. I'm just going to be a glorified house sitter, aren't I?'

Quinn didn't answer for several seconds. When he finally did, he said, 'No, Nate. You're going to be a cleaner.'

# Acknowledgments

Help with this novel has come from various sources, some old, some new, and some I'm sure to forget to mention. Thanks to Jon Rivera, Helene Cariou, Lorena Philp, Jim Hardwick, and Tammy Sparks. All have provided assistance and support in abundance. And to Kelly for the same and more.

A huge thanks also to the sanity squad: Robert Gregory Browne, Bill Cameron, and Tasha Alexander. Not only did they help me focus, but they also gave valuable feedback and suggestions throughout the writing of this book.

And to team Quinn at Bantam Dell in the U.S.: Sharon Propson, Sharon Swados, and Nita Taublib. And at Preface in the U.K.: Rosie de Courcy, Trevor Dolby, Ben Wright, Paula Hogben, Nicola Taplin, and all the rest. And, of course, my agent, Anne Hawkins. But most of all, thanks to my wonderful editor at Bantam Dell, who makes everything I do better, Danielle Perez.

Finally, I couldn't have done this without the love of my three children — Ronan, Fiona, and Keira — who make life meaningful.

As far as any mistakes you might find in the story, I'm told that I'm supposed to take the blame. Guilty as charged.

We do hope that you have enjoyed reading this large print book.

Did you know that all of our titles are available for purchase?

We publish a wide range of high quality large print books including:
**Romances, Mysteries, Classics**
**General Fiction**
**Non Fiction and Westerns**

Special interest titles available in large print are:
**The Little Oxford Dictionary**
**Music Book**
**Song Book**
**Hymn Book**
**Service Book**

Also available from us courtesy of Oxford University Press:
**Young Readers' Dictionary**
**(large print edition)**
**Young Readers' Thesaurus**
**(large print edition)**

For further information or a free brochure, please contact us at:
**Ulverscroft Large Print Books Ltd.,**
**The Green, Bradgate Road, Anstey,**
**Leicester, LE7 7FU, England.**
**Tel: (00 44) 0116 236 4325**
**Fax: (00 44) 0116 234 0205**